D0209845

Renewing Your Church Through Vision and Planning

Library of Leadership Development

Leading Your Church Through Conflict and Reconciliation
Renewing Your Church Through Vision and Planning

9612

269.4
R41L

LIBRARY OF Leadership DEVELOPMENT

Renewing Your Church Through Vision and Planning

30 Strategies to Transform Your Ministry

Marshall Shelley, General Editor

BETHANY HOUSE PUBLISHERS
MINNEAPOLIS, MINNESOTA 55438

Renewing Your Church Through Vision and Planning
Copyright © 1997
Leadership/Christianity Today

Scripture quotations are from the HOLY BIBLE, NEW INTERNATIONAL
VERSION®. Copyright © 1973, 1978, 1984 by International Bible Society.
Used by permission of Zondervan Publishing House. All rights reserved.
The "NIV" and "New International Version" trademarks are registered in
the United States Patent and Trademark Office by International Bible
Society. Use of either trademark requires the permission of International
Bible Society.

Scripture quotations identified KJV are from the King James Version of the
Bible.

Scripture quotations identified TLB are from the Living Bible © 1971
owned by assignment by Illinois Regional Bank N.A. (as trustee). Used by
permission of Tyndale House Publishers, Inc., Wheaton, IL 60189. All
rights reserved.

All rights reserved. No part of this publication may be reproduced, stored
in a retrieval system, or transmitted in any form or by any means
electronic, mechanical, photocopying, recording, or otherwise without the
prior written permission of the publisher and copyright owners.

Published by Bethany House Publishers
A Ministry of Bethany Fellowship, Inc.
11300 Hampshire Avenue South
Minneapolis, Minnesota 55438

Printed in the United States of America.

Library of Congress Cataloging-in-Publication Data
Renewing your church through vision and planning : 30 strategies to
transform your ministry / by Marshall Shelley, General Editor.
     p. cm. — (Library of leadership development)
     Includes bibliographical references and index.
     ISBN 1–55661–965–0 (cloth)
     1. Church renewal. 2. Church growth. 3. Pastoral theology.
I. Shelley, Marshall. II. Series.
BV600.2.R43   1997
253—dc21   97–4696
CIP

Contents

Renewing Your Church through Planning
Part 3
Strategizing

Part 4
Decision-Making

Part 5
Reassessing

Introduction

*Vision is a snapshot of the future in the mind of a leader
that simply will not fade.*

—David L. Goetz

My church just voted to start a second Sunday morning service.
The new service will feature contemporary music. That doesn't
seem like such a big deal these days, almost thirty years after the Jesus
People. But for our family of believers, steeped in tradition and proud
of it, the change is huge.

My church is a fifty-year-old, wealthy congregation with a complex latticework of committees, boards, and task forces. The church
has plateaued for thirty years, spiking occasionally to the 400-mark
but then dropping back to 300. It took more than five years of meetings to write a mission statement, develop a long-range plan, and decide to implement the plan.

The vision was ignited when the church hired a senior pastor who
said while candidating, "Don't vote for me if you don't want to reach
out." The church voted yes, of course, not knowing what they were
doing. Throughout the five-year process, many said, "I don't want to
lose our family feel. That's why we love this church." They wanted
to reach out without the sacrifice of reaching out. Now it appears as
if they are ready to make the sacrifice.

That's the power of vision.

Every church needs vision. And every church needs a plan to
achieve its vision. It is to this that *Renewing Your Church Through
Vision and Planning* is dedicated.

But what is vision, anyway?

It's that penchant some have to see a more glorious tomorrow, to conceptualize what the church could be like. It's a snapshot of the future in the mind of a leader that simply will not fade.

Some leaders burn white hot with vision; they have one thing on their mind: the vision. The rest (perhaps the majority) of us leaders, however, have skills in other areas of leadership; all we need is a little encouragement and help to think in visionary terms.

The good news: Visionaries can be developed. That's the assumption of *Renewing Your Church Through Vision and Planning*.

I hope you feel "I can do this" after reading this book, and I hope you find practical ideas that will bring renewal and revival among God's people.

—David L. Goetz
Senior Associate Editor
LEADERSHIP Journal

Contributors

Leith Anderson is pastor of Wooddale Church in Eden Prairie, Minnesota, a suburb of Minneapolis. A contributing editor of LEADERSHIP, he is author of *Dying for Change* and *A Church for the Twenty-First Century*. He is also coauthor of *Mastering Church Management, Who's in Charge?* and the tape series *The Best Is Yet to Come.*

Ken Blanchard is founder and chairman of Blanchard Training and Development, Inc., a management consulting and training company whose clients include AT&T, Hewlett Packard, and McDonnell Douglas. He is author of the *New York Times* bestseller *The One-Minute Manager, Leadership and the One-Minute Manager,* and *We Are the Beloved: A Spiritual Journey.*

Stuart Briscoe has been pastor of Elmbrook Church in Brookfield, Wisconsin, for more than twenty years. Before entering the ministry, he was a banking official in England. He has also ministered with Capernwray Missionary Fellowship of Torchbearers. He has authored numerous books, including *Fresh Air in the Pulpit,* and coauthored *Mastering Contemporary Preaching* and *Measuring Up.*

Kennon Callahan is founder of the National Institute for Church Planning and Consultation in Dallas, Texas. He has served as a consultant for nearly forty years. He was also Minister of Evangelism and Minister of Finance and Administration at Lovers Lane United Methodist Church in Dallas, Texas. He is author of *Twelve Keys to an Effective Church,* and *Effective Church Leadership.*

Don Cousins is founder and director of T.D.I. (Team Development, Inc.), a nonprofit organization that assists church leadership teams in carrying out their ministry. Before that he was associate pastor at Willow Creek Community Church in South Barrington,

Illinois. He is coauthor of *Walking With God, Networking*, and *Mastering Church Management*.

Max De Pree is chairman emeritus for Herman Miller, Inc., an international office furniture manufacturing company. He is author of *Leadership Is an Art, Leadership Jazz*, and *Dear Zoe*.

Peter F. Drucker is founder and honorary chairman of the Peter F. Drucker Foundation for Nonprofit Management. He has been Clarke Professor of Social Science and Management at the Claremont Graduate School for over twenty years. He has authored numerous books, including *Managing the Nonprofit Organization* and *Managing for the Future*.

Ted W. Engstrom is president emeritus of World Vision. He has authored numerous books, including *The Pursuit of Excellence, The Fine Art of Mentoring*, and *Integrity*.

Carl F. George is a consultant and church analyst. He is author of *Leading and Managing the Local Church* and *Prepare Your Church for the Future*. He resides in Diamond Bar, California.

David Hansen is pastor of Belgrade Community Church in Belgrade, Montana. Before that he pastored yoked congregations in western Montana. He has written *The Art of Pastoring*.

Jack Hayford is pastor of Church on the Way in Van Nuys, California. He is the author of many books, among them *Worship His Majesty* and *Rebuilding the Real You*, and is coauthor of *Mastering Worship* and *Who's in Charge?*

Howard Hendricks is distinguished professor at Dallas Theological Seminary and chairman of the Center for Christian Leadership. Prior to the seminary, he was chaplain for the Dallas Cowboys. He is author of *Confrontation, Conflict and Crisis*, and *Church Management Manual*, and is coauthor of *As Iron Sharpens Iron*.

Joel Hunter is pastor of Northland Community Church in Longwood, Florida. He is author of *The Journey to Spiritual Maturity, The Challenging Road*, and *Prayer, Politics, and Power*.

Paul Johnson is pastor of Woodridge Church in Wayzata, Minnesota, and director of church planting for the Baptist General Conference.

John Koessler is assistant professor of pastoral studies at Moody Bible Institute in Chicago, Illinois. Before teaching, he served as pastor at Valley Chapel in Green Valley, Illinois. He is author of *No Little Places: The Untapped Potential of the Small Church*.

Bob Moeller is a contributing editor of LEADERSHIP and interim pastor of First Baptist Church in Elmhurst, Illinois. Previously he was director of communications at Trinity Evangelical Divinity School and has served as senior pastor in Arizona and Minnesota. He has written *For Better, For Worse, The Stirring,* and *Love in Action.*

Terry Muck is professor of comparative religion at Austin Presbyterian Theological Seminary in Austin, Texas. Before that he was editor of LEADERSHIP and executive editor of *Christianity Today.* He has written, among others, *Alien Gods on American Turf, The Mysterious Beyond,* and *Theology and Ministry in a Global Age.*

Larry Osborne is senior pastor at North Coast Church in Vista, California, a suburb of San Diego. He is author of *The Unity Factor* and coauthor of *Measuring Up.*

Ben Patterson is dean of the chapel at Hope College in Holland, Michigan. Before that he pastored Presbyterian congregations in New Jersey and California. He is a contributing editor to *Christianity Today* and LEADERSHIP, author of *Waiting: Finding Hope When God Seems Silent,* and coauthor of *Mastering the Pastoral Role* and *Who's in Charge?*

Eugene H. Peterson is James M. Houston Professor of Spiritual Theology at Regent College in Vancouver, British Columbia. He is a contributing editor to LEADERSHIP. His many books include *The Message: The New Testament in Contemporary English* and *The Psalms: The Message.*

Wayne Pohl is pastor of St. Paul Lutheran Church in Trenton, Michigan. He serves as a contributing editor to LEADERSHIP. He is coauthor of *Mastering Church Finances.*

Dennis Sawyer is pastor of Church By the Side of the Road in Seattle, Washington. Before that he pastored at Philadelphia Church in Chicago, Illinois.

Lyle E. Schaller is research associate for the National Evangelistic Association. Before that he was parish consultant for the Yokefellow Institute. He is author of numerous books, including *Strategies for Change, Twenty-One Bridges to the Twenty-First Century,* and *The Interventionist.*

Fred Smith, Sr. is a business executive living in Dallas, Texas. He is a recipient of the Lawrence Appley Award of the American Management Association. He is a contributing editor to LEADERSHIP and serves on the board of directors of Christianity Today, Inc. He has written *You and Your Network* and *Learning to Lead*.

Roger Standing is pastor of West Croydon Baptist Church in London, England. Prior to West Croydon Baptist, he pastored for six years in Leeds, Yorkshire. He serves on the Academic Board and College Council of Spurgeon's College.

John Vawter is president of Phoenix Seminary in Scottsdale, Arizona. Before that, he was pastor of Wayzata Evangelical Free Church in Minneapolis, Minnesota.

Charles L. Yarborough recently retired as minister of First Christian Church in Albany, Kentucky. He currently lives in Hookerton, North Carolina.

PART 1

Dreaming

1

I'm the Leader, Now What?

Pastors who lead effectively must be willing to risk the ship repeatedly for the sake of the gospel.

—Leith Anderson

I t was May of 1969. I had just crammed three years of seminary into two and couldn't wait to reap the rewards of surviving my education: full-time ministry. The church I had been serving part time asked me to become their associate pastor. My wife, Charleen, and I were ecstatic.

By the end of that summer, the senior pastor had resigned, and I was named his successor. At age twenty-four, I was handed the reins of a local church.

Most of my training prepared me for the one hour on Sunday morning. The first few months, I studied and planned until lunch. After lunch I headed for home. With my parishioners working during the day, I had nobody to visit, so at first I took afternoon naps or caught up on the soap operas! I returned to work in the evenings, visiting or attending church meetings.

A lot has changed since then—I now work afternoons. But regularly I'm faced with the same question: as a leader, exactly what am I supposed to do? This is especially relevant for the first days of a new pastorate (or during the transition into a new chapter of church life). What should I do with my time? Where exactly should I lead the church? And what are the first steps I should take to lead them into the future, whatever that might represent?

Recognize your swirling emotions

I enjoyed baseball as a boy. Once while playing catcher, I stood up to grab a wild pitch. As I stretched for the ball, the batter swung, hitting me on the back of my head and laying me out across home plate. After that, I became a reluctant catcher.

Pastors can also feel reluctant to stretch in a new direction, fearful of risking their neck in the process. Many emotions swirl within us as we begin a new ministry. These emotions are neither good nor bad. But we are wise to monitor them so they don't undermine our work.

First, we may begin to wonder if we're using our time wisely. I felt guilty for not working afternoons during the early days of my first pastorate, even though I studied at the office until noon and attended church meetings in the evenings. It never dawned on me that I didn't have to work from 7:00 A.M. to 11:00 P.M.

We are wise to be aware of the emotional tug to be busy, making sure our emotions don't pressure us into patterns of ministry that will raise false expectations. Some pastors, especially in smaller communities, feel the pull to visit every family in their congregation during the first year. This can have enormous value for pastors' immediate credibility, but it also raises expectations that can destroy them later.

People will expect to be visited regularly and have a special friendship with the pastor. When that doesn't happen—and it can't over the long haul—pockets of dissension about not being nurtured surface. Relationships with members, important though they may be, can consume an inordinate amount of our energies. This can undermine our ability to lead the church effectively.

I wound up filling many afternoons by reading biographies of famous Christians such as Robert Murray McCheyne, Charles Haddon Spurgeon, and David Brainerd. I gleaned much from the trials and successes of these great people.

Another powerful emotion is the desire to be accepted by the members. When Patti Hearst, a member of a wealthy California family, was kidnapped in the 1970s by the Symbionese Liberation Army and held for ransom, no one suspected she would surface with a submachine gun, robbing banks in Northern California alongside her captors. Through her long ordeal, she was sucked into acting like them. She *became* one of them.

The Patti Hearst syndrome can also affect pastors. Wanting to be accepted and liked by our congregations, we can become too much like those we're trying to lead.

One Saturday morning, while I was standing in my Colorado church parking lot, a man walked up to me and handed me a copy of the church constitution. Pointing to the section regarding pastor's responsibilities, he had highlighted my duty to do pastoral care.

"I think you're neglecting the elderly in our church," he said. What he really meant was "I want my own elderly parents to be visited more."

"Visitation is only one of my many duties, Bob," I replied, "and I believe the bases are being covered." I, too, felt pastoral care was important, but I refused to let it become the driving force of my ministry—it isn't what I'd been called to emphasize.

I also felt the pressure to offer altar calls at the end of each church service. But I believed it to be counterproductive to evangelism, making it more difficult for the people in our community to believe.

I wanted to be liked, but I resisted the temptation to blend in with the members' ways of doing things just to please them.

A third strong emotion is our eagerness to succeed. I am the son of a successful pastor. Thirty years ago, few Protestant congregations could boast a thousand Sunday morning worshipers. The church my father pastored, located near New York City, could. It bore many of the external trappings of success, including a sizable staff and a large budget. This became to me an unwritten standard of success.

Financial considerations intensify the pressure to be successful. When Charleen and I left seminary, we needed a washer and dryer, so we drove to Sears and charged them. We also needed a new car, so we obligated ourselves to car payments for three years. In short, I couldn't afford to lose my job.

Tangled up in the emotion of wanting to succeed is the fear of failure. I still feel this fear. I sometimes wonder if a reason I'm still at Wooddale is my fear of not being able to repeat success in another church. Ultimately, I'm convinced Wooddale is where God has called me, and frankly I'm excited about what He is doing in this church. But periodically, a subtle fear of failure lets itself be known.

Finally, there is the fear of inadequacy. Even though I had grown up in a parsonage, I wasn't prepared for the emotions that stirred within me when I dealt with people's problems. When I was a young pastor, a woman came to see me about her difficult marriage. In addition to her marital struggles, she had physical and financial problems. Her list of maladies seemed to be endless. I helped her as best

I could. I prayed with her and even called a local physician to make an appointment for her.

One afternoon, after hearing about her tragic life again, I drove home, laid down on my bed, and wept. I felt so inadequate to deal with her problems.

Entering a new phase of ministry can raise latent fears about our capabilities. When we've admitted these emotions, we're ready to tackle the tasks of leadership.

Do first things first

When entering a new ministry, we've got to do some things, and that means not doing other things. But of the multitude of possibilities that exist, what are the essentials, the wisest investments that will yield the greatest return?

First, I do the things that the culture of the particular church demands.

A pediatrician in our church completed a short-term mission service in Africa. She was the only physician on duty in the African hospital where she worked. On one occasion, she admitted a woman who couldn't deliver a baby normally and needed a Caesarean section. Though the pediatrician wasn't skilled in delivering babies, much less by Caesarean section, she performed the operation, saving the lives of both the mother and child. The doctor did what she had to do.

The same holds true for pastors. There are certain things that pastors must do—whether we are experts at them or not, and whether or not we like them.

Some pastors might say, "I'm not a morning person." But if they are ministering in communities where people rise early for work, they too must turn on their office lights at 8:00 A.M. Otherwise, they will be perceived as lazy, even if they work late into the evenings. The church culture demands that only after their credibility as hard workers has been established can they revert to their preferred routine.

When I became a full-time pastor, I recognized that something needed to be done about evangelism. Although my father was a pastor and I a seminary graduate, I didn't know much about evangelism. So I started reading books on the subject until I thought I had the principles down pat. One of these was training laypeople. So I found a layperson, dragged him with me for my first evangelistic visit, and made a complete fool of myself.

Evangelism wasn't—and still isn't—my gift. But it needed to be done. The context dictated that I begin a program, even if evangelism wasn't maximizing my own personal giftedness.

Doing what has to be done initially runs counter with today's emphasis of focusing on one's gifts. I also subscribe to Peter Drucker's principle of going with our strengths, not our weaknesses. Beginning a new chapter of ministry, though, requires us to do what needs to be done, priming the engine and then fueling it later with someone who is gifted and much better at it than we are.

We must resist the temptation to build a twenty-year strategy based on our weaknesses. Still, we must be driven by mission and purpose rather than personality.

Second, I try to get some successes under my belt. Success will give us credibility we'll need later. One way to success is visiting revered, elderly people in the congregation. Another may be asking a beloved predecessor to speak some Sunday, validating the church tradition that preceded you.

Planning and executing church programs with a high probability of success is also important. During my first summer of full-time pastoring, I proposed a four-week series of evening films called "August in the Park." We gathered at sunset in a nearby city park and showed Christian films on a large screen. Hundreds came from the church and community. The effort multiplied Sunday evening church attendance, communicated that we were interested in outreach, made parishioners feel good about their church, and bolstered my pastoral credibility. Everyone was a winner.

Preparing for the long haul

As I take care of these two essentials, I'm already beginning to think about how I want to lead for the next few years. That to me is what it means to be a leader on day one, day two, and the rest of my ministry at that church.

To lead, the pastor must create vision for the local church. Vision has to start with someone, and that someone is often the pastor. Years ago, when Wooddale relocated to our present facility, no one believed it could be done. As a leader at Wooddale, I was responsible to voice the vision to build a facility.

Someone with vision lives in the future. I "lived" in our new building at Wooddale for years before the church actually moved in. The pastor, as a visionary, is like an architect who intimately knows each room in the building he or she is designing long before it's actually constructed.

Though the pastor takes initiative, the vision is honed and further developed by others. The others may be talented staff members or gifted lay leaders who make real the dream God has given, giving it sophistication, expanding and developing it in ways the pastor never could.

Tailoring the dream

A visionary pastor faces a big challenge: creating a dream that is rooted in the timeless truth of Scripture and then tailoring it to reach the local community for Christ. Here is a framework to begin:

Develop a theology of ministry. My basis for local church vision is grounded in the birth of Christ. By invading time, the Son of God risked all, inaugurating the recovery of paradise lost by coming to do the work of the Father. Christ is our model, the prototype for taking risks and planning to reach our community to do God's work in our locale.

This transcends New Jersey, Minnesota, or California. The vision for a Colorado community corralled by sugar beet fields and cattle will look different than one for downtown Minneapolis, which is inhabited by universities, corporations, and hospitals. But the underlying theology is the same: to do the work of the Father.

Discover the church's values. In addition to rooting our vision theologically, we also must understand the community where we live. The pastor must function like a physician diagnosing a patient's condition. Often this requires digging into the past.

One of the first things I did in Colorado was read the minutes of the various boards and committees covering the entire history of the church. I also visited families in the congregation to hear their perceptions about the church. Such research pays rich dividends.

Recently I talked to a pastor who ministers in a 140-year-old congregation. Flipping through the church's minutes from over a hundred years ago, he discovered that the last names of those making and seconding motions were often identical to those making and seconding motions on his present board. The grandparents and great-grandparents of his congregation dealt with the same issues the same way their children and grandchildren were dealing with them. The church's problems, he realized, had less to do with the issues and more to do with the families who dominated the church.

Discovering the values of a local church is usually learned the hard way—through experience. Wooddale's previous pastor was a gifted musician who led the church successfully for nineteen years. I, on the other hand, took piano lessons for eight years as a child but never finished the second lesson book. So when I arrived at Wooddale, I couldn't match my predecessor in many areas. Even though I had carefully researched my compatibility with Wooddale, I endured criticism for my inabilities.

Become an ethnologist. Several years ago, a California church pursued me to be their senior pastor. I discovered later that they had hired an FBI-type person to research me. I also was surprised to find out that he knew so much about me. That church was committed to matching someone to their specific culture.

I had this same commitment coming to Wooddale—only I did a background check on a church, not an individual. In a library, I scanned the history of Minneapolis. I familiarized myself with the local schools as well as the local economy.

I also found another candidate whom Wooddale had previously interviewed, and I talked with him at length. Before I ever agreed to a first interview, I had a general picture of the church and the community in which it was located.

Begin studying the local subculture. While construction was underway for our worship center at Wooddale, a visiting church consultant, leading a group from his local seminar, walked through our partially completed building and remarked, "Here is a good example of how not to build a church. It looks like a church—a turnoff to today's generation."

He assumed what worked in Southern California would work in Minneapolis, Minnesota. In our research, though, we discovered that people in our subculture wanted a church to look like a church, a value embedded in the heritage of the community.

As a new pastor I studied and analyzed the local subculture immediately. During the candidating process, this cannot be done in depth. But it is essential in the early phase of a new ministry. We cannot discover our church's priorities without understanding the culture in which we minister.

Put it all together. As I think about my theology of ministry, the church's values, and the culture of the community, I ask myself: what would the church look like if these three elements were combined?

The vision for a church includes imaginary people (who they are and how they relate to each other), imaginary programs that touch the community with the gospel, and imaginary facilities that allow the ministry of the gospel to penetrate the local subculture. Long before we relocated and became a church that reaches out, we "saw" ourselves reaching new people through a new program of support groups. To some it was an idea on a list. To those of us with the vision, we could almost see the faces, hear the voices, and watch people pull up chairs in a room.

Investing in momentum

Actually, putting those three ingredients together doesn't solve my problems. It probably produces more ideas than can possibly be accomplished in a three-, five-, or even ten-year plan. Next is to decide which idea should be tackled first.

Go with your strengths, individually and corporately. Too often, churches invest heavily in weak programs, never developing the momentum needed for growth. If a church is strong in worship and weak in Sunday school, the worship must be promoted and expanded first. Later the Sunday school can be nurtured, fed by the resources of a healthy worship service.

Not long after I arrived at Wooddale, we inaugurated a small-group ministry and various social activities, emphasizing our strength in fellowship. Our people were good at relationships, and so focusing on their gifts became an effective means of incorporating new people.

Often right choices run counter to peer pressure. Designated gifts to bolster weak areas, for example, can undermine this strategy. It's tempting to accept these gifts. But just because someone donated $1,000 for refurbishing Sunday school rooms doesn't mean the church should make plans for renovation.

Find the quickest return. One year we faced the important decision of whom to add to the staff. One faction in the church lobbied heavily for a counseling pastor.

But our counseling program was weak. Our singles ministry, however, was already up and running. In addition, the Minneapolis metropolitan area provided many resources for Christian counseling, while a largely unreached singles population existed in our community. So we went with a singles pastor. As a result, our singles ministry exploded, reaching many unchurched singles in the community and adding excitement to a growing congregation.

In American culture, most suburban and urban churches need a critical mass of people to develop growth momentum. To reach that critical mass, which hovers near three hundred worshipers in most suburban settings, pastors must invest in programs with quick returns, targeting ministries with high impact and immediate results. Churches today need an irreducible minimum of resources—people and money—to attract newcomers. Basic programs like children's and youth ministries are needed to draw the people that will enable the church to grow.

Shifting gears

Creating a local church vision is one thing. Implementing that vision is another. Small churches function on a hub-and-spoke model of operation. The pastor is the hub, and the church members are the spokes, relating directly to the pastor.

One frazzled pastor was at the end of his rope. He had led his church to exciting new growth—700 attenders filled the sanctuary on Sunday mornings—but now he couldn't keep up the pace. During our long conversation, he complained about his unmotivated congregation and the problems on his elder board.

"There's nothing wrong with your church," I said, when I finally got a word in. "The best solution may be for you to leave, to hand the reins of leadership to someone who can lead a church of that size."

As his church grew, I discovered, this pastor wasn't able to change his leadership style. He started working harder, still trying to operate on the hub-and-spoke model. He ended up logging eighty-hour workweeks.

When I pastored a small church, I frequently stopped by the hospital on my way home from work, just in case someone I knew was there. When a baby arrived, I was the first to know, even if it was 2:00 A.M. "It's a girl" or "It's a boy," I'd often hear as I'd pick up the phone in the middle of the night.

Few call me today. I had to relinquish close relationships with a majority of the congregation so that their needs could be met by someone else and the kingdom of God could be expanded. I had to move from being the hub of the wheel to being the axle, moving from a direct to a more indirect relationship to the congregation. New systems of leadership had to be developed, distributing relationships and power to other pastors and leaders in the church.

Risking the ship

In 1990, when Wooddale was building its worship center, I was convinced we should be planting churches to reach the community for Christ. If we were serious about evangelism, then we needed to grow new churches, one of the most effective means of evangelism. A church building was merely a means to an end, not the end itself.

Some thought I was crazy. They argued that we'd be committing financial suicide by planting a church in the middle of a building project—we needed all the money and bodies we could muster.

"Wait until we have more people," I heard over and over again. "Plant a church after we move into our new worship center."

By planting a new congregation, I felt we would make a powerful statement about our purpose: we were willing to risk crippling a major church project to reach people for Christ. The leadership got on board, and finally the congregation voted to plant the church, which in the end didn't sabotage our building project.

Recently, while sitting on an airplane, I glanced at the aeronautics magazine the passenger next to me was reading. A picture of a Boeing 777 accompanied the article. The headline read, "Boeing Risks the Company Again."

I discovered Boeing had risked the company in 1957 when it unveiled the first commercial jet aircraft—the 707. Boeing gambled again in the late sixties by producing the first wide-body plane—the 747. Now they were planning to do it again with the 777.

I realize there will never be a time when I'm not carrying out these principles. While these issues are most acute in a new situation, new situations never really go away. Pastors who lead effectively must be willing to risk the ship repeatedly for the sake of the gospel. In one sense, we'll never stop asking, "I'm the leader, now what?"

2

Visionary Jazz

Rarely does too much vision tire a church out.

—Max De Pree

M any years ago at Herman Miller, Inc., we invented a product that revolutionized the office world—the open office. When we were ready to introduce it in 1968, however, our sales department said, "We can't sell that. That's a dumb product. Nobody will want that."

To get that product to market, we had to bypass our own sales department!

One key person in the sales department, Joe Schwartz, thought the open office was a work of genius. He said, "I can sell it. This is absolutely needed."

Joe invited facility managers from major corporations to come together for two days of meetings, and he asked them on the first day what problems they faced.

When they arrived for the second day of meetings, he restated the problems they had talked about the day before. Then he showed them how this new system could create solutions to their problems. They began to buy the product directly from him—bypassing the normal sales process. Joe is retired now, but his ability to capture a vision helped change the office furniture industry worldwide.

Most of us tend to see life the way it is, not the way it could be. It's somehow simpler to see life as though we were looking into a mirror. Seeing reality is difficult day by day, and it's even more difficult to see it five years from now. How can we be leaders of vision, and how can we help those in our churches become followers of that vision?

Carrying a vision

Some people have a gift for being visionary, but most of us don't. A leader, however, doesn't have to have a gift for vision or be the author of the vision. Vision can come from a number of sources. But the leader should be the carrier of the vision—explaining and illustrating it. Leadership, in some ways, is like teaching third grade—the significant things need to be repeated.

A demanding vision energizes people. But it's not unusual in the church that we'll call up somebody at the last minute and say, "Sorry we're so late with this, but we wonder if you would like to teach the eighth grade Sunday school class? It doesn't take much preparation. It's not a lot of hard work. You can do it. We know you can."

Believe me, there are better ways to help people reach their potential. It's lazy leadership to offer people easy work. Few things in life are more insulting than to be offered an easy job.

Many years ago my wife and I attended a church that was having some special problems with a high school class. Those kids were tough to handle. The Sunday school superintendent asked a capable, experienced woman in the church to help. "Mary," she said, "we'd like you to take this class. They're unmanageable, and we don't know what can be done with them." The superintendent challenged her in a wonderful way.

Mary replied, "I'll take the job on one condition: that you ask Max De Pree to teach it with me." "Why don't *you* ask him?" the superintendent suggested. So Mary did—and caught me completely by surprise. She impressed me when she said, "This is the toughest job in the church. I've agreed to do it only if you'll help." She created the right environment, and I accepted her challenge. We put together a program for those kids. She had a lot of good ideas, and we did a number of things that turned out beautifully.

Rarely does too much vision tire a church out. When a church is worn out, it may be that it's not being renewed. When people work in second gear all the time, never getting into overdrive, dealing with random trivia year in and year out, they get tired. But usually we're not worn out by tackling meaningful challenges. As a matter of fact, a leader ought to give high-performing people tougher challenges. Keep nudging them toward their potential. What makes us weary is the lack of satisfaction from work well done and well rewarded, followed by new challenges.

Developing vision

If I were the new pastor of a church, I'd start the process of developing vision by going to a few faithful area ministers and asking what they do in ministry. I'd ask for their thoughts about the church I'd been called to, about the community and what I needed to know about it.

I might invite three or four people for coffee and dessert and say, "I've got this thing on my mind. Give me some help. I want to run the risk of saying some foolish things, but give me your reactions."

One of the great failures of leadership is the inability to ask for advice. Many people know a great deal, but we have to ask them to tell us what they know. Generally, people are not going to volunteer advice on how you can save your hide.

When I was young I was transferred into the sales department. One day I had lunch with a friend who had been running the New York sales office for years. As we walked back to the showroom, he took me by the arm and said, "You're off to a good start, Max. But one thing you have to keep in mind: If you want help, you're going to have to ask for it."

Our culture sees asking for help as a sign of weakness, but it's not. It's a sign of strength.

Pastors can take several steps to improve their ability to understand and mold vision. Books and education can help, but in the game of leadership, you learn best when you're out there actually risking something. Talking to peers who share the same kind of risks helps connect you to vision, not just to ideas. If a pastor links up with other pastors who have similar problems, they can help one another evaluate what they plan to do.

Focusing on a vision

A church's vision should be both general and specific. There are general, overriding visions. For instance, the congregation of which

I am a member has a motto: "To know Christ and to make him known." That's a wonderfully broad, overarching vision. We will never fully achieve it, but that's okay.

On the other hand, significant parts of a vision should be achievable. A company may have a vision for a specific product—something that can be manufactured within a certain time. Likewise, a congregation may decide to build an orphanage in Albania or Romania, for instance—a marvelously specific vision. Part of the vision ought to be achievable, within budget and on time.

There are, thank goodness, different kinds of visions.

My wife and I recently attended an evening service at a megachurch. They were receiving into membership more than a hundred people. There was a crowd there, and the event was led by three pastors—very efficient.

Some time later, we had several people join our own church: the teenage son of our senior pastor, two people who had just returned from lifelong missionary service in Japan, two widows aged seventy-plus who had recently moved into town, and a family from Kenya. Our pastor introduced each person—including his son—talked about each one's family background, and helped us get to know all of them.

The lesson is that there's more than one way to skin a cat, and there's more than one cat to be skinned. The great thing about diversity in the church is that there's a place for all of us.

Avoiding myths about vision

There are several myths about vision.

One is that a good idea makes a vision. If risk isn't connected with it, you probably just have an idea. Risk, like inconvenience, is a standard part of vision.

A second myth is that having a vision makes it possible to do anything. Believing such a thing can lead to serious consequences. One immediate consequence is feeling frustrated when you can't achieve your dream. No one has the talent, the budget, or the time to do everything.

The discipline to stick with a game plan is crucial. If we stray, a big percentage of our work can be thrown away. Usually we get trapped because somebody told us we had to answer our mail within two or three days and pay attention to what everybody sends us. But just because people send it to us doesn't mean we have to do it.

Since we can't do everything, we need to stay focused on the vision at hand. Leaders need to understand who and what is presently important, because not everything is. Vision says: "We are going to do some things well." But this implies that we are not going to do certain other worthy things, or we're going to bypass other worthy people. To resolve the tension between "focused vision" and "ministry to all," we need to acknowledge that we can't do everything. We have to decide what it is we're going to do.

Pastors may find this difficult because, in a sense, the parishioners are helping pay their salaries; parishioners have some right to assign work to their pastors. Even if pastors find it difficult to delegate work, there are still ways to tell people to get somebody else for the job when what they are suggesting is not on your list.

Suppose a member says, "I really want you to get behind this community prayer breakfast." It would be good to say, "Great idea. Let's talk about it a minute." Then you'd ask about that person's hopes for the prayer breakfast: "What would you like to achieve? What are your expectations?" Together you'd discuss who might be the best persons to deal with those things. Maybe you'd end up with three names—people who would be really good at it.

As long as you work with them through that process, people usually don't feel snubbed—they feel involved. You're helping them find the help they need to succeed.

The moral of the story is that not everybody has the right to assign work to you. Examine carefully all the well-meaning requests for help. Sticking with priorities is a choice for which we are all accountable. We can also learn to recognize the great deal of junk in our lives—junk phone calls, junk advertising, junk meetings. Junk will sap our energy.

Implementing a vision

In some organizations, people feel they have more to gain by following a visionary leader. But in other organizations, people seem to think vision will make things harder. In some churches we find many non-participators—people who like to remain anonymous. One thing that draws some people to large churches is that they can remain unknown. It's more difficult to challenge them with a vision.

They are less inclined to identify with it and take ownership of it.

But church leaders need a critical mass of people to become advocates. There's a simple two-step path to that: First, everybody has to *understand* the vision. Second, they need to *accept* it.

When you're making your vision understood, you start by taking everyone seriously. Treat people as adults by making both the benefits and the costs clear. We can't have a great vision unless there are risks. A vision is going to be hard work. It's going to cost us something. It's going to take some time. We're going to make mistakes.

At the second step, we can fall into a trap: We think we need to have *agreement* on everything. We don't. What we need is *acceptance*. We adults do many things we don't agree with but do accept. Leaders need to recognize that.

If pastors meet initial resistance to their ideas, they need to find out if there's anyone in the church who feels a compelling need for change. If the general attitude of the congregation is that their programs are fine, they're doing okay, maybe working on a vision is not the thing to do. It's hard to effect change in an organization unless people feel a compelling need for change. If you're a pastor who works best out of vision, perhaps you should not accept an invitation to a church that has no soil for change. Find a church that relates to your strengths, interests, and goals.

But if you're already in a church with a long history, it's still possible to cultivate the soil, turning it over a little bit—almost creating a desire for change. You start by asking questions that help people see different horizons. What would people like? What do they wish for? What legacy do they desire to leave? Instead of telling them, you simply ask enough questions so they'll discover for themselves that they have some problems. If you get enough signals that there's room for something more, then, with a lot of participation, you can start to develop a vision.

When implementing a vision, leaders can make several critical mistakes. One is not being vulnerable. If I feel my position as a leader means I don't need help, it's going to be difficult for me to implement a vision. If we protect ourselves because we're afraid of the creative person or afraid of change and innovation, we can't really lead.

Another problem arises when we can't separate our egos from an issue. If I identify too strongly with a project or a church, I can't be objective about it. Everything that comes up touches who I am, affirming or threatening me. We have to learn how to separate ourselves from the issues of the church; some things happen that don't involve us.

But even good leaders with good visions sometimes fail. Sometimes nothing can help a vision. When the leader or the people lack resources or are untrained or incompetent, then they're not the right people to implement that vision. Sometimes the organization's structure cannot contain the vision, and it has to go outside the organization.

Right-sizing a vision

My brother-in-law came off an Iowa farm and went to seminary when he was around thirty-five. He pastored middle-class Protestant churches until he moved to Bushwick, New York, where he pastored an inner-city church for many years. Then he retired and moved to Grand Rapids, Michigan, where he bought a church building in the heart of a poor black community.

The primary thrust of this church is the after-school program for the children of the neighborhood. More than 100 children show up. He recruits people to teach sewing, accounting, remedial reading—whatever is needed. Then in the summer, he leads an all-day, six-week course concluding with graduation exercises. He's doing all this—even the janitorial work—though he's now in his seventies.

But every Sunday he holds a service and preaches a sermon. At the most, eight people attend. One day somebody asked him, "Isn't that kind of hard, preaching to only eight people?"

"Nothing hard about that," he said. "The Lord called me to preach. He never said anything about how many."

It takes a lot of maturity and grace to have that sense of calling and that kind of vision. Sometimes those of us with big vision can act as though we're on the moral high ground, while everyone without a vision is teetering on the edge. Yet for a pastor keeping forty families together in South Dakota, perhaps the most wonderful vision is doing just that. Great visions come in all sizes.

3

Church of Your Dreams

Ideal churches and visions for ministry often look and feel the same. Both consist of mental pictures, or images, of good churches—except one is a projection of the ego and the other is the product of the indwelling Spirit of God.

—David Hansen

The serious Christian, set down for the first time in a Christian community, is likely to bring with him a very definite idea of what Christian life together should be and try to realize it. But God's grace speedily shatters such dreams. —Dietrich Bonhoeffer

Each member of the board was a friend. Confident they would understand, I planned to tell them the truth. As their pastor I had listened to their pain in time of need; I knew they would listen to me in mine. After the business part of my pastor's report, I shared my situation.

"I'm really tired," I began. "The doctor says I have pneumonia. My load here is hardly bearable at times."

I went on about my problems. One board member began fidgeting. His face reddened and wrinkled. He held his thoughts as long as he could (which wasn't very long).

"We're all tired," he said. "We're all stretched to the limit. Your job is no more difficult than ours. . . ."

His comments, which began civilly, degenerated into acid.

"I'm offended," he continued, "that you think you work so much harder than we do. You need to understand us. You don't know what *we* face out there."

I defended myself by attempting to describe my unique respon-

sibilities. Pretty soon I realized I was playing into his hand. The other
board members were becoming offended by my defense. I didn't
mean for any of this to happen. I just wanted to tell them how tired
I was. I didn't mean to imply that I worked harder than they did. How
did this turn out so badly?

During a lapse in his volley, I turned from the member who was
first offended and said to the board, "I have spent many hours with
each of you in private, listening to you express your frustrations and
tiredness. Have I judged any of you or your work as you poured out
your heart to me? Why are you attacking me now? All I expected tonight is that you would listen to me as I have listened to you."

That sort of ended it. The board and I exchanged perfunctory,
conciliatory remarks, and the meeting went on as if nothing had happened.

I didn't sleep much that night.

The next day I chopped wood. The meeting was still hot in my
mind. Internally I alternated between tirades at the board, well-prac-
ticed I'm-quitting-this-stupid-job soliloquies, attempts to think
through the whole thing with prayer, and a mental game of assem-
bling the ideal church that I wished I pastored. In this mythical
church, the board supports me through my insecurities; my happi-
ness is their mission.

When I'm mad at the church and my feelings are hurt, I like to
crawl into a spot in my brain reserved for my ideal church. This imaginary church masks the parish I serve, correcting the faults in my present situation. I pretend it's Jesus' church.

Jesus vs. Barney

The process reminds me of a kids' show designed to introduce
children to the solace that imagination can provide. Its hero is a purple velvet dancing dinosaur. Barney teaches children how to with-
draw into an imaginary world in which waistline-challenged reptiles
are adored, everyone has fun, and everyone follows the rules.
Barney's rules, of course.

Sometimes I want Jesus to be like Barney. I want him to lead me
to an imaginary church where everyone loves everyone, everyone
has fun, and everyone follows the rules. My rules.

The fact is, Jesus dwells in the church that actually exists, not in the ideal church that exists in my mind.

The actual church is made up of sinful people and served by a sinful pastor. The actual church is where Jesus lives, the church that Jesus is building, the church that Jesus died for. We have no reason to believe that Jesus cares about our ideal church at all.

Vision or fantasy?

Ideal churches and visions for ministry often look and feel the same. Both consist of mental pictures, or images, of good churches— except one is a projection of the ego and the other is the product of the indwelling Spirit of God.

How can we tell the difference?

There is no sure way. Real visions do not come with holograph-certification seals; ideal churches don't come with purple velvet dancing dinosaurs. In this realm, we all stumble through, making mistakes along the way.

But as I'm trying to sort through the myriad pictures, ideas, and leadings, I pay attention to some warning signs.

If an image of an ideal church comes when your feelings are hurt, don't give it the time of day. The debacle with my church board hurt my feelings, and it set my mind to wandering. *If I just had a board that understood my needs, I would thrive in pastoral ministry.*

This is a lie.

Even given the fact that the board didn't handle my exhaustion well, my mental retreat to a church that would care for me was nothing more than a projection of an insecure ego. After the pain was gone, I was able to think and pray through the situation and I realized most of the board members were hurting as badly as I was. Christ was in the middle of the meeting the whole time. He wanted us to see that it wasn't *my* board, it was *his* board that exists for all of us.

Seeing it as *our* board is a lot more complicated. That means that everyone's feelings count, not just mine. It means that bad board meetings will happen again. That's the real church. That's the church in which Christ dwells.

If an image seems too good to be true, it probably is. An ideal image works in a perfect world; a vision works in a sinful, unpredictable world. The test comes when we're shooting the breeze with friends and we spill our plans and dreams.

I've never heard a pastor describe an ideal church that didn't sound biblical, that didn't sound like it would do great ministry, and that wouldn't be a great church to pastor. But I get skeptical when all the pieces seem to fit. When in theory the church should run like a Swiss watch, I can never believe it's watertight. Sin can always leak in. It doesn't take a Charles Manson in your church to goof up your best ideas. Sweet old Aunt Bertha on a bad day can trash a sure-fire plan to build the ideal church, even if it is backed up by the best-thinking church experts in America.

Vision, on the other hand, never comes with all the answers. It doesn't promise to fix anything. Vision is, by definition, seeing something beyond the present possibilities, so it never seems as if it's going to work. But vision works in the sinful church. It has a way of working in and through disparate personalities, theologies, and indigestion.

When the failure of an image threatens your call to ministry, be glad it failed. An ideal emerges from a self-established call to ministry; a vision emerges from prayer.

It is a big problem when our ideal church gets fused with our call to ministry. It's something like a Cartesian perversion of the pastor's call. Rene Descartes' famous proof of self-existence was "I think, therefore I am." (My favorite form of the proof comes from a fisherman's T-shirt someone gave me: "I fish, therefore I am.") The pastor's twist goes something like this: "I know my call, therefore I am a pastor." It's a common way to view the call to ministry, and so is its corollary: "If God has called me to pastor a church, then the church I am called to pastor must exist."

Naturally, the church that we assume must exist, since we are called into ministry specifically to pastor it, is our ideal church.

When reality smacks us in the face that our ideal church does not exist, this logically affects our sense of call: If our ideal church does not exist, then perhaps our ideal call does not exist. The argument sounds far-fetched, until you ask yourself if you know any pastors who have left the ministry because they could never find the church of their dreams. They wanted the church in Acts, but all they ever got was the church in Corinth.

Our call to ministry, however, is not based on specters in our head; our call is based on the Word in our ears. When we hear Jesus say, "If anyone would come after me, he must deny himself and take up his cross and follow me" (Mark 8:34), and we know that he is calling us, then we realize that our supposed call to an ideal church is silly.

If an image comes from a previous ministry, make it do fifty push-ups at a council meeting. My first church staff position was at a large Presbyterian church in Southern California. We pulled off a junior high ministry that was bigger than some of the churches I've served. We built it on some simple concepts of ministry: love the kids, have fun with them, teach them the Word of God, and pray for them. Not too complicated. Of course, it had to have a structure too.

In the twenty years since, every time I have tried to conduct ministry on those principles, that ministry has succeeded; every time I have tried to duplicate the specific programs we used, that ministry has failed. The insight is not difficult: Churches are different. Things that work in one place don't work in another. But scratch a little deeper, and we discover that our ideal church is often filled with images of our past successes.

If we want to try something in a new ministry that worked in an old ministry, we should submit it to the ruling board. They may affirm it, or they may send us back to the (mental) drawing board.

Whereas an ideal church is a myth, a vision for ministry is an incarnation of the will of God in a particular place. God often wants to do something new, and that can't happen if we bog down everything with past successes.

If an image carries even the slightest scent of envy, let it bleach in the sun until it looks like a valley of dry bones. Then see if it rises again. Much of what we call "vision" today is nothing more than envy. It's worth remembering that the apostle Paul lists envy—as common as corn flakes among pastors—among abhorant sins: "The acts of the sinful nature are obvious: sexual immorality, impurity and debauchery; idolatry and witchcraft; hatred, discord, jealousy, fits of rage, selfish ambition, dissensions, factions and *envy*; drunkenness, orgies, and the like" (Galatians 5:19–21).

We visit successful churches and listen to tall-steeple gurus. Do we come away with an influx of inspiration or an adrenaline rush of covetousness? There's a big difference between "I *can* do that," and "*I* can do that." We need to glean ideas from others who are conducting unique, productive ministries. The question is, how do we harvest vision and remove the taint of the sin of Cain?

Samuel Rutherford tells us: "Our pride must have winter weather to rot it."

Instead of implementing mental images, we must abuse them. Lean them up against the fence in the backyard, expose them to sun and rain and frost, and when they are good and weathered, look them over to see their real skeletal structure. Frequently there's nothing left. But sometimes it's like Ezekiel 37. We see the bones, clues to a solid idea. We pray, and the bones begin to rattle.

An ideal church is an idol; a vision for ministry is a prophecy.

Communion of the (real) saints

The council meeting meltdown happened a long time ago. But things like that still happen. I still dream about the perfect church when my feelings are hurt. In weak moments, I'm positive I know the system that will solve the church's problems. When my ideas get drubbed, I wonder if I'm really called into ministry. That I still envy goes without saying. But I've learned to see my church differently, and that helps me sort things out.

A few Sundays ago I was serving Communion. Standing behind the table, I speak a few sentences before the sacrament, my eyes scanning the congregation. As my mind gathers each face and forms them into a congregation, I see the communion of the saints; but this time my efforts fail at a few sets of eyes. My spirit gets stuck on some people who are mad at me, and some people who are bickering.

That kind of thing aggravates me. It irritates me that I fixate on the dumb little things in life, the inevitable things, the quirkiness and crankiness that seem to go hand in hand with being human. My first reaction is, *How can I fix this? Whom should I call on? What should I say? How can I solve this?*

I realize there is nothing I can do now, or probably ever, so I continue the liturgy and return to my seat as the elders serve the elements.

During the deliciously spiritual minutes in the service when the elders are administering the broken body of our Lord and I am all alone in my seat waiting and praying, it flashes through me that I have been granted the extreme privilege of serving a real church. The church isn't splitting. It isn't collapsing. The ups and downs and rights and lefts of our fellowship of the Spirit are as old as the New Testament and as contemporary as Uncle Grump and his oversensitive pastor. With joy and with love, I see what we really are—a real church, united not in my dream but in Christ's plan, not in my work but in the body and blood of Jesus of Nazareth.

Sitting up there in my big chair during these solemn moments, I see the servers, who have finished administering the elements, returning up the aisle to the table. They will arrive soon (our aisles aren't very long), and I need to get up and walk to the table to meet them. But I force myself to sit a little longer and take a moment to be grateful for the fact that the work is really finished—the church is one in Christ.

The irony makes me smile. The whiners are living proof that I pastor a real church. The fact that there isn't a whole lot I can do about the problems points to the fact that Christ is in charge. This makes me relax because, to be honest, it takes a monstrous amount of mental effort to continually re-imagine the church. Barney really is a slave driver.

4

Clearing Your Vision

*The most compelling reason I have for going away to pray
is to find what God is saying to our congregation
in the context of the larger church.*

—Joel C. Hunter

When I first came to my present pastorate, I wanted a vision à la Proverbs 29:18 ("Where there is no vision, the people perish," KJV). I wondered, *What does God have in mind for our church?*

For several months, though, I concentrated on building relationships, establishing credibility, and hearing the leaders' ideas about the church. Before long my days were spent in disjointed attempts to repair programs or solve people-problems. I became bogged down in routine. My hope of finding a vision, a long-term goal for the church, never materialized.

I looked to the elders for leadership, but they spent all their time, like me, solving problems instead of providing vision.

In the midst of my frustration, however, I had two hit-yourself-in-the-head realizations.

First, in twenty years of ministry I had never seen a committee receive a vision. Committees had offered wonderful methods to accomplish a vision or reach a goal. They had confirmed and refined an individual's insights. But I had never seen vision originate in group process—not in the Bible, not in the church.

Second, the problem was not my inability to discover and articulate a vision. My problem was more basic: interruptions and distractions hindered me from seeing where God was leading.

These distractions were good and necessary elements of ministry—daily devotions, sermon research, pastoral care, and administration. But they hindered me from discovering God's larger purpose for this church.

Like most pastors, I enjoy being accessible. It makes me feel useful, almost indispensable. And after years of experience, I'm pretty good at overseeing the operation of the church. But there is a downside. Always being available drains me. When I'm drained, I lose perspective. I begin to think God's kingdom is our local church, and our church is one problem after another! Then vision is hard to come by.

Also, the more I'm available to people, curiously enough, the less they seem to respect me, mainly because I'm not taking care of a crucial element of my calling. Years ago a man said to me: "Why are you always here when I call? Haven't you got anything more important to do than hang around the office? If we had wanted a crisis manager, we would have hired a fireman."

The itch I sensed in me and my congregation was twofold: (1) we wanted a long-term goal larger than our routine, and (2) we wanted our purpose to go beyond our local church.

Unspoken plea

Though they may not be able to articulate it, church members sense a need for long-range planning. Like the second law of thermodynamics, congregations tend to unwind and break down. I've found that the typical way to get a congregation jump-started and focused toward the future is to begin another building program. But I've also found building programs can be divisive, costly, and a poor substitute for a deeper vision. We need vision that does not rely on facilities, additional staffing, or a new program.

The most compelling reason I have for going away to pray is to find what God is saying to our congregation in the context of the larger church. Local church projects are fine, but they often don't fulfill our highest priorities. New church program emphases are good, but so often they lack a sense of the eternal. Even emergency projects leave laypeople wondering, *Is there a broader point to all this?*

After five years as pastor here, I still hear questions such as: "Where are we going? What vision do the leaders see for our church?" Such specific questions cannot be answered by our mission statement: "The mission of Northland Community Church is to bring people to maturity in Christ." We have to offer more than that, because people need specific answers to these questions before they are willing to fully commit themselves to the congregation.

It's natural for the congregation's most immediate needs to capture our attention. I could not escape the emergencies. In sermon planning I thought about what people needed to hear now. In program planning I thought about what activities people needed now. Even though many were concerned with the next stage of their lives, I focused on what they needed from Sunday to Sunday.

But the immediate frustrated my attempts to find the eternal. Until I learned to get away, I struggled to reconcile the immediate needs with a larger vision.

These insights culminated in a decision to simply get away from the church and its routine, even if only for a few days, to do what I—and no one else in the congregation—am called to: gaining vision for the future.

Risky retreats

Moses heard God on the mountain, but I had trouble taking time to separate myself as he did to be with God. Besides my busyness, I recognized that getting away entailed some risks. Here are some concerns I faced:

Something traumatic will happen in the church while I am gone. If so, people will be angry with me for not being available, or they will breeze through the problems and discover they don't need me as much as they thought they did!

I will be misunderstood. "Yeah, I wish I had a job where I could just go and dream all day," parishioners may say. Or the staff might ask, "Wait a minute—you get paid more than we do; why are we left to hold the church together while you go off to a condo?"

I will go away and come back empty. What if I think, pray, and wait, and the Spirit says nothing?

My vision may get vetoed. What if the church leadership says no to the vision I come back with? How could I handle the embarrassment and disappointment?

Nonetheless, by not setting aside time for envisioning, I became increasingly frustrated, a CEO (Consumed by Everyday Objectives) who fell far short of my potential as a leader. I could not tell the congregation where the church was going because I did not know.

I went ahead with my plans to get away. I felt if I didn't take such risks, I'd never gain a vision for the congregation.

My first attempts to hear from God were neither long nor far away. I wanted to see whether a day in a library or a walk on the beach would benefit me. Through those early experiences, God confirmed two things to me.

First, I sensed that we were not too far from the mark. God used the quiet to give comfort and peace about the church. I began to appreciate the good things: the congregation's earnest desire to love God more, our outstanding staff, our very adequate facilities, and our people's desire for vision, rather than being satisfied with just fixing problems.

Second, I began to see that the work of the kingdom is not left to us alone. The Baptist church is literally the friendliest church in town—it's not just their slogan, it's their gift! The Assemblies church focuses on healing and confidence, restoring bruised people. The Presbyterian church concentrates on a rich heritage of Reformed theology and distinguished tradition. God offers all of these churches to our community. Our church need not try to imitate any of them. We can simply add another facet to the diamond.

These came to me not as staggering revelations to the mind, but as balm to my spirit.

A number of these brief times away convinced me that God was involved in the present. I could then begin to concentrate more on the future.

On a trip to a lake house, I outlined three months of sermons. Later, I perceived a theme we should develop through an entire year. In addition to monthly goals, I plotted each week's sermon topic for the entire year.

After my third long-range planning trip, almost three weeks in Colorado, I was ready to offer the church leadership a way to fulfill our mission of bringing people to maturity in Christ. It would be a ten-year process toward Christian maturity. Rather than accumulate biblical principles for specific problems, the process would spend a year weaving one major biblical theme (purpose, faith, reason and revelation, holiness, witness, worship, among others) into people's character.

What changed

As a result of my times away, both the church and I have changed the way we approach ministry. The elders, for instance, are now asking practical and helpful questions about the long-range plans of the church: "If this ten-year process is progressive, what will happen to those joining us in years to come? Will they understand the foundation we laid at the beginning?"

The other pastors and staff are working on the implications for their areas. For instance, in youth ministry, we're asking, "Should we write a curriculum to take teenagers through the process?" In pastoral care, we're asking, "How does our home group ministry change in light of a long-term church focus?" In the area of leadership development, we're discussing, "What kind of congregational leadership will we need for such a process?"

In addition, my preaching and planning now are markedly different. They are, I trust, still relevant to current issues, but they also paint with a broader stroke. People have a sense of anticipation as well as a sense of history. Planning around a larger theme allows latitude even as it insures consistency.

For example, I will begin the emphasis on maturity with a series on "Paying Off the Past," exhorting people to reduce their debts—whether financial, emotional, or spiritual—so they can be free to move into the future. I know the messages will have specific application, given the current consumer debt load in this nation and knowing how unresolved emotional problems cause most counseling needs. At the same time, the broader perspective of what we can become serves as our primary motivation.

Long-range planning, then, is more than practical; it is inspirational. It does more than fix; it fulfills.

On another level, three things in particular have amazed me about my times away. First, I found that prayer never diminishes the amount of work I can do; it multiplies my accomplishments. Sometimes I return with so much for my secretary to type that it seems I haven't taken time to pray. On the contrary, it was because I had time to pray that the ideas flowed.

Second, my time away has also increased my pastoral effectiveness. I used to be easily distracted from conversations, thinking about work I wanted to do elsewhere. When I take time now to chart progress and direction, I can give more undivided attention to people as I meet with them.

Finally, instead of resenting my going away, the church leadership and staff appreciate someone taking the time needed to consider our future. They know they will have input without having to create vision in committee.

In the details

I've noticed that if I pay attention to certain details, my time away is more productive. To help me concentrate, I try to eliminate distractions beforehand. I need to know the church is covered, my family is secure, and that no one is overburdened. My secretary reminds me in advance of any such details.

The setting where I go can distract me if I don't select it carefully. It helps if I know no one there, if there is no TV, and if food and reading—two of my favorite activities—are kept to a minimum. I usually take only a Bible, a writing tablet, and several mechanical pencils.

Studying and praying before I leave on a trip probably prepares me for my time away better than anything else. Faith seems to come more easily when I assume in advance that God wants to reveal his plans for our lives.

While I'm away, I try to call home every night. Calls earlier in the day would tempt me to think about church routine or my family. My wife, Becky, fills me in on messages or events. I have not yet been brave enough to go somewhere without a phone. Besides, because I miss my family, a nightly call helps me sleep and concentrate on the next day.

Also the very way I pray while I'm away makes a difference. For instance, I find it more productive not to pray about a specific agenda but simply to pray for a sense of God's love and leading in my life. For me, thinking things through in the presence of God prepares me to discover his agenda.

Some years ago, I had a disagreement with one of my denominational officials. At the same time, a man in our congregation verbally attacked me and my wife. After weeks of trying in vain to put this experience behind me, my wife scraped together enough money for me to get away to pray.

During those days away, God began healing me, showing his love to me. I began to see the incidents in perspective and realized what God could build in the future. I was able to come back, submit willingly to the denominational officials, and love the man who had attacked us.

I am grateful my wife saw a need in me I could not perceive. That time away not only gave me perspective on the future, it was a time of healing.

Another added benefit of getting away is that it allows my creative juices to flow. My weekly routine is not creative. Study time, small-group meetings, counseling, calling, and administration comprise routine in my ministry. I enjoy these activities; they all add something valuable to my life and ministry. Yet they do not provide much chance for creativity.

I find it necessary to pray and fast in order to be creative. I must fast from conversation. I must fast from normality. I must fast even from religious activity.

During a recent planning retreat I found myself writing ideas for dramas in worship. I've never done that in my life! Whether these dramas are performed is beside the point. I realized that even after years of established patterns, completely new aspects of ministry can be born within me during planning retreats.

For years I pastored churches by problem-solving rather than planning. No matter how many problems were solved, however, I never felt we made progress. The size and number of the problems set the pace of the church and the pastor. I remember leaving church board meetings knowing that the church was afloat but somehow adrift.

My perspective has changed. Immediate problems are opportunities to adjust our long-range course, a destiny we eagerly anticipate. More important, we're no longer in a hurry. Our goals are not emergencies. So we don't worry. We have heard from God, and we will, in time, get to his goal for us.

BETHEL SEMINARY WEST
LIBRARY
6116 Arosa Street
San Diego, CA 92115-3902

5

Hope in a No-Growth Town[1]

*It was in the church's history that we found
hope for the future.*

—Charles L. Yarborough

G rowth in this little church seemed impossible.
The First Christian Church in Albany, Kentucky, was started
by sixteen people in 1834. Descendants from two of the original families are still members. The original church building was destroyed
by fire on March 20, 1926. The congregation, broke and in despair,
made their own bricks, built a new church, and moved into it November 6, 1927. Today that same building is in use.

The church suffered a split in the late 1950s. By the late 1980s,
attendance had dropped to an average of twenty. The Sunday school
was in the low teens. The youth program had two members (a
twelve-year-old girl and a five-week-old boy). Most members were
retired.

This small church is located in a non-growth town. Albany (pop.:
2,500) is in south central Kentucky. While the scenery is breathtak-
ingly beautiful, there is little industry, and unemployment runs high.
The nearest medium-size city is fifty-five miles away. Almost all our
young people leave town when they graduate from Clinton County
High School.

I asked church members how long it had been since the last family
moved into the area, and no one could remember. This church was
only two or three funerals away from closing.

---

[1]Adapted by permission from *Jump-Starting the Small Church* by C. L. Yarborough, 104
Church Street, Hookerton, NC 28538.

My assessment of this church's potential, however, needed to factor in the power of the Spirit of God. That power touched the small group of mostly senior citizens left in the Albany church. They decided enough was enough. They decided to grow.

Ours is not a rags-to-riches story of church growth. It is a story of a small church that struggled to stay alive under the leadership of a new but aged pastor who should have been thinking about retiring instead of leading a small church in a no-growth town.

In our first four years of effort, we added fifty-seven members. Now, we keep struggling to maintain our growth, hoping and praying for just one more new member. They keep coming from somewhere. It's not a mad rush, but growth is steady. Sunday worship attendance is now in the fifties rather than at twenty. There are twenty youth active today. The congregation purchased a new Allen organ and new choir robes. An old garage next to the church was purchased, and renovation is planned to connect it to the church building.

For what they're worth, I'd like to pass along the simple ideas that put our church into action and broke the bonds that held us back.

Draw on history

Three weeks after I arrived, I was looking through some church files when I found some old record books. I read that "Raccoon" John Smith, one of the founding fathers of our denomination, preached in this church. He and fifteen others founded the church. His grandson helped make the Communion table and pulpit, which are still used every Sunday.

I could not believe this great church, a house of worship and a community landmark since 1834, was so close to closing its doors. Yet I wasn't certain I had the energy to lead the people in a church growth program, or sure the congregation was up to it.

It just doesn't seem right that this church should close its doors, I thought. *If it is closed, who will have the dubious honor? Me? One of the relatives of the founders?*

Throughout an afternoon of tears and prayer, I came up with the sermon I needed. That Sunday I preached on, "Who's going to turn off the lights in The First Christian Church?"

During the sermon, I read this statement from the display case downstairs: "From the beginning it was a church of vision, a church that tried and succeeded in living out the gospel set forth by Jesus. They lived through some of the toughest times in American history. They survived. Their flames may have flickered as the winds of the Civil War blew around them, but the light remained bright, and has continued to burn."

Then I said, "We will not say to our children, 'The last one out, blow out the lamp and sell the building. It's all over.' Let us never let that happen. Instead, let us say to them, 'Take this lamp and handle it well, because it will light your way as it has for those before you.' Let history record these words, 'In 1989, a small group of servants known as The First Christian Church in Albany, Kentucky, fought back. Because of them, the flame of the lamp glows brighter than ever!' "

When we sang the hymn of commitment, "O Jesus, I Have Promised to Serve Thee to the End," nine people came forward, saying, "We shall never close this church." The first to come forward were the descendants of our founders.

It was in the church's history that we found hope for the future.

Most small congregations feel threatened by growth. They may lose their identity: "Do we want these new people coming in here and taking over?" Or they fear, "If we grow, I may have to give more money and do more work." Some people are just opposed to change. Change is difficult for many, and we do what we can to not hurt them, but we still must build Christ's church.

I tried to help people see what would be reality if they *didn't* grow. I told people, "Don't be afraid to become involved in church growth! Instead, be afraid of a declining church. Church growth is a lot more fun than turning off the lights in your church."

Build friendliness

I've used a modern retelling of Luke 5:17–20 to encourage people: "Be like the four friends who brought their neighbor on a stretcher to Jesus." I tried to help people see the positive motivation for church growth—to bring others to have an encounter with Christ. This has become our theme.

Before growth can occur, you must have prospects, and you cannot get prospects if you don't have a friendly and receptive church. Visitors who come to a cold, unfriendly church are not likely to return.

Most small churches are quick to tell you, "Why, we're the friendliest little church in town." Most actually are friendly to their own members, but in truth, they often ignore the lonely visitor. They're so busy being neighborly to their neighbor, they pay no attention to others. For some reason, many small-church members are afraid they are going to bother the guests.

To break the ice, we began having people greet others during worship. Following the opening hymn, I'd say, "Would you please remain standing and greet those around you, especially our guests."

The first Sunday I tried this, people looked at one another and no one moved. So I stepped down from the pulpit and greeted two people in the second row (my mother-in-law and father-in-law, who were visiting with us).

The next Sunday I again asked people to greet each other, particularly guests. My wife, Linda, greeted someone, and then two choir members and two from the congregation joined in, and we were off and running. Now people look forward to this time of greeting.

I've also learned that if you don't have a record of your visitors, you can't follow up your best church-growth possibility. Many small churches use a guest register, which is a great idea for funerals and weddings but a total failure in churches. I know how beautiful the gold-lettered guest book is, and it was given in memory of Aunt Ada, but many guests walk past the register and never see it. Those who do sign it usually list only their name and city.

We began having deacons or ushers pass out visitor cards, along with pencils, during the time of welcome. The cards give our guests' full address, ages of children, and more.

We follow up with what we call "pie evangelism"—taking a pie, cake, cookies, or home-baked bread to the person. We don't, though, let the person who baked the pie take it to the prospect.

For instance, the delivery people say, "Hi, we're John and Kathy from First Christian Church. We just wanted to stop by and tell you how happy we are to have you visit our church. We keep saying we're the friendliest church in the world, and to prove it, we brought you a delicious apple pie." People say thank you, and then our delivery people have their opening. They say, "I'm just the delivery person. Mrs. So-and-so baked this pie for you. I'll be happy to point her out to you this Sunday." That way, the prospect meets two church members rather than one.

For us, this has been the best way to reach prospects who visit our church more than once. And it has helped us to build friendliness, which is the foundation for growth.

Hold special events

Anytime you have a crowd in a small-town church, it's a big deal. It gives you a positive appearance in the community.

One event that helped us was Friend Day. We used the program from Church Growth Institute (800–553-GROW). At first, I had my doubts about the program, but that one day (and the follow-up) did more for our growth than any other single event.

A committee of our best workers met every Monday night for eight weeks prior to the target day of April 1. After the first meeting, I announced to the congregation that we were going to have a Friend Day on April 1. They all smiled; they had heard this kind of thing before. The next week, I said that our goal for Friend Day was ninety people. One lady said, "You'll never get ninety people in here." I agreed with her that we should change the goal; we made it 110.

Then, every Sunday I began to read letters from the town's VIPs— the mayor, county judge, school principal, and bank vice-president— who were accepting invitations to Friend Day. The program began to gain credibility. On that Sunday, after having twenty-nine people Sunday after Sunday for nine months, 151 showed up! We followed up Friend Day by making seven contacts with each prospect within seven days.

Teach members how to reach neighbors

Most people don't feel comfortable evangelizing their neighbors. I'm often told, "Pastor, he's my neighbor, and he's definitely not interested in being a member of our church."

So we have tried to relieve that pressure by teaching people how to bring their neighbor to an encounter with Christ.

We tell our members: "Bring people you know. *You* will be most effective in reaching your mother, father, brother, sister, son, daughter, cousin, co-worker, or friend. No one in the world can reach this group as well as you."

The process takes time. We have found that it takes an average of thirteen months for a visitor to unite with our church. In these old foothills, people are slow about making commitments.

Then we teach members to ask a simple but specific question: "Do you attend any particular church on a regular basis?" The last four words are key. We don't ask, "Do you belong to a church?" or "Do you go to church anywhere?" Most people belong to some church, even if they haven't attended in the past forty years. If a person responds, "On a regular basis? No, we don't attend church very much," you can talk about your church.

Minister to young people

On my first Sunday evening service at First Christian Church, I asked our congregation, "What changes do you want to see in this church?"

The majority said, "We want a lot of young people."

I then asked, "Who will work with them?"

The excitement came to a crashing halt. No one, including the preacher, wanted to take on the role of youth leader. I had served a large church as minister of music and youth, but that had been twenty-two years ago, and there's a great difference between being a thirty-six-year-old youth worker and a fifty-eight-year-old youth worker.

I finally realized, *Our problem is not a lack of leadership. Our real problem is finding young people.*

There is one sure way to attract young people: take them on a trip. Albany is about five hours from the beautiful Smoky Mountains, so we decided to hold a youth retreat in the Smokies. I'm still not sure where they came from, but we found six teenagers for our retreat. Following the retreat, all six were baptized and received into the church.

In addition, we incorporated a children's sermon into the worship service. Parents go to a church where their children are happiest.

Reaching young people has been our most difficult task. But over time, things have happened. We now have youth activities, three children's Sunday school classes, and a nursery.

Improve the music

A well-prepared organist truly lifts the spirit of worship. Yet so often we try to get by with a person who can't play adequately, and the music program is stuck until he or she is replaced.

We often continue to use incompetent musicians because of relationships. "Aunt Ada has played for us for sixty-five years. She was good enough for us in the past when nobody else would help us, so why not now? She would never think of charging us to play. Now you want to spend all this money by paying an outsider when we could continue using Aunt Ada for free."

Aunt Ada has been a dedicated servant to her church music program, and we need more like her. And a servant should never be hurt and made to feel unwanted. Still, sometimes a pianist or organist is simply not musically or physically able to continue.

Hiring a pianist could solve the problem. Use organ and piano together. Select choral music that will challenge the older musician to work harder. One of two things will happen, and both are good. Either the extra practicing will make her a better musician, or she will decide it's time to retire. If she makes that decision, host a church-wide retirement dinner in her honor. Award her with a certificate of appreciation and a nice gift. If she has played free for many years, the church owes her a great debt of gratitude.

Here are some ways to make a small choir sound great:

- Start singing simple unison music, if need be.
- Hold an optional music school to teach people to read music. This could be held immediately following each choir rehearsal for about six weeks running.
- When the music calls for a soprano solo, and you don't have a soloist, use all the sopranos, or all the women, to sing it.
- Select music that employs a big sound. It's easier to sing out on "Onward Christian Soldiers" than on "Nearer My God to Thee."

Motivation for growth

Our growth committees are diverse: some people are in their eighties, some in their fifties, and a few are younger. But all are dedicated to one goal: "Bringing others to have an encounter with Christ." Although some people are opposed to change, almost everyone has enjoyed seeing our church come alive and grow—even those who might have originally been opposed to it. An unusual thing has happened in our community: even people from other churches are enthusiastic about our growth. The talk around Albany is, "First Christian is really on the move." That gave our congregation a lift. It's a pretty encouraging statement for a small church in a no-growth town.

6

Rekindling Vision in an Established Church

*Battling for change is less productive than letting
the need become obvious.*

—Dennis Sawyer

The warmth of the autumn sun through the bedroom window
aided my mellow reflection. Sunday afternoon naps were a luxury. I had resigned a productive but stressful pastorate ten months
before to slow down, do some thinking, and await further direction.

The phone rang. I reached across the bed to answer it.

Eric Pearson introduced himself as an elder of Philadelphia
Church in Chicago, two thousand miles away, and then inquired
whether I would be interested in candidating for the position of pastor.

I took a deep breath. "Before I answer that, Eric," I replied, "I
need to ask two questions. First, are you planning to stay in the inner
city, or move to the suburbs? Second, if you opt for staying, are you
willing to make the necessary changes to reach the community for
Christ?"

"I can answer both of those now if you like."

"Actually, I'd prefer an official response from the church leadership," I said. My insistence grew out of what I knew about this
particular congregation. It had begun under the name *Filadelfia
Forsamlingen* in November 1925, in a storefront building three
blocks south of Wrigley Field. A haven for Swedish immigrants, it had
named itself after the mother church in Stockholm. For the first fifteen
years, almost all of its services were in Swedish.

The church had grown steadily, made the transition into English, moved into a large building easily seating seven hundred—and filled every seat. But in more recent times, things had changed. An average Sunday morning was now less than 200. The neighborhood was still called "Andersonville," but as you walked along Clark Street, the few remaining Swedish bakeries were widely separated by Korean, Thai, Mexican, Japanese, and Lebanese restaurants. Senn High School nearby was reportedly the most diverse student body in the nation, averaging between forty-nine and fifty-two nationalities attending. Many of the church's third-generation Swedes now lived in Evanston, Skokie, or Niles, leaving behind the second-generation stalwarts, some new residents from around the area, and a few "colorful" urban types.

Was there a future to match the notable past of this congregation?

Eric Pearson called back a few days later to convey the leadership's response: "We want to stay in the city, and we are willing to make the necessary changes."

The only remaining question was whether I had enough of what it would take, God helping me, to lead this 56-year-old church into the 1980s.

Hard-way learning

If so, the lessons of the previous six years would have to be maximized. Our church in the small village of Hammond, Oregon, had grown from 150 to more than 600 during that time, with Easter crowds of up to 1,200—but not without periodic upheavals. I remember the quarterly business meeting where I suggested that qualifications for membership be clearly stated in the constitution, not simply left to oral tradition. The atmosphere soon became electric. Verbiage flew back and forth across the room like a meeting of the Teamsters union. *Maybe this church needs a different pastor*, I mused, *someone who doesn't care about the future*. It became the kind of night that knots your stomach and makes you promise you'll never try to initiate another change as long as you live. The establishment reactions were the usual:

"I like it the way it is."

"I don't think it's necessary."

"I heard about a church that did something like this, and it was a disaster."

And then, of course, the old standby: "We've never done it that way before."

In spite of resistance, we made progress. I had begun as the only paid staff person, and we gradually grew to five full-time pastors. But the repeated struggles over ingredients of the vision—going to two Sunday morning services, dividing the midweek service into home meetings, or enlarging the staff—drained me and often damaged individuals in the congregation. Eventually I grew tired enough to resign, take a job teaching public school, and try to analyze the successes and failures of my leadership style.

Any kind of growth in any kind of church, I saw, would require constant change. I began seeking for "natural birthing" procedures that would allow future changes to be more positive and less painful. What wisdom could I take with me to the next pastorate?

The call to Chicago was the test of whether or not I had learned anything. I would be only the second non-Scandinavian pastor in the church's long history. But they said they were ready for a new vision. How would it go?

My family and I have just begun our third year of ministry here. The church has grown steadily since our arrival, and the congregation exhibits a multiplicity that matches the neighborhood. There's an air of excitement and expectancy. The fact that transitions have been smooth can be largely attributed, at least from where I sit, to the following:

The printing-press lesson. Back in Oregon, I had come to the deacon board one night with an irresistible bargain. "A single-lever, self-washing offset press in good condition for only $500—we'd be crazy to pass it up." I cajoled until finally I convinced them we couldn't live without this soul-saving boon to literature evangelism, and that they would be wise men to authorize the purchase.

It never occurred to me that to utilize an offset press, one should first secure an operator. Five years later, the press still stood unused in the attic, a silent reminder that church leaders must promote qualified people with a vision, not just good ideas or programs. A bus without a driver, an audiovisual library without a librarian, and an organ without an organist are worthless. My best idea, plan, or solution is void of life until shouldered by a person with a genuine vision for how God can use it to further his kingdom.

When we support the person with a burden, we reflect the current concern of the congregation, not the burden of someone who died ten years before. If the burden dies, we should let the program die a quiet death as well. Otherwise, some well-meaning member of the church (or the pastor!) will be exhausted trying to maintain something for which he or she has no heart. This not only wastes valuable resource people but prevents them from enthusiastically entering an area of ministry for which they are perfectly suited.

I didn't necessarily want a preschool in the Oregon church, but Jan Rea did. She and her husband visited our service while they were camping at Fort Stevens State Park nearby. I remember shaking hands at the door, and Jan asking if we had ever thought about having a preschool. I said we would if we had a person with a vision for such a ministry. The next Sunday as they were leaving she brought up the subject again, only a bit more fervently. I gave the same answer, and they left us to return to their home in Arizona.

I was surprised to see them again late that summer. I asked how they were able to take another vacation so soon.

"Oh, we're not on vacation," Jan replied. "We've moved here so we can start a preschool; we just love the church."

I outlined all the problems and resistance she might encounter, but she was undaunted. I had to admit she was capable. She had soon done all the research on community needs, licensing, building codes, and so forth. She made presentations to various civic groups, the church board, and committees. She and her husband even dug the post holes for the needed fence.

The truth is that for more than five years now, that church has had a successful preschool because it has had Jan Rea.

Axiom: In rekindling vision, support people, not programs.

The chandelier lesson. This lesson came not from pastoring but from my earlier days as a teacher. I had been hired as a "specialist" to bring order to a junior high class that had already gone through four teachers in three weeks.

As the principal led me into the room, I caught sight of one particular student amid the chaos. From his perch on the bookcase, he sprang upward, caught the light fixture, and trapezed out into the room, dropping to the floor.

"Students, this is your new teacher, Mr. Sawyer," said the principal, making a quick retreat.

Where should I begin?

So many things needed changing *instantly*, but some were of higher priority than others. It simply would not do for me to call out "Hey! You on the chandelier, spit out your gum!" I had to prioritize the needed changes, starting with the most obvious or intolerable, and work down the list. Gum chewing would be somewhere near the bottom.

The new pastor of an established church quickly sees many changes that must occur if the church is to regain its vibrancy. But everything can't be overhauled at once. If we take time to think through the problems and prioritize them, we will make far more headway.

A friend of mine came to a church whose building was in poor condition. Paint was peeling inside and out. The carpeting was so worn that it was actually a hazard to women wearing high-heeled shoes. Noisy folding chairs were used instead of pews.

The wise newcomer knew he couldn't change everything. He elected to try to inspire one very visual change, in the hope that everything else would look so shabby by comparison that people would then clamor for a transformation. He asked the church board for permission to form a committee to investigate the *possible* need for new carpeting.

The selected committee agreed that such a need existed. A new committee began studying how much of the building to recarpet. A different committee decided quality and cost. The final committee, based on the recommendations of the others, selected the color. By this time, nearly everyone in the church had taken part in the Great Carpet Project.

Soon after its installation, people began to paint, scrub, redecorate, and repair. They even purchased pews. An air of excitement and change blew like a fresh breeze through every area of church life.

Axiom: For effective change, prioritize carefully.

The lighted-cross lesson. When I was only twelve years old, my pastor came to me with a serious statement: "Dennis, I have a problem, and I think you're the only person who can help." I was dumbstruck. Here I had been coming to Brookside Baptist Church in Oakland, California, just a few months and was the only church attender in my family. What could Reverend Appleberry possibly need me for?

With deep lines of concern in his face, he convinced me that no one else in the church could possibly be entrusted with the task of watching from the back pew for his secret signal, then creeping silently out the sanctuary doors, down through the basement, back up the baptistery steps, and turning on the switch to illuminate the cross while the Sunday evening congregation sang its customary benediction, "Jesus, Keep Me Near the Cross."

I didn't even know people *went* to church at night. Nevertheless, I accepted the job, and for nearly five years I assumed my assigned seat on the last pew, awaiting my secret signal. Of course, I was also drafted into the youth choir, helped in the Sunday school, attended youth meetings, and grew spiritually. The church became my ballast as I navigated the stormy teenage years.

Wise old Pastor Appleberry knew that everyone needs to feel important.

Here in Chicago, there's a faithful member named Sigrid Peterson. We know she's somewhere in her eighties; she doesn't tell her exact age. She sang in the choir until just a few years ago, when it became difficult for her to stand for long periods of time. But she needed to be needed. That was when I began hunting for a genuine need (not a make-work job) she could handle. Sigrid now has a mail receptacle in the church with her name on it. All intrachurch correspondence goes to her for delivery before and after the Sunday services. She has an important task—important to us, and most of all, important to her. She is part of the new vision at Philadelphia Church.

Axiom: Everyone needs to be needed.

The keys lesson. Several years ago in Hammond, a young man named Danny volunteered to take care of the church lawn. I gave him a set of keys to the building and storage areas and told him his offer was greatly appreciated. He began doing an excellent job.

Then one day, I found him digging up the front lawn.

"Say, Danny, ahh, what's going on?"

"Oh—I was hoping you wouldn't see this till I'd finished. I wanted it to be a surprise."

"Yes, well, it's still quite a surprise. What are you doing?"

"I got this great idea," he explained. "Wouldn't it look great if we had a large cross of flowers growing here, surrounded with white rocks and log ends?

"I've already bought the rocks and flowers. Don't worry—I used my own money, so nobody could complain."

I began listing in my mind all the people who, along with me, would not be excited about Danny's landscaping. But wait a minute—it was Danny's responsibility to see that the area was well groomed, and he was volunteering the time and energy.

At that moment I created a homespun piece of church algebra: Responsibility+Time+Energy=Privilege.

That served me well when George approached me one day and stated that he didn't like the location of the Sunday school picnic. I asked him if he'd like to be the picnic chairman the next year. No, he wasn't really interested in that.

"Well," I responded, "generally it's my feeling that the person willing to shoulder the responsibility should have the privilege of making most of the key decisions."

Yes, there must be guidelines and limits, but in general, this approach turns on a congregation. People in Hammond began saying "my church" instead of "the church." There was a marked increase in volunteering, and that's when we began handing out keys by the dozen. Laverne needed one so she could arrange the altar flowers late on Saturday afternoons. Francis needed a key to have her bread and coffee warm before Sunday school. Delbert needed a key because he wanted to relieve the custodian from "doing windows." Eighty percent of the new activity was valuable body ministry; 10 percent was all right but nothing special; the remaining 10 percent required close monitoring, correction, and sometimes cancellation. But it was worth it.

The giving of keys not only enhances feelings of ownership and commitment, but it also dilutes the established pockets of power in a church. In my present church, we probably have more than forty keys outstanding—which is crazy, given our inner city location. But people are changing, learning how to work together, exercising patience and forbearing one another in love.

Axiom: Responsibility+Time+Energy=Privilege.

The platform lesson. If the vision is valid, if the cause is just, it will often demand a hearing on its own. The best idea in the world, if presented prematurely, takes a great deal more effort to bring to fruition. But when people discover a need themselves, they feel a greater sense of responsibility to rectify the situation.

When Wes Niles became the Oregon church's first minister of music, he did an excellent job of building up the ministry. Several times he said to me, "Pastor, we can no longer fit the choir, orchestra, piano, organ, and pulpit on the platform and still have room for you and me to function. You've got to get the deacons to remodel the platform."

Finally I said, "Wes, as soon as you can, try to use both the choir and the orchestra together on a Sunday morning."

"They'll never fit, Pastor—that's what I've been trying to tell you. I haven't used them together for months."

"I know," I said. "But just squeeze them together anyway."

He gave me an exasperated look. "You're going to have people and music stands falling all over the place. There won't be any room for you at all!"

"I know—but go ahead anyway. I'll sit on the first pew instead."

We followed my suggestion, and I must admit things were pretty chaotic. But before the week was out, several deacons stopped by with rough sketches of how the platform might be expanded to accommodate the growing needs of the music department.

On the other hand, I pushed that church into adopting a much-needed new constitution. It took months of heated discussion. People simply didn't see how the old system of checks and balances was too cumbersome for a growing church. The new constitution, when finally approved, streamlined the decision-making process, but the cost was high.

Here in Chicago, the same changes were needed. I wrote a new constitution more than a year ago, gave it to the elders—and now I am waiting. We still function under the old document. Whenever I can, I point out how much easier a procedure would be the new way. Lately, the elders have been pushing to get the new constitution approved and operational. The impetus is not the fact that the pastor wants it but rather that growth is demanding it.

The key to getting a nursery remodeled is to outgrow it. If your nursery is already overcrowded and the decision-makers don't seem to care, make sure they (or their wives) have the opportunity to serve a few nursery duties. Additional people create the need for enlarged vision by their very presence. Thus, evangelism is not the only result of a church's vision; it can also be the catalyst. As you bring in the unchurched from your community, their mere presence casts many things in a new light.

Axiom: Battling for change is less productive than letting the need become obvious.

None of the above is meant to demean the power of direct proclamation as an instrument for change. I believe in openly sharing my vision for the church and community. I work it into sermons, prayers, fellowship times, and casual conversations. As James reminds us, "A tiny rudder makes a huge ship turn wherever the pilot wants it to go, even though the winds are strong" (3:4, TLB).

Some may think this is manipulation, but it is not—it's leadership. The difference between manipulation and leadership is *motive*. Yes, if *I* want a big church, if *I* want a large Sunday school, if *I* want convert totals to notch into the spine of my leather Bible, it is manipulation. But if my motive is solely that the Lamb receive the reward of *his* suffering, that is leadership.

The first-grade teacher does not complain that the children do not know how to read. He teaches and inspires. He builds their self-esteem and helps them see their potential. By his words, he opens up a whole new world. "The tongue has the power of life and death" (Proverbs 18:21).

So we teach that everyone has a place in the body of Christ. We teach that everyone has been gifted in some way for the benefit of the whole church. We teach that everyone is important to God. We also teach that Christians often work themselves out of a current job in order to move on to something more. We train our replacements, thus seeding greater growth in the future.

Rekindling vision in an established church is not just a matter of following a recipe. It is a developing of relationships—between the people and God, between the pastor and the people, between one Christian and another, and between the church and the waiting world—to be the force God envisions to do his work.

7

Leading Into the Future

An appropriate, specific mission grows out of the knowledge that God is leading his people into the future.

—Leith Anderson

As soon as people walk into a church, they can tell if it is oriented toward the past or the future. They don't discover that by what they see as much as by what they *hear*. When I visit a church or catch conversations in my congregation, I listen to how people talk about one subject: the greatest days of the church.

At one well-known midwestern church, for example, visitors may hear people say: "I remember when folks lined up to get into evening services. Conventions of major national associations were held here. When people came to town, they attended here." Their glory days are past, not future. The result for both the listeners and people speaking is an overwhelming feeling of sadness.

When I came to Wooddale Church, people spoke similarly: "I remember when we used to . . ." "I remember when attendance was growing instead of declining." I found it emotionally difficult to be involved in conversations in which people quoted somebody else's sermon, said the music or the ushering was better before I came, or pointed out that this week's attendance was lower than the previous week's.

I knew, as every pastor does, that which direction the people are looking is of enormous importance. But how could we move from looking backward to looking forward? How could I shift people's wistful gaze at the past to an expectant peering into the future?

The God who transcends time

It takes a great deal of faith and courage for a pastor to switch the direction in which people look. It demands waiting it out and working it out. There is not one simple answer.

But the starting point for any answer lies in God. Vision is rooted in God. God transcends time: He is the God of the past, but repeatedly in Scripture he is the God of the future. We need to fix our attention on who he is and what he wants to do.

Theology, in the Scriptures, is not a doctrinal discourse but the record of God's revealing himself through history. We must assume God will continue to reveal himself in the future. We can't, therefore, live only in the past, because God is calling us to something. There's always something out in front of us.

Harry Truman visited Oliver Wendell Holmes when Holmes was in his nineties. When Truman walked into the room, the retired justice was reading Plato's *Republic*. Truman asked him, "Mr. Justice, why at this point in life would you be reading something like that?"

Oliver Wendell Holmes replied, "I may be old, but I haven't stopped growing."

If somebody can have that perspective about law and philosophy, ought we not all the more to have that perspective about the church of Jesus Christ?

Eventually, this general vision of God's purposes for the local church needs to become specific: What mission has God given our particular congregation?

Too often successful mission is immediately interpreted to be numerical growth. But for a church in the iron range of Minnesota, which has had unemployment as high as 80 percent in recent years, decline is not the barometer of whether the church's mission is being fulfilled. Just surviving the economic stranglehold is considered success. On the other hand, Wooddale is located in a city that has grown from 24,000 to 34,000 in the last five years. If we weren't growing, it would be hard to believe we are fulfilling all of our mission given by God.

In either case, though, the appropriate specific mission grows out of the knowledge that God is leading his people into the future.

Present needs, not past success

What causes a church to settle into past-directed thinking is not so much present difficulty as past success. Churches don't longingly remember defeats and conflicts; they grow nostalgic over past victories and expansions. Past success can become a staggering weight. What, people wonder, can they possibly do to surpass those days?

A similar dynamic occurs for any person successful early in life. Consider Jonas Salk, whose pioneering medical research led to the development of a vaccine for polio. His achievement immortalized him. What possibly could he do next?

Recently, however, Jonas Salk is in the news again—not because of polio, but because of AIDS. He's working on a vaccine. Here is a person who said, *Yes, I've had past success. But there are needs in the present.* He's using the skills he has developed to help his present generation.

In a similar way, a church lifts the burden of past success when it focuses instead on present needs: What do the people in this community and subculture need? How can we provide that?

At Wooddale, probably 99 percent of the people would now say the greatest days of the church are ahead, because they see present needs they can help meet.

One man who led our junior high program became a missionary to the Sundanese. Of the thirty million Sundanese in West Java, only one hundred are believers. Yet in this man's two and a half years of ministry there, fourteen more have come to Christ. It's phenomenal and almost unprecedented.

In a morning service he told the congregation, "This is not because I'm a great linguist; it's because you prayed." He read from letters he'd received from people in the church: "I pray every day." "I run five miles every morning, and as I run I pray for the Sundanese people." An eleven-year-old had written, "I get down on my knees every night and pray for the Sundanese."

The people at Wooddale think that in the next ten years, thirty million Sundanese are going to be won to Christ. They're not talking about yesterday; they're talking about tomorrow. Why? They have been gripped by the needs of these Sundanese. Past success fades in the light of present needs and opportunities.

A few people of vision

Most people are not persons of vision. In a church of hundreds or even thousands of members, a leader would find only a few.

Part of the reason is generational. The baby-boomer generation has, until now, been present-oriented. The generation, as a whole, has given little concern to traditions or to the future. But foresight won't necessarily come from the older generation, either; the elderly may be more prone to look to the successes of the past.

Some leaders lament the paucity of people of vision. But to move forward, an institution requires only a few. Robert Kennedy put it this way in his great quote: "Some people look at the way things are and ask why; others look at the way things could be and ask why not." A church needs only a few such people—ideally, a pastor and one or two laypeople. If they are leaders, others will follow.

Many pastors, serving a tradition-entrenched congregation, wonder how it can ever move forward. *There aren't enough people with vision. No one sees how things could be.* But usually there is one other person, or two, who can envision greatness, and gradually that influence can spread.

People with vision don't even have to be on the cutting edge of ecclesiastical innovation. The field of medicine provides an analogy. Most U.S. physicians are not researchers (and most hospitals are not teaching hospitals). Rather, most doctors treat patients on the basis of what they learn at seminars or read in journals.

Similarly, a few pastors and churches in the United States pioneer new structures, approaches to evangelism, and methods of outreach. But the vast majority minister on the basis of what they learn at seminars or read in journals. A church's few persons with vision may not be on the cutting edge, but if they are willing to learn, evaluate ideas, and adopt some of them, they can move the church forward.

Your role

What is the pastor's role in all this?

A few years ago a magazine ad pictured a man standing in his office, looking out the window. The caption read: "Why would a company pay this man $100,000 a year to look out the window?" The point: Every organization needs someone who looks out the window, outside the organization, to the world and to the future. A pastor helps the congregation by looking out the window.

But how much time ought a pastor devote to dreaming of the future, especially with a multitude of immediate concerns?

The answer varies with each situation, obviously, but much of the answer is determined by how long a pastor has been with the current congregation. Strangely, natural tendencies work against effective vision.

Typically, when pastors come to a church, they are not vested in the programs. Therefore, they can be objective: "We shouldn't be having this many services," or, "We shouldn't be doing vacation Bible school this way." Most pastors start with a burst of energy in envisioning how things could be. (In addition, when pastors come to a church, few members call or trust them with information. This frees time to look ahead.) But new ministers' ideas often are not readily accepted by the people. Even a good vision can die because people haven't yet learned to trust the pastor.

But after pastors have been in a church five or ten years, most programs reflect their ideas or bear their imprimatur. Their schedules are jammed, so they have little time to dream about the future. Momentum shifts to maintaining the programs they have built.

We need to reverse the process.

When we start in a congregation, most of our time should be devoted to the current program, not looking ahead. Then, gradually, we need to slide the scale until we spend more time on future projects. Why? Because a congregation won't follow a pastor in looking forward unless it trusts that pastor, and building trust takes time.

I know one pastor who went to a church that was ready to build, change its constitution, and reach out. He accomplished more in his first year than I accomplished in my first seven or eight. But that doesn't happen often. Most pastors enter situations in which people remember the past and problems exist. These pastors have to build credibility. The best way is to concentrate on the existing program. As a pastor works hard inside the given structures, the congregation develops the trust that later allows the pastor to lead people forward.

It's taken a quarter of my life to reach this point, but now I am able, during many weeks, to spend more time on future possibilities than on the current program. This week, for example, I have concentrated on a variety of dreams: starting a daughter church, providing a Saturday night service, expanding staff, and helping new missions projects. Now, these are fitting tasks, but they probably would not have been when I began at Wooddale.

Pastors need to look out the window, but in the early years particularly, it pays to spend more time at the desk.

Role obstacles

Every pastor would like more time to look out the window. But that requires overcoming significant obstacles. First, we hands-on types may find looking forward painful, because there is so much present work demanding attention. Second, a more hidden, formidable obstacle is our need for affirmation. Planning doesn't receive much recognition, at least not nearly as much as direct ministry does.

When I devoted most of my time to hands-on ministry, I could see my impact. When a baby was born, the parents called me, often before they called the grandparents. When someone was dying, I would spend a whole night at the hospital. When a family made a decision about shutting off a respirator, I watched the switch being thrown.

Because of the congregation's growth, however, we may have three or four babies born in one week. I can't be there for them all. In order to fulfill our mission, I have to make sure somebody will be there, but it can't always be me. My role increasingly is to look ahead for the entire body—to look out the window—and that means I have to give up many wonderful strokes from hands-on ministry.

Having said that, however, every pastor must give direct, hands-on attention to some areas. Which ones? The few most essential for the congregation right now.

Recently, for example, our staff discussed the prayer life of Wooddale Church. Although there is much prayer in various cells and subcongregations, I'm convinced, by my own observation, that the vast majority of that prayer is for personal needs. People are praying earnestly for kids struggling with drugs and adults fighting cancer. But I sense we are not doing as well in praying for the fulfillment of our mission, for the services of the church, and for missions.

So the question came up: Who will lead the midweek prayer meeting that draws only a handful of people? I volunteered. I thought, *If I stop people in the hallway and ask "Will you pray with me on Wednesday night?" they are likely to come.* Our congregation won't move forward without corporate prayer, so right now I'm giving it hands-on attention.

Strategy specific

It is not enough, of course, to look ahead in a general sense. Vision must translate into specific strategies.

Have people think next year, not this year. At the start of school, Greg Weisman, our minister to junior high students, has planned his program for the entire school year. He has in print every time the group will play miniature golf. He knows when and where they will hold retreats, who the retreat speakers are, and which bus is scheduled. With the program completely planned, what's left for Greg to do?

Minister to kids.

He doesn't have to worry about a topic for next Sunday's lesson. He doesn't have to reserve the bus. He doesn't have to schedule a camp for the junior high Breakaway. Living week to week consumes energies for ministry. It is painful not to know what you're going to do next week. But planning ahead releases ministry, and that moves a congregation forward.

Further, as members see the pastor planning, they do the same. That spirit permeates the organization. Wooddale's treasurer, for example, doesn't sign checks. He looks at how we're going to fulfill the purpose of the church financially through 1997. He concentrates on modeling projected income, expenses, and debt service. That way, when an opportunity appears on the horizon, we know in what ways we're able to respond.

Spend time as a cultural anthropologist. Pastors benefit from keeping their ears to the ground of culture. For example, one shift I failed to foresee is that people increasingly are choosing not to be classified by marital status. Whether they are single, divorced, separated—it's irrelevant to them, or at least they don't see that as a primary point of identification. Traditional categories—single and married—have become fuzzy because there are so many new classifications: living together, once divorced, separated but acting like a single, and others.

By listening for these rumblings, pastors can be ready for the eruption. We are asking serious questions: Is it time to reorganize singles ministry? Should we group according to preferred learning style? Or solely by age? Or more likely, should we group people by the age of their children? Already, we have placed no restrictions on which Sunday school class someone attends, and many singles attend classes composed primarily of couples.

In an increasingly pluralistic society, it's wise to offer options. (If I had my way, I'd lead one service in a sweatshirt, a second service in a suit, and a third service in a robe.) Baby boomers are highly tolerant of pluralism and comfortable with diversity. By studying culture—through seminars, books, and conversations—we can provide options when they're needed.

Plan for opportunities rather than problems. This principle, advocated by Peter Drucker, helped the congregation about ten years ago, when we were ready to add a staff member. The choice narrowed to either a minister for counseling or a pastor of singles. The church couldn't afford both. Which position would most directly fulfill Wooddale's mission?

When we looked at projections for the area's singles population, we were stunned. The number of singles was going to increase rapidly. We said, "That's where the opportunity is. Many Christian counselors exist in the region, but who is going to seize this opportunity for singles?" We hired a pastor of singles.

Related to this is the well-recognized principle that a church staffs to grow, not because of growth. If the church-growth experts are right that a typical congregation should have one pastor for every 150 parishioners, then the time to add the second pastor is when the congregation reaches 151, not 300.

Emphasize ministry rather than structure. When we were building a new sanctuary, which we had anticipated for years, we couldn't wait until it was completed. If I want to upset people, all I have to talk about is "when it's time to sell this building and move." The idea stuns them, but it makes the point wonderfully: I am not beholden to this building. If in five or ten years our sanctuary doesn't fit the ministry God has called Wooddale to, we should move on. It is ministry we're concerned about. As we emphasize that, people are better able to let go of structure and move ahead.

Purpose-driven

I don't think of myself as a futurist. I prefer to think of myself as "purpose-driven." Looking to the future is part of that. But being future-oriented is not the end; it is only one means to the end of fulfilling Wooddale's congregational mission: "To honor God by bringing lives into harmony with him and with one another."

Consider, for example, if the United States were to have a depression or nuclear disaster. There may not be any future, or at least only a painfully difficult one. To fulfill the purpose God has given us, we might be setting up bread lines or providing help for people with radiation burns. But that would be looking forward, with purpose.

Mother Teresa is future-oriented, even though many of the street people she touches are going to die. But she is driven by a purpose. She is doing what's necessary to live as Jesus Christ would in the streets of Calcutta.

Karl Barth says that Christians are to be the "provisional representatives of a new race." Would that all our churches were driven by that wonderful concept. We are provisional in the sense that we haven't arrived, but we are called to live as a new race of believers.

We are a future-oriented, purpose-driven people.

PART 2

Facing Reality

8

Turning Vision Into Reality

Leadership is not something you do to people;
it's something you do with them.

—Ken Blanchard

I once asked Don Shula, longtime coach of the Miami Dolphins, "What are your goals next year?"

He said, "I think goal-setting is overrated."

"What do you mean?"

"Everybody in professional football has a similar goal," he answered. "If they have halfway decent players, they want to win the playoffs. If they have good players, they want to win the Super Bowl. So I haven't won more games because I have better goals. I've won more games because I'm willing to roll up my sleeves and do whatever it takes to make it happen."

Leadership demands that we have the ability to realize our goals—to turn vision into reality. Those who have given themselves to leadership know how difficult this is. But effective leaders have a way of getting to the real issues.

Vision alignment

The challenge for every pastor is to match his or her vision for the church with the congregation's. It's easier to match your vision with the church's when you create a church, like Rick Warren did in Orange County and Bill Hybels did outside of Chicago. The pastor creates the vision and then invites members who want to buy into the vision. It's more difficult in churches that have been around. Many churches don't know what business they're in; they try to be all things to all people. When the pastor creates a vision, it can go against the vision of the people who hold power. Then the pastor gets fired.

I have been working with a minister in San Diego who has the potential to turn around a church, but it will be difficult. The older crowd wants hymns; the baby boomers want different kinds of messages. Especially in that situation, I'm not sure a minister can pull a vision from the crowd. Moses didn't go up the hill with a committee; if he had, he would never have come down.

My advice to ministers: be clear about the vision.

When you are in the process of developing a vision, the first secret is to decide what you want. What's your vision of perfection? Every great organization I know has somebody at the top who has a clear vision of perfection and is willing to put it to work. If reporters came to your church because of the excitement there, what would they see? What would the youth see? What would the members see? What would the staff see? What would this church be like?

Developing clear vision takes time—something many pastors feel a shortage of—but that perceived shortage is the result of faulty values. A woman said to me yesterday, "In America, we don't value thinking." If people walked by the office here and saw the two of us talking, they wouldn't interrupt. But if they walked by and I was sitting alone, they'd knock. They'd assume I'm not doing anything. We don't legitimize thinking. Most people have a sign on their desk that says, "Don't just sit there, do something." What they need is a sign that says, "Don't just do something, sit there."

We need to think things through, create a strategy and a plan, and stick with it.

In the process of setting the vision, it's important to find out what the congregation wants. But notice that this is second. In business, many people ask, "Why wouldn't you first see what the customers want?" Well, because the customers don't have the big picture.

Every time you get a suggestion from the congregation, you see where it fits into your picture. The reality is, you can't include everything in your picture. For example, you cannot get a tablecloth and candlelight at McDonald's. It's not part of their vision. Some would ask, "Wouldn't McDonald's want to attract everybody who is going out for dinner tonight?" No, if they tried to attract everybody, they'd get nobody.

After you create a vision, the people will probably want to tweak it, but they're not going to change it significantly. If the first person says, "Yeah, but you didn't think of this," and you snap back, communicating, "This is a closed deal," you're in trouble. The biggest problem in implementing change is when you think, "If it wasn't invented by me, it's not worth considering."

Journey of change

Much has been written in recent years about the central importance of vision, and some people wonder whether vision is overrated. I don't think so, but vision alone can't get it done. Too often we spend all our time on vision and none on implementation. At some point you've got to move.

Managing the journey of change is more important than announcing the destination. Often we announce a destination: "Here's a vision; here's what I want to do." Then we use a delegating leadership style and don't roll up our sleeves and get in there. Why don't New Year's resolutions work? Because people announce them and then don't do anything.

Disney Corporation invites their competition to Disneyland to observe and take courses. How do they feel safe doing that? Because they know nobody else will follow through on the vision. People imitate Disney's rides because they think that is the key. But they miss that the key is follow-through on the details—the friendliness of the staff, the cleanliness of the park.

The question every leader and organization needs to ask is, Are you committed to reaching the vision or are you just interested? A lot of people are interested in improving, but they aren't willing to pay the price. A person interested in exercise will wake up in the morning and if it's raining, say, "I'll exercise tomorrow." A person committed to exercise gets up in the morning and if it's raining says, "I'll exercise inside."

Follow-through is so important. I asked Max De Pree, former chairman of the board of Herman Miller, "What is your role in the vision of your company?"

He said, "The top manager should be like a third grade teacher: You repeat yourself over and over until people get it right."

Managing the journey means coming up with the vision and the direction, and then implementing the vision: coaching, supporting, giving directions, praising progress, and redirecting.

The leader who best models this is Jesus. I told Tom Peters and Robert Waterman, who wrote *In Search of Excellence*, "You didn't invent management by wandering around. Jesus did."

He wandered from one little town to another, and people would say, "How do you become first?"

Jesus said, "By being last."

People would ask him, "How do you lead?"

"By following."

How many people do you know who go to their boss's house for dinner and the boss says, "Take off your shoes and socks and let me wash your feet"? Managing the journey of change is servant leadership. We must get our egos out of the way and praise, redirect, reprimand—anything it takes to help people win.

Bumps along the journey

Organizations resist change because people get comfortable with the way things are. They prefer what's familiar.

Adding to the problem is the fact that most leaders of change don't understand the concerns people have when they go through transition. Their first concern is for information: "Tell me what you've got in mind; let me ask questions about it." The second concern is personal: "Will I be able to survive? Where am I going to fit in?" The third concern is implementation: "Okay, now I know what you are talking about, and I think maybe I can live with it. How is it going to be done?" The fourth concern is impact: "What's the result? What's the benefit?"

Notice that not until the first three concerns are answered do people care about the benefits. That means a leader cannot announce a change and explain its benefits and expect people to support the change. When you ask people to do something different, they focus on what they have to give up, not on what they are going to gain.

I went into several divisions of AT&T just before it broke apart into seven companies. The chairman was talking about all the great benefits—more entrepreneurial activity, more initiative. But nobody was giving the employees a chance to deal with the loss. So we created "mourning" sessions and brought in crying towels and let people talk about what they were giving up, which was a lot—prestige, lifetime employment, status. If you let people talk honestly about their concerns, often the concerns are resolved.

Situational leadership

To determine the most important qualities of a leader, people have done tons of research over the years and found there are no constant ones—except for integrity. The qualities needed in a leader depend on the situation.

For instance, the issue of how pastors should relate to board members—employee to employer, leader to follower, or friend to friend—depends on the structure of the board. If the board has hiring and firing capability, you work for them. Your job is to figure out what their needs are and to satisfy them.

It's important to understand whether a board member is high on dominance, influence, steadiness, or compliance—as the Disc instrument measures. Board members high on dominance fear losing control. If you know that, you can battle the person appropriately. A person who scores high on influence fears rejection. Such people are not going to give you a hard time because they want you to think they are good people. The High S person—steadiness—fears change. They'd like the church to stay the way it is. Board members high on C, compliance, fear having their work criticized.

A very important trait for a minister dealing with a board is not to need to be right. You're crazy if you get into a win-lose confrontation with key board members. My experience has been: the people who get fired have let their egos eat their brains. Jesus knew he was right, but he didn't waste a lot of time proving it. He didn't get into a lot of win-lose confrontations, even with those who wanted to kill him.

I've come to think more and more that leadership is not something you do to people; it's something you do with them. Leadership is more of a partnership; unless the follower is willing to follow, you don't have much leadership.

Turning vision into reality is something leaders do *with* their followers. Leaders must be committed to both develop a vision with their people and then walk with them through the difficult journey of implementing change.

9

Running Into Reality

The greatest reality affecting our vision is always God.

—Wayne Pohl

The story is told of a major corporation that launched a new brand of dog food: Through research, they developed the most sophisticated, most nutritious dog food to date and poured millions into marketing it.

But it didn't sell.

Out of frustration, the corporation gathered in a Chicago hotel. The national sales manager got up and said, "What's the problem? We have this nutritious product that is cheaper and better marketed than our competitors' product. Why is nobody buying it?"

There was a long, uncomfortable silence. Then, from the back of the room, a salesman from Iowa drawled, "The dogs don't like it."

Vision, it seems to me, is overrated. As this story reminds me, it's no match for reality. I've discovered this truth in the only institution that teaches it: the school of hard knocks.

Several years ago, our church purchased fifteen acres of prime real estate along a main artery in the Detroit metropolitan area. Our current three-acre site was constricting our growth, and so we saw this purchase as a way to fulfill our vision of reaching the lost.

Shortly after purchasing the property, however, we discovered that the cost of building a new facility was prohibitive. To build a facility the same size as we currently had would have cost over $14 million—and we needed to expand. We then stumbled upon the fact that our present church facility would not be easy to sell.

To top it off, we discovered our new property lay 400 feet outside the city of Trenton. It might as well have been 400 miles. Our church identifies itself with the town of Trenton; we couldn't move without altering our personality. So, after some huffing and puffing, we opted for staying put; we hired an architect and added space to our current facility.

Reality rarely matches our dreams. Perhaps that's why I'm a little skeptical about all this recent talk of vision in the church. Typically, anyone who pastors a large church is said to have vision. But many pastors who have seen growth, when pressed, will confess, "I'm not sure how it happened. I was just trying to do ministry."

I suspect that most pastors have more than enough vision, even too much vision. The pastor leading the megachurch and the one struggling to shepherd 75 people both have dreams. What most of us need, then, is not more vision but a greater grasp of reality.

What follows is the fruit of years of learning the balance between vision and reality.

The draconian twins

Pastors who dream face two draconian realities:

First, church culture is just about the toughest soil in which to nurture vision. The CEOs of major corporations work with board members who at least agree upon what makes their stockholders happy. Pastors work with volunteer boards that have a hard time agreeing about why the church exists. The diverse backgrounds of board members only complicate matters.

Let's say you have one board member who formerly lived in Southern California where he and his family attended a church of 5,000. He expects your church to have all the amenities of a large church.

But another board member grew up attending a church of 75. "Pastor," he says, "aren't we big enough already?" He expects a staff member to be present during all three hours of his wife's gall bladder operation. That's what his former pastor would have done.

Both members deserve to serve on the board if they're spiritually gifted and qualified to lead, yet their philosophies are as far apart as the north and south rims of the Grand Canyon. Add to the board another half dozen people who are just as diverse, and it's no wonder they don't read off the same page. To make matters worse, just when you've developed consensus among the board members, their term is up. Suddenly, the board is filled with new faces who don't share the vision.

A second difficulty for visionary pastors is that the subculture is constantly in flux. Our community of Trenton, for example, is pricing itself out of the reach of young families. Only older families, buying their third or fourth home, can afford the mortgages. Many women in our church, in order to send their kids to the best colleges, have gone back to work. As a result, we're losing our adult volunteer force.

Today, many church attenders feel more concerned about time than money. They'd rather pay Chem-Lawn $40 to spread fertilizer over their lawn than take an hour to do it themselves.

In these changing times, the pastor who clings to the same approaches to vision for more than two years simply isn't living in the real world. Of course, the church's core mission to reach the lost never changes, but the way in which that mission is accomplished should constantly be up for revision.

Winning traits

Given the above realities, it's not surprising that the number of churches rallied behind a clear vision are few.

But people-rallying visions are possible. Successful visions seem to possess several characteristics. Here are three to consider.

Solid in core. People rightly get frustrated when the reason the church exists changes. St. Paul Lutheran Church, for example, has this primary mission: "We will live the Great Commission." (See Matthew 28:19–20.) Although our church ministers to the poor through our food pantry, feeding the poor isn't why we exist; we exist to reach the lost for Christ.

Let's say, though, I decided to swap our vision of reaching the lost for feeding the poor. Every program would have to be altered; every mission statement would have to be rewritten. That would put a heavy strain on our people, who enlisted under our present mission. People don't like the core vision to be radically shifted.

Ways to achieve the core mission may change, but the core mission needs to be set in concrete. A fixed mission is the church's ballast during times of upheaval.

Flexible in execution. We use every means possible to interest unchurched people in the gospel. For example, sports are a good opportunity for Christians to interact with non-Christians. So our church sponsors a men's hockey team, which plays in one of Detroit's city leagues. This nontraditional church program has helped us evangelize. (We confess, though, that one of our associate pastors led the league in penalty minutes.)

A realistic vision must also allow for all sorts of creativity.

Local. In the early 1980s, one ecclesiastical rage was satellite churches: a church would operate as the hub of other churches it began nearby. Each "campus" would share staff and money with the main campus. This model was touted as the wave of the future.

So I traveled to various churches piloting satellite campuses and then convinced my leaders that we needed to do the same. Suddenly, we had a vision. We planned to start four satellite campuses in various Detroit suburbs: Woodhaven, Grosse Ile, Gibraltar, and Riverview. Our timing seemed impeccable.

When we were ready to launch the first campus in Woodhaven, we gathered together the people from our church who lived in Woodhaven. "Here's what we've been dreaming about," we said. "We're going to buy an old school in Woodhaven and start St. Paul of Woodhaven. We'll serve you with the staff of the main campus and pay their salaries. You'll have to worship in a school gym for a while, but we'll upgrade your meeting space as the church grows. We'll be the same church, just in two locations."

"What a wonderful idea, Pastor," they said. "But why don't you make Grosse Ile the first campus?"

Not a bad idea, I thought. So we gathered the Grosse Ile members and delivered our spiel. They responded, "Great idea. But why don't you start the first campus in the Gibraltar community?"

To make a painful story short, we scrapped our vision, or should I say, someone else's vision. I had to learn what now seems obvious: you can't necessarily import a vision created elsewhere. Vision is local.

Preemptive strikes

There are myriad reasons why a vision doesn't catch fire. Sometimes it's a problem with the vision; other times it's a problem with how it's presented. Here are several ways to avoid setbacks.

Admit your failures. When I arrived at St. Paul in 1974, this congregation was long on potential but short on commitment. We had more than 500 people on the rolls who hadn't attended in the past year. As an energetic, thirty-three-year-old pastor, I set about correcting the problem. I created a program called "My Brother's Keeper." The program attempted to match the committed with the uncommitted, the attenders with the Christmas and Easter crowd, helping both grow up in Christ.

At the program's inception, a lay leader named Harold said, "Pastor, I want to tell you that this won't work." Harold was not a crank operating on the church fringe; I respected his opinions. But I wasn't swayed by his criticism and pressed ahead. After two years, however, the program died. At a Sunday evening service shortly thereafter, Harold stopped me and said, "I told you so."

He was right, which was hard on my ego. But I smiled back and admitted his genius. Harold turned out to be one of my most energetic supporters until he retired and moved away.

Few of us married the first person we dated. We had to go out with a few dates before we found our one true love. The same is true of vision: A church will probably need to court several visions before the one true vision is found. In the process, its leaders will stumble a few times, so we'll need to say, "Boy, I really blew that call."

That's not easy for many pastors. Yet for the lay leader, there's something almost alchemical about hearing the words "I was wrong." People trust a pastor who 'fesses up when he's wrong.

Challenge your people. On Sunday mornings, an adult Bible class called Breakfast Bible meets in our church gym. Besides biblical insights, the class offers a continental breakfast: coffee, doughnuts, bagels, and fruit. It meets during the Sunday school hour, and the children who pass by the gym where the class meets occasionally grumble that they never get to eat any of the goodies.

So the Sunday school department issued a challenge a week before Friend Sunday: if the kids brought more unchurched friends than the adults did, for the month of April they got to eat the food—while the adults watched in envy.

You can imagine who won. At St. Paul we're not afraid to challenge our people to fulfill our vision of reaching the lost.

In a recent sermon before Friend Sunday, I said, "The only people who shouldn't bring a friend on Friend Sunday are those who don't have a friend. There are only two options: either you won't speak to your friends about Christ, or you don't have a friend. If you don't have a friend, you're in real trouble, and we'll pray for you."

My intent wasn't to shame but to challenge my listeners. Visions often fail because the leader fails to rally the troops around the cause. Our culture is filled with people dying to find significance. The gospel is worth giving our life to, and when challenged with its eternal significance, people will rise to the occasion.

Offer skills to reach vision. One Sunday I said, "If I could get every man in our congregation to spend one tenth of the time talking about Jesus Christ to his friends as he does talking about the NCAA tournament, the whole downriver area of our city would be converted."

I put the onus on the leaders of our church: it is our responsibility to train people to share their faith. People have a right to expect us to give them the tools needed to achieve the vision.

Connect ministry with mission. In many churches, nursery workers are recruited with the line, "Boy, we need somebody to take care of the screaming kids. Would you do it?"

With that approach, you may find someone willing to serve, but not for long. Guilt is a poor motivator.

Our church has 430 nursery workers, all volunteers, so to fill every slot is not easy. We attempt to connect the job of nursery worker with the mission of the church. When we ask someone to volunteer for nursery duty, we say, "You know, maybe next Sunday a young couple who has drifted away from the Lord will be here. They've got a youngster who needs special attention. Through your ministry, this couple will have the chance to hear God's Word."

In that light, our volunteers are not baby-sitters; their work contributes directly to the church's mission. Consequently, fewer people respond, "I did my turn in the nursery when I had kids, but now my kids are grown."

Whatever their niche in the church, people must believe their work has eternal significance and contributes to the church's mission.

Stay around. One of my professors in seminary said, "It takes three years for a congregation to know a pastor, another two for them to love him, and then another two for them to trust him."

Most pastors give up too soon. If their visions aren't executed within three years, they move on "to some church that will appreciate me."

It's trite but true: the failure of local church vision can often be traced to a string of abbreviated pastorates. Stability enhances the chances of vision's success.

The reality of God

Surely vision is important. Without it, the Bible says, the people perish.

But the longer I'm in ministry, the more I'm convinced it's important to face and accept reality. For it's in the reality of church life—even its painful limitations—that we grow.

Several years ago we kicked off a campaign to raise money for a new facility. Shortly thereafter, the bottom dropped out of the Detroit economy. The automotive market slumped, and many people attending our church lost their jobs. Our timing couldn't have been worse. Not surprisingly, the final pledges came up short—25 percent short. The reality of the economy had taken a huge bite out of our vision.

But we plunged ahead anyway, and I spent a few sleepless nights worrying about our financial future.

Because the economy was so lousy, however, builders all across Michigan were hungry for work and scrambled to bid on our project. The competition drove down the bids, and, as a result, the final cost ended up being 25 percent lower than our projections. It matched our 25 percent shortfall!

It was clear who had engineered the final outcome. The lesson was not lost on our church: the greatest reality affecting our vision is always God.

10

Clarifying the Pastor's Role

For the sake of an effective and growing ministry,
I needed to function as an initiating leader.

—Larry Osborne

N avigating my way through unfamiliar streets, my thoughts darted
between the task at hand—finding a pancake house at the edge
of town—and the opportunities ahead of me as the new pastor of a
small, Southern California church.

After eight years as a youth pastor and assistant pastor, I was excited by the challenge. As I pulled my Toyota into the restaurant's
parking lot, I was full of ideas, energy, and enthusiasm. The chairman
of our board had been in Europe while I candidated and was called,
but at this pancake house we finally would have the chance to get
acquainted.

After initial pleasantries, the chairman asked me what I had in
mind for the church. For thirty minutes, I shared my dreams and
vision.

When I finished, he leaned across the table. "Son," he said, "don't
get too many fancy ideas. You just preach and pray. We'll run the
church. And don't dig your roots too deep, either, because it's a good
idea to move on every three or four years."

I was stunned. Based on the interviewing process, I'd assumed
people were looking to me to set the direction for our ministry. But
it was painfully obvious that as far as he was concerned, I was an
employee, not a leader. And something told me his opinions weren't
to be taken lightly. Maybe it was the three offices he held: board
chairman, treasurer, and finance elder.

What's my role?

Driving home, I knew we had a serious problem. Each of us saw himself as occupying the same role, the initiating leader.

Many, if not most, leadership teams experience such role confusion at one time or another, particularly when there's a new group of lay leaders or a new pastor has been brought onto the scene.

I asked myself questions like: *Am I supposed to be the leader, taking charge, setting the agenda for ministry? Am I supposed to be the church's employee, waiting for orders? Or am I the chaplain, carrying out the spiritual duties assigned by the board without getting involved in the decision-making process?* All my instincts told me that for the sake of an effective and growing ministry, I needed to function as an initiating leader. But before this could happen, the board and I needed to answer three key questions.

Whose church is it?

When a pastor finds, as I did, that some of the lay leaders don't want him to lead, it usually indicates that they see him as an outsider, a hired hand to take care of spiritual chores. And no one who cares a lick about his church is going to hand it over to an outsider.

Obviously, a church doesn't belong to anyone. It's the Lord's alone. But there is a legitimate sense in which people speak of a church as "their church." Those who have poured significant time, money, and energy into a local congregation rightfully feel a sense of ownership. After all, they have demonstrated love and concern for it.

A new pastor usually has an easy time leading these people—as long as he leads them along the same road. But let him (or her) suggest a change in direction, and he'll quickly learn how little real leadership he's been granted. It doesn't matter if the changes are significant or minor; people will soon start asking, "What's he trying to do to *our* church?"

How important that pronoun is! Until the leaders are convinced it is as much my church as theirs, they will not let me function as their leader. A respected, influential, and honored outsider, perhaps, but an outsider nonetheless.

To overcome this, pastors need two things: time, and a personal commitment to that local body.

There isn't much we can do about the passage of time. And exactly how much time is needed depends on factors such as the age of the church, the length of the previous pastorate, and our age in relation to the other leaders' ages.

But demonstrating commitment to the church is totally up to us. Until the board members are convinced the pastor is as committed to the church as they are, they won't let him lead.

Perceptions are sometimes more important than reality. When we came to the church, my wife and I were committed to the body and the community for the long haul, for better or for worse. We often said as much during the candidating process. Yet, even after I had been around long enough to expect trust and tenure, I found some board members still resisting my leadership role.

Why? Because no matter what I said, their past experiences led them to believe I wouldn't stick around. Our board chairman, for example, had seen many a pastor come and go during his years of committee and board work. And since our church was small and struggling, and I was young and "on my way up," it's no wonder he was hesitant to turn over the reins. In his position, I would have been, too.

The board members had to see me demonstrate my commitment with my finances, my use of time, and my decision to stay with the church even when opportunities to move came along.

Lay leaders may give lots of other reasons for resisting a pastor's leadership, but the real issue is usually a concern that he isn't as committed to the long-term ministry of the church as they are.

Frankly, they are often right. When a tough crisis comes, many pastors bail out. One denominational study found a pastoral crisis occurred every year and a half. Not coincidentally, pastors from this same group moved on an average of every eighteen to twenty months. We may speak of a calling, but if our resumés reveal something that looks strangely like a career track, our lay leaders will know it.

Obviously, many pastors can't stay for the long haul, due to personal, geographical, or even denominational constraints. That's okay as long as we don't usurp the authority and leadership of those who will be there for the long run. If, for whatever reason, we know our stay will be short, we need to let someone else take on the role of primary, initiating leader. A more appropriate role for us might be that of an influential consultant.

Aaron, for example, serves in a denomination that moves him to a new parish every three to five years. He sees no reason to battle for the reins; he knows he would lose. So when he arrives at a new church, he quickly tries to find out who the real power brokers are. Then he pours his life into theirs. He knows that long after he's gone, they'll still be running the show, so he tries to influence rather than lead.

Pastors who want to take the responsibility of strong leadership have to give up the privilege of loose commitment. Only adequate time and our demonstrated commitment will help boards see that the church is not only theirs, but also ours.

Who is best qualified to lead?

Even if the pastor is as committed to the church as the rest of the board is, most lay leaders will want to know why the pastor should be the leader. Why not the chairman of the board, another layperson, or the entire board working together?

The answer is easy. In most cases, the pastor is best qualified to lead, not necessarily by virtue of age, intelligence, spirituality, or force of personality—for many board members can surpass their pastor in these areas—but by virtue of two key factors: time and training.

As a full-time pastor, I'm immersed in the day-to-day ministry of the church. Unlike any of my board members, I'm thinking about our problems and opportunities full time. I have the time to plan, pray, consult, and solve problems.

To lead, a person needs to know the organization inside out—how the parts fit together and how each will be affected by proposed changes. And that takes time, lots of it. In all but the smallest churches, it can't be done on a spare-time basis. In a church with a multiple staff, Lyle Schaller claims, it takes between fifty and sixty hours a week.

Not that our board members are incapable of leading an organization. That's what a number do for a living. But they do it on a full-time basis. None would think of trying to do it in his or her spare time. Yet that is exactly what happens in a church where the board or a powerful lay leader tries to take on the primary leadership role.

I also have a decided advantage when it comes to training. Like most pastors, my formal education and ongoing studies have equipped me specifically to lead a church. Add to that a network of fellow pastors and church leaders, and I have a wealth of information from which to draw. When a church faces a tough situation or golden opportunity, the pastor is the one most likely to have been exposed to a similar situation. If not, he'll usually know where to find out what the experts recommend.

By contrast, most board members are limited in their exposure to other ministries. They don't have the time to read the literature. And their network of experts is usually limited to a previous pastor or two. Because the church is spiritually centered, volunteer-run, and educationally focused, it's different from any other organization, and, as a rule, the pastor has more training in how to lead it than anyone else.

Are there exceptions? Certainly, but that's the point: they are *exceptions*. A friend tried to model his church after one with an incredibly strong and competent group of lay leaders. In his model church, the pastor simply prayed, taught, and counseled, while the elders took care of everything else. There was no need for strong pastoral leadership, he told me, if you picked the right people and discipled them properly. But he failed to notice that the key elders in his model church were self-employed and independently wealthy. They had all the time in the world to lead, and they attended seminars and seminary classes and read in their spare time.

His elders, on the other hand, all had jobs that called for fifty to sixty hours a week of their time. They had neither the time nor the training to take a strong leadership role. As long as my friend waited for the elders to take charge, the church floundered.

What about pastors who feel they aren't cut out to take a strong leadership role?

In a smaller church, a key layperson might be able to fill the role. While it's not the ideal (due to the time and training constraints we've just looked at, as well as the problems it might create for the next pastor, should he want to take back the reins), it sometimes has to be done if the church is going to move ahead.

A staff member might be another option. I know one church where the associate pastor was a stronger leader than the senior pastor, so the senior pastor let him lead. They had known each other for a long time, and they had a great deal of mutual trust and respect, so it worked well for them.

One thing won't work: The pastor can't be a Dr. Jekyll/Mr. Hyde leader, someone who abdicated leadership and later jumps in to take over. That only confuses, embarrasses, and annoys the people who have been pushed aside in the attempt to rescue the situation.

In short, the role of primary leader needs to be filled on a protracted basis, and usually the pastor is the best person to fill it.

Can a strong leader be controlled?

Before being allowed to take a strong leadership role, most pastors have to clear one more hurdle: the fear of domination. It doesn't matter how committed or qualified a pastor might be, his or her leadership will be resisted if people think it smacks of domination.

Most people fear a dictatorship, even a benevolent one. Nearly everyone has a horror story of a strong leader gone bad. And the fear is even greater in churches, like mine, that have a heritage of congregational government. To some folks, strong leadership and domination are synonymous. Before they'll let a pastor lead, they have to be thoroughly convinced that appropriate checks and balances are firmly in place.

As far as I'm concerned, those fears are justified. I know my sinful nature too well to want *carte blanche*. I've committed myself to follow three key guidelines—not only to keep me in line but also to allay the fears of those who are most suspicious of a strong leader.

1. *I present first drafts, not final proposals.* I don't mean that I offer half-baked ideas or suggestions off the top of my head. My first drafts are carefully thought out and forcefully presented. But I don't confuse them with God's final revealed will on a subject. That's something the board and I will determine together.

It's easy for a strong leader to make it sound as if every idea he has came directly from God, completely developed, needing nothing but the board's approval. But that puts the board in an awkward position—not fellow leaders seeking to know God's will, but arbiters passing judgment on God's ideas. When that happens, boards that hate conflict become a rubber stamp. Those that fear domination dig in and become adversaries.

When Don sought to lead his board, for example, he presented his ideas as straight from the Lord. Fearing domination, some of the board members began to resist his leadership. Even when they might otherwise have agreed with his proposals, they put up a fight. It was the only way they knew to keep him from taking total control.

In Don's eyes, the board was carnal. After a few years, he left to go to a church where people were more open to God's leading. But he soon found the same thing happening again.

Sadly, the resistance wasn't so much to Don's ideas as to his style. If he had offered the same ideas as first-draft proposals, many of them would have been supported.

2. *I keep no secrets from the board.* When I keep something from the board, perhaps because of it's sensitive nature, I'm putting them at a decided disadvantage. If they make a different decision than they would have with all the facts, they've been duped and manipulated.

For instance, I used to see no reason why the board needed to know the details of the spiritual and moral struggles our people went through. That was privileged communication between pastor and parishioner. But when it came to making decisions about people, the board and I had two sets of information.

I now ask most people who come to me for help if I can share the situation with the elders if I need to. I'm not the least bit apologetic. If it's a significant issue, I simply say, "The elders need to know about this. Can I tell them?" Almost everyone says yes. If not, I honor their request, but I also suggest they go to someone else for counsel because the elders and I jointly shepherd the flock, and we can't do our jobs if we keep secrets from one another.

To my surprise, no one has ever gotten upset or angry or left the church over this. In fact, most folks seem to appreciate it.

That doesn't mean I share every gory detail or all the little problems that arise, but I have permission to share information the board needs to know in order to make wise decisions.

I learned the importance of this guideline the hard way. During my third year at the church, I found myself accused of misleading and manipulating the board. Though my motives were pure, I stood guilty as charged.

We had hired a staff member who wasn't working out. During his first year, I received numerous complaints about his failure to follow through on plans and commitments. I kept the comments to myself, figuring it was my role to be a staff advocate. But before long, the board heard some complaints on their own. At a later budget meeting, a couple of elders suggested we let this staff member go. During the discussion, I made no mention of the calls I'd received or my own growing frustration. Instead, I pointed out the good things he had done (and there were many). We ended up giving him a raise!

But, a year later, I realized things weren't going to work out. Along with the other problems, now the staff member and I weren't getting along. So I went to the board and told them I thought we should make a change. They were perplexed. How could I defend his work one year and ask for his release the next? When I explained what really had been going on, some board members became indignant. Why hadn't they been informed before?

The truth was I didn't trust them to deal with the information. I was afraid they might overreact. But that only revealed the hollowness of my claims to believe in a leadership team. I had taken on the role not of a strong leader but a manipulator. I promised myself it would never happen again.

3. I follow the board's advice. Some people confuse leadership with infallibility. They assume that submitting to others means abdicating their own leadership role.

Jim is a case in point. Whenever his board resisted an idea or asked him to go in another direction, he found a way to get around their advice. It never occurred to him that God might want him to follow the board's direction. It's no surprise that Jim constantly complained about his board's unwillingness to follow his lead. What he called *leadership*, they called a refusal to cooperate. They never did develop a relationship of trust.

I've committed myself to follow the board's advice not only because I want to avoid the resistance that comes with a domineering leadership style, but also because I want to be a wise leader. Both life and Scripture have taught me that wisdom is found in heeding counsel, even when I think it's wrong.

Even when I'm right on an issue, I can be wrong on the timing. Often, the Lord has used the board's hesitancy as an impetus to slow me down. For instance, the board's caution caused me to move much more slowly with changing our worship music from traditional to contemporary. The switch was accomplished without even a minor church fight because it was done at the right time and at the right pace. Submitting to their will, rather than looking for a way to get around it, has kept many a great idea from premature birth.

There are only two circumstances under which I wouldn't submit to the board's direction. First, if they wanted me to violate what I understood to be the clear teaching of Scripture, as happened to one pastor whose board wanted to financially support an organization that was pro-abortion. Second, if they asked me to disobey what I understood to be the clear and unmistakable voice of the Lord. In the last nine years that's happened only once.

I was pushing for us to hire someone from within the body to fill an associate pastor position. While he was a gifted and anointed man of God, at that time he lacked a seminary education and had never worked in a church. Understandably, some of the board members were hesitant; they wanted to hire someone who had been around the block before.

But one night, driving home from a meeting, I felt God made it absolutely clear to me that we were supposed to hire Mike. It was one of those supernatural moments when you know beyond a shadow of a doubt that God has spoken. So I went to the board and told them, "I strongly feel that God wants us to hire Mike."

Some of them were taken aback, but they didn't argue. "Fine," they said, "we'll present him to the congregation."

It turned out to be one of the most important decisions we've made. Within months, even those who had voiced the most concern over his qualifications were singing his praises. Yet I'm sure the board never would have gone along with me if I hadn't followed their direction previously, even when it differed from mine.

I've found the more successful and experienced we become as leaders, the easier it is to ignore those who disagree. But anyone who's tempted not to follow the board's advice should consider the options. If he is lucky, the board members will dig in their heels, providing a check against tyranny. If he's not, they'll let him have everything he wants, a fate much worse than staunch resistance. Sooner or later, he'll make a terrible decision, and there will be no one to stop him.

Research has shown that strong pastoral leadership is a key ingredient in a healthy and growing church. But it can't be demanded or taken. It has to be granted. The board needs to be convinced that (1) we are committed to the church, (2) we are qualified to lead, and

(3) we desire to lead, not dominate.

Addressing these three issues as questions, and thoughtfully answering them, will help lead us to more effective pastor-board relationships.

11

Understanding the Three Church Systems

God values the means over the end.

—Fred Smith

This is a very personal opinion that comes from observing and participating in many churches for more than fifty years: Most churches are run on the poor human system, a kind of system with which you'd run a marginal business.

There are two other systems with which churches can operate: the good human system, and the spiritual system. Only the last is the one on which the church of Christ should be run.

Poor human system

In a marginal church you have a "Mom and Pop" operation, and both "Mom and Pop" are tired, harassed, and limited. One may serve different functions than the other, sometimes not even properly classified functions. Sometimes Mom is a better financier than Pop, so she handles the cash register. Pop may have more energy than Mom and so when he's on the premises, he keeps the store open longer. He may sit at the front door while she sits at the back, or they may reverse it.

I see churches run this way.

The pastor and his wife are running a "Mom and Pop" operation. The church will not pay Mom, although they expect her to work. She runs the missionary society, helps with the catering, makes calls with Pop, and usually plays the organ. If she's really strong, she may teach a class and even quietly help him prepare the sermon. Though she is not paid, she comes under the same review as "Pop." These operations never grow very big because Mom and Pop have to see to everything and do everything.

Some insidious things usually start to happen. Mom and Pop often learn to like this management style and they become attached to the location, or at least they don't know of another place to go. And, being human, security becomes important to them. If Pop isn't the greatest preacher on earth, then the people he invites in to preach have to preach worse than he does—Mom's going to see to that! This is so human that we can quickly appreciate it and understand it.

Now, what happens? Mom and Pop inadvertently form a small clique. They want control of who is on the board of deacons, who is doing everything—even the janitoring—so the janitor will be sure to come and tell them what he heard from the members who didn't know he was listening. This control system is initiated out of a desire for security. It is one of the most limiting factors that can exist in an organization. Directly or indirectly, many smaller churches are controlled by Mom and Pop, and you'll find they come in varying degrees of attractiveness. Sometimes Mom and Pop are pretty hard to get along with; sometimes they're great; sometimes they fight with each other; sometimes they are a wonderful team.

The poor human system of administration has nothing to do with doctrine, which can be anything from super-fundamentalist to liberal. The poor human system is a management style, a style that can be spotted the moment you walk in the front door. Pop leads the singing, makes the announcements, prays the prayer, preaches the sermon, pronounces the benediction, and runs down the aisle to shake hands with the people at the door. He does everything—just like a small business owner—because it is *his* little operation. It's the only system he knows. And God bless Mom and Pop! A vast number of Christians would not be blessed if they did not exist.

I've often wanted to sit down with a Mom and Pop team and say, "Do you know there's another system? Do you know there's a way to do all this and not work yourself to death?"

Laypeople help in perpetrating this human system. They enjoy the familiarity with Mom and Pop. It helps them know their place in the congregational mix. They like the paternalistic, benevolent feel that comes from Mom and Pop, and they develop their own form of clout by being part of Mom and Pop's personal family.

We have to be careful when we talk about the poor human system in a church. Poor human system doesn't mean poor Christian experience. Some of the finest, most meaningful Christian experiences one can possibly have will be found in a church run by poor human administration. This is true because there is no system where humans are able to accomplish what only God can do.

Good human system

The key to a good human system is a dynamic leader. This is a person who could make it in business, ministry, or almost anything. He or she has that rare combination of abilities to preach, teach, and administer. When I say good human system, I'm talking about good human management, the kind that can be learned through an MBA program.

Good human managers are organized and understand organization. They understand human nature. For example, Napoleon's strength was that he understood what men would do in war. A good human system preacher understands what people will do in a religious context as well as in a human context. Thus he knows how to motivate them. A good human leader understands that any successful operation is run by a small oligarchy, and that the oligarchy is controlled by one person. Egotism plays a big part in any human system.

The leader understands how things get done. He doesn't argue with it or philosophize about it; he accepts it. He isn't always apologizing, "Well, I hate to get things done this way, but . . ." He genuinely believes that he knows the way to get things done, and he sees it happen time and time again. He knows how to utilize people's strengths and buttress their weaknesses. He knows that people don't essentially change. People enthusiastically do what they can do well, and they drag their feet on what they can't do well.

For example, the good human system requires that you divide work into its logical parts. Then, you put somebody in charge who has the capability of doing it. When the good human leader starts using a new person, he always *assigns* rather than *delegates* to him. Assigning means telling him what you want, what time you want it, and how you want it done. And you expect him to do it himself while you watch the task get done. As you develop experience with this person, you find there are certain things you can delegate to him. Delegating is the second step; you simply tell him what problem you'd like to have solved, and he develops and implements the solution. *But you must have working experience with somebody in order to move from assignment to delegation.* I've seen people who bypassed the assignment process, delegated prematurely, and then wondered why the delegation system didn't work. We have all seen new Christians, particularly wealthy or famous ones, hurt by overuse before they mature—God can wait for them to mature; it's the rest of us who get overanxious to use them in our programs.

Motivation in the good human system is identical to the motivation used in any other successful human process. Participation, recognition, rotation, the feeling of belonging, moving up through the ranks, one title after the other—all of these principles are the same anywhere.

A person gets tired of teaching one grade level, so you move him to another grade level so he won't lose interest in teaching. If a person's tired of being on one committee, you put him on another committee to keep him excited. Also, you protect the organization by rotation. You keep someone from sitting in a job until he thinks he owns it (squatters).

With a good system you must set up feedback networks. You must find your troublemaker and remove him. However, the good human system leader never goes head to head with him. You develop people whose specialty is removal procedures. In business they are called hatchetmen. Transferred to the church, this process takes on more of a spiritual tone. It's like a hive. The queen might want a drone removed, but she never stings the drone. The other bees do. The whole transaction may be couched in very pious tones, involving even public prayer.

Privately, the men I know in the good human system are very candid with their close associates. However, they take a long time to move a person into the inside group. I noticed that former Texas governor John Connally said, "I have very few close friends and I take a long time to make one." What he may be saying is, "There are parts to my life or organization I don't want anyone to see until I trust them."

Good human leaders are lonely, but they don't necessarily try to avoid loneliness; they accept it as part of the price. I mentioned this one time to the president of an architectural firm, and he said, "You've just identified all my problems. Because I hate to be lonely and I'm always telling my associates about my half-baked plans, bad things begin to happen to me." He didn't realize that everyone who would be helped by his half-baked plan began to support it, and everyone who would be hurt by it started to work against it—before it was formulated! Confusion and polarization were born out of his desire to talk.

In the good human system, great leaders appear open but are often closed. In fact, in the good human system, hypocrisy is often a requirement. This is one of the reasons I do not feel it is a system that God would prefer to use. For example, if the leader wanted Deacon Smith removed, he would publicly shed great tears about the "trouble" in the body, and how the Lord had helped him to identify this problem, and how the Lord needed to help him help these "people." Invoking the Lord is a smoke screen. It is the "good" human system working in its best and worst fashion. And this is the hypocrisy that bothers me.

But keep in mind that I'm convinced God's going to use whatever system is around. I think this is part of his sovereignty. I also think it is part of his humor. Remember the old saw, "God can use any kind of vessel except a dirty one"? Well, from my experience, that is the only kind he can use. We are sinners.

As an aside, there are certain principles I have accepted that have given me a kind of relaxation about these matters. I am convinced of the sovereignty of God. God doesn't need me; God loves me. This is so different from human ways because we love only people or things we need. God doesn't *need* us and *still* loves us. That's another thought too big for my mind. It can be understood only by my heart. When I really believe in the sovereignty of God, and the fact that God doesn't need me or anybody else, and that his plan is going to be ultimately successful, it gives me a relaxation that cancels a lot of fear and anxiety.

People inevitably say, "Well, how are you going to get God's work done? How are you going to motivate people to evangelize?" You see, they're humanizing. What is really being said is that God's work cannot be done any way except by the human plan. It's part of our love of legalism; it's part of our humanizing of God; it's part of our lack of belief in the sovereignty of God.

The motivations in the good human system are absolutely human. The politics are human. You bring in the people that you can count on. You never let a person into the inner circle until you have his vote in your pocket. You never take a chance on a person who might vote on an issue as he sees it. The system admits a person who will question the issue but is sure to vote with the group.

There is always a subtle relationship between motivation and manipulation in effective human leadership. Motivation is moving along together in *mutual* advantage. Manipulation is moving along together for *my* advantage. If I were going to write a book on motivation and expected it to be a big seller, I would title it, "How to Get People to Do What I Want Them To." It wouldn't be about motivation; it would be about manipulation. Motivation is letting people recognize joint interest and then moving with them toward that mutual interest. In the spiritual system, you only need motivation. In the good human system, often manipulation and motivation are combined.

It all boils down to this: we value the end over the means. God values the means over the end. His purpose for us isn't that we "succeed." His purpose is that we mature, and we mature by the process. Therefore, the process must be pure.

But man doesn't see it this way. Man says the end is a successful church. The end is numbers, the end is respect, the end is "stars for the crown." And in all of these varying concerns about the end, we become careless about the means, because we don't recognize that the means is the method by which God is developing us. His end is our maturity, not our "success."

For example, if you ask any pastor, "Will money make any difference in the hereafter?" he will say no. And yet in subtle, almost subconscious ways, many pastors will snuggle up to the rich in the church because they represent the means to achieve certain ends. I can almost hear some rich person say, "Pastor, will my wealth make any difference in the hereafter?"

"Absolutely not."

If the rich were open enough, they would then ask, "Then why does it make so much difference here in the church if not in the hereafter?"

I believe God wants to get us as close to maturity as he possibly can. Here in America we are basing a great deal of our Christian success on the good human system—a system taken right out of industry and entertainment. In many cases ministers could be replaced with non-Christian executives. This scares me.

You watch a human system leader and he will often slowly start to satisfy his ego off of the organization instead of sacrificing his ego to the organization. He eventually comes to that dangerous turning point where he goes from cause-orientation to self-orientation. When he begins his leadership he may be very cause-oriented, but as he sees the cause prosper, he starts to embezzle from the cause—either praise, credit, position, or money. The things that should have gone to God he starts to take. His actions say, "I'm motivating these people to bring these things to the altar; therefore I ought to have a little of it. I ought to get a commission."

Once he starts this process his commission begins to climb, and soon he has gone from one percent to 15 percent to 50 percent. In extreme cases, he finally says, "Well, God really doesn't need it, and since I'm God's man, I'll just take it all." Thank God these people are few in number.

The human system is built on ego. For example: It almost always removes time for meditation and time for God. When you talk to many of these human system leaders, they seriously and sincerely decry their need for more time to personally pray and study the Bible. They study the Bible to preach, but they don't study it in order to live. These leaders have a great tendency to never find this kind of time because of "the system." They have committees to attend and meetings to run. Have you ever noticed how these people have a great dramatic sense for appearing at every committee meeting as though it were the Second Coming? They have this sixth sense for dropping in and blessing the place with their presence.

The people of India have a word—*darshan*—that blesses where the spiritual leader stands, and the people walk under his shadow. The human system leader has many ways of doing this. Have you ever heard someone say, "At three this morning, I awoke and the presence of God was upon me and God was saying to me . . ."?

You see, everyone who hears this tends to think, "Stupid me, I was sound asleep. No wonder this man is a man of God—he's talking to God at three in the morning." This is a means of establishing authority.

Or he says, "I am convinced that building this edifice to God is God's will." And the followers meekly set in marble the date and the name of the pastor. And if that doesn't get the job done, they'll also chisel in the committee names. You can go to the airport and find the same thing. Good human leadership qualities always leave the same identifying marks, whether they be found in industry, politics, or the church.

The thing in the human systems that we're most proud of, we should be the most ashamed of. In the first century it was impossible to unite thousands of Christians in one body and fail to revolutionize—not a city, not a state, but a country. The very fact that we can proudly put thousands of born-again people together and not make much more than a ripple on the life of a neighborhood shows our weakness, not our strength. What is our pride should be our shame.

Spiritual system

While the good human system is based upon a dynamic, highly motivated, competent leader, the spiritual system is built *around*—not *upon*—a shepherd whose purpose is to develop mature Christians—not a facility, a memorial, or a human organization. He looks at a facility as helpful but not vital. Organization is part of the process—for himself as well as for the flock. In human systems the individual leader doesn't tend to mature spiritually because his purpose mitigates against spiritual maturity. In the maneuvering and the manipulations and the passing out of the accolades, the human system leader is forced to claim more spiritual maturity than he has.

But the leader of the spiritual system is different. By definition, he is not an administrator. He's a shepherd. The shepherd is involved in administration, but it's one of the functions of the church—not his personal function. He doesn't train the sheep to walk in tens and twenties or by age groups with the separation of men and women because he knows that isn't too important. He knows how many sheep there are, and he is prepared to take drastic action if one is missing. But his function does not revolve around personal power. A function that is saturated with responsibility is very different from a function that is saturated with power.

A pastor told me he was going to Africa with his staff, and I asked him how many he was going to take. He said, "All of them. All the personnel—eleven ministers." I asked, "Who's going to run the church?" He said, "The same laypeople who are running it when we're here."

His job wasn't to run the church. His job was to minister to people. I don't know of very many human systems that could stand the strain of every paid worker being gone for six weeks. The place would fold up.

The spiritual system utilizes people by their gifts. Its function is ministry and its object is maturation. Spiritual system leaders push the dynamics of growth and leadership toward their people for the people's benefit, rather than pull from the people the dynamics of "growth and leadership" that will ultimately benefit themselves.

If I were pastor of a church I would have to take as my first concern the spiritual vitality of the leadership. I would try to see that the lay leaders took seriously what we together claimed to profess. If I saw that they did not take it seriously—and I don't think it's very difficult to find out whether a person takes faith seriously—then I would see it as my task to individually help them. I would not pour guilt on them, because I've become convinced that I can make a man feel dirty, but only the Spirit can make him want to be clean. I would make every effort to help each one come to a genuine belief in the hereafter and the judgment of God, and the availability of God.

The late Ray Stedman, pastor of Peninsula Bible Church in Palo Alto, California, used to do something that I never understood until recently. The elders board would make no major decision until they got absolute unanimity. Not a majority vote, but a unanimous vote. I told him that was totally impractical. Then I started to see what was happening. Think of the tremendous responsibility of being the only person who kept something from being done. If you really believe in the judgment of God and the hereafter, and this belief affects your day-to-day relationship with God, you will take your lay leadership quite seriously. So I see a totally new reason for this kind of decision making I had never seen before.

I think Ray did it because he felt it was scriptural, but I see the practical reality. It wouldn't work if the people didn't have a spiritual vitality, because they would get a great satisfaction out of having the power to stop the whole process. Here, instead of having the right to stop it, they have the *responsibility* for stopping it. It's a totally different dynamic.

As a pastor I would also ask the lay leaders to be monitors of my spiritual vitality. I can't assume, because I'm the pastor, that I will always have spiritual vitality. I would appreciate it if one of my leaders came to me and said, "Pastor, I sense that you're a little low. I came to pray with you. May I read Scripture with you?"

For your lay leaders to talk to you about your spiritual vitality, and you to talk to them about theirs—that would be the heart of a successful church operated on a spiritual basis.

If we really believed the church belonged to God, we wouldn't want to "bottom line" it. But because we really believe it belongs to both God and us, we want to numerically evaluate it. We want to see how we're doing so we can be proud of it. We all know the temptation of figures. I've never met anyone in religious life who underestimated numbers pertaining to his organization. It's an accepted practice to puff a little air into the numbers.

Wouldn't it be different to hear a preacher say, "I want a church whose size will be determined by the maturity of the individual members"? It would mean that he has control of his ego. He can't have his eye on the big church or the bishop's job. Both pastors and laypeople have become so busy and so traditional and so habit-bound that we don't stop and ask, "Is this God's or is it mine? Am I treating it as God's or am I treating it as mine? Am I motivated by ministry, or am I motivated by desire and human ambition?"

When I read Ray Stedman's book *Body Life*, I didn't think it was a complete statement of what went on. While riding with Ray back to an airport I said, "You left the heart out of *Body Life*. What you have written won't work."

Naturally Ray was surprised and he said, "I tried to be honest." You couldn't make Ray defensive, which to me is one of his saintly qualities.

"What you have left out is what most of us can't do," I told him. "You have gained control of your ego. And without control of the ego, the Body Life system won't work."

I don't think it would have disturbed Ray if he were to be called into business or medicine or anything else. I think he could have walked away from Peninsula Bible Church and not expected them to build a big building and name it the "Stedman Memorial Auditorium."

I have a suspicion that at some time in Ray's life he dedicated his ego to God. This is not to say Ray wasn't human. But I believe he came to the place of saying, "This ministry is God's."

12

Rising From a Glorious Past

*"You took a big risk," somebody told me. But it would
have been a greater risk to do nothing.*

—Roger Standing

D escending the steps from the platform, I sighed in relief. My first
Sunday as the heir to a portion of history was over. As I made my
way to the door, I again took in my new surroundings. The imposing
Victorian preaching house, the three-quarter gallery, the labyrinth of
narrow corridors and stone stairwells were daunting. Beyond all that,
the 125 years of accumulated evangelical witness was intimidating.
Many denominational worthies had preceded me as pastor.

Not the least of my spiritual ancestors was the founder of the
church, James Archer Spurgeon, whose china bust looked on stoi-
cally while I prayed before the service with church leaders. James
Archer was also associate pastor at the Metropolitan Tabernacle, pastored by his more famous brother, Charles Haddon Spurgeon.

My first weekend as Spurgeon's heir had been hectic. A welcome
service the previous day (complete with a busload of friends from
our former church), our homesick young children, and a full slate of
Sunday preaching activities made me eager to get home so I could
enjoy a cup of tea.

At the door I said farewell to the last worshiper and then stepped
back into the sanctuary. What would the future hold? I wondered. I
had no ideas, no schemes, no ten-point plan for growth in a downtown church. I knew God had called me to this place, but the inex-
orable decline in numbers for the past seventy years had left the
church a shadow of its former self.

The last upsurge had been in the 1950s under the ministry of a pulpit giant whose preaching had begun to fill the gallery again. But those days were gone. The area around the church had changed as well. Large-scale immigration had seen many West Indian families move into the area. To the credit of the church, the immigrants had been welcomed, and they now made up around a third of the congregation. Indeed, the members' roll contained two dozen nationalities.

The challenge was not to recapture the past, but to move into the future. But how? That was too big a question to answer after such a heavy weekend. I chose instead to go home to tea and football.

Seeking a vision

My questions returned later that week, however, when I recalled my Sunday evening sermon. I had preached from Habakkuk on the importance of having a vision—a theme I had used frequently during my days of hit-and-run itinerant ministry. Now, with a fresh set of pastoral responsibilities, I needed to find appropriate and practical ways to express a vision.

I knew that a new pastor couldn't make any grand pronouncements of a newly discovered vision. I couldn't impose my agenda on this church. They had lived with the fruit of the initial vision long before I had come on the scene. I wondered what I could say to our church leaders.

At my first deacons' meeting, I told how my sermon had affected me and how I longed to discover what God wanted for the future of the church. (What Mr. Spurgeon would have thought, I do not know. The china bust was as impassive as ever.) Our leaders, though, listened with interest. Before I accepted their call, they had impressed me with their openness to change. But now our discussions were no longer abstract. These exchanges could lead to major shifts in the life of the church.

I had determined to lead by consensus: the leaders would have to agree that changes were needed. I soon found that this approach, coupled with their desire to halt the decline, made them receptive. They had seen better days, and they did not want to continue the way they had been. They offered constructive suggestions and encouraged me to give it a go.

Gradually, and together, we found several things that helped us implement a new vision for our historical church.

Grassroots growth

The church leaders and I decided that if the people in our older church were going to own a new vision, they would have to help discover it. This would have to be a grassroots vision. Some members, however, found it hard to comprehend that we would give them a central part in this planning effort, called "Catching the Vision." Repeatedly, I explained that, like Habakkuk, we wanted to put ourselves in a position to hear what the Lord might say: "I will keep watch to see what he will say to me" (Habakkuk. 2:1, NRSV).

I preached a series about vision in the New Testament. During the evening services we studied the seven churches in Revelation, to see what God had said to other churches. Our midweek fellowship groups were assigned topics related to vision. We asked people to pray about the future of the church: What is the Lord saying to the congregation? Where is he leading us?

We printed a small brochure outlining our quest for a vision. The back page was a response sheet for people to submit their ideas of what God was saying about the direction for the church. Gradually, people became convinced that we actually wanted their input. Even more important, they sensed they were involved in hearing from God for the direction of the church.

Sifting expectations

Progress seldom comes without setbacks or obstacles to overcome. Even as our hope and expectations rose, we began to encounter challenges.

One day a member asked to see me immediately. Distraught and confused, he spilled out that his wife was involved in a three-year adulterous relationship with the previous associate pastor. Worse, she was unwilling to end the relationship.

A somber atmosphere fell over the congregation the following Sunday as they heard the news that their former associate pastor was resigning from his new church. Still, despite the sadness, we sensed God's holiness among us. "See what happens when we invite the

Lord to take charge of our future?" someone said later. "He starts to get us sorted out." That word proved to be more than an observation; it was a prophecy.

We gathered around the Lord's Table and sang Luther's "A Safe Stronghold Is Our God Still." And though the song speaks of the devil's "watching to devour us," it affirms the sovereignty of God. As the deep bass tones of the organ reverberated through the sanctuary, our hearts stirred with determination to face whatever lay ahead.

Realizing we were in a spiritual battle seemed to raise the stakes. A sense of momentum gathered, and the members began to make the process their own: this new vision would be one the Lord had given to us, not just another bright idea from the pastor. We placed a "Vision Box" at the rear of the sanctuary, and it began to fill with responses.

The thread of God's will

In January I met with a small group of leaders to begin sorting the written responses. Our buildings can be imposing and dark on a cold winter night, but we felt light in our spirits as we picked through the replies. Some people had submitted extensive, detailed plans. Others offered simply a Bible verse that had spoken to them. A few had drawn pictures they saw while in prayer. Still others shared tentative impressions they had felt.

Research by the Bible Society shows that, on average, only 16 percent of the people in any congregation in the United Kingdom are forward-looking. We received 55 responses out of about 150 active members, double that percentage.

It would not be easy to find the thread of thought winding through the responses. We decided to follow God's instructions to Habakkuk: "Write the vision; make it plain on tablets" (2:2). We pulled all the thoughts together into a nine-page summary for the leaders, which was further condensed for public distribution. The process clarified our understanding and made the vision accessible to everyone, rather than just a select inner circle.

Talking about our process later, somebody said to me, "You took a big risk." No doubt. But it would have been a greater risk to do nothing.

Still, asking the entire congregation to seek a vision from God posed two major risks:

1. We might follow a faulty vision. We would have to sort through many, perhaps conflicting, ideas. Would we be able to discern God's leading?

2. We might stir up division by rejecting an individual's personal vision. No one wants to hear that others have judged his insights to be out of touch with what God is saying. We would have to be sensitive with people.

We sought to avoid such problems by establishing some ground rules at the outset. For example, we were not to think of our individual ideas as the vision for the church; rather we were offering provisional thoughts, our impressions of what God might do. We were to see our individual contributions as part of the process that would help the whole body discover vision for the future. While we as individuals might see things a certain way, none of us could claim to be infallible. But we all could add color to the picture; the outcome would be a blending of hues. And even if one idea might run contrary to the others, it still would help us get closer to what the Lord wanted for us.

Despite such precautions, some lively discussions could not be avoided. One idea, for example, posed an extraordinary challenge. Our church sits on an unusual site—a large traffic island in the middle of a major intersection. Though we own just part of it, somebody saw a vision of the whole island with a banner around it that said, GOD'S ISLAND. Several people interpreted this to mean we were going to buy up all the real estate on the island. The idea caught the imagination of a number of people.

When we pursued that angle, however, it became apparent the cost to implement such a vision would be several million pounds. Others balked: "Even if God helps us raise those funds, is that really the best way to spend the money? Just think of all the ministry we could accomplish with that amount." Eventually, someone pointed out that while the vision could be genuine, our interpretation might be wrong. We came to see that if we faithfully served God on our corner of the island, our ministry, rather than our property, could give the traffic island the reputation that it belonged to God.

Mop-up operations

Even after our vision was written, we faced challenges. Greater numbers had joined the church than had for decades, including many new believers, and many new opportunities for ministry had appeared. Yet complaints still surfaced.

The church had had a history of poor conflict management. It had never handled differences of opinion well, often avoiding the problems rather than dealing with them. Prior to my arrival, some members had been bruised by destructive leadership styles. People were still tripping over issues that had been swept under the carpet. Though I continued to work at building trust and understanding, a few key people withdrew from the fellowship.

One day another complaint came, this time from a friend and supporter: "It's been twelve months that we've had this vision, Pastor," said this person. "But we've gone nowhere, and we're going nowhere. What are you going to do about it?"

I found my stomach tying itself in knots. I now had to defend myself to friends. Was there something wrong with me?

At times I could hardly bring myself to preach and lead worship. Long-standing differences of opinion over music and worship style intensified the pressure I felt. The vision to "grow and go" had not changed people's feelings about classical organ music or guitars and drums.

To my comments about quitting or moving on, my wife, Marion, listened patiently and pointed me back to the Lord. She prayed with me and refocused my attention. I also sought the counsel of respected leaders outside of our situation, and their support and insight encouraged me to go on. God sent blessings at just the right time to lift my spirits: a conversion here, a healing there.

I was convinced I was where God wanted me to be, but "Catching the Vision" turned out to be tougher than I had imagined. Patience was critical. Instead of expecting situations I felt were wrong to be resolved overnight, I've learned to wait for the Lord. I've learned that waiting for the vision to unfold is a normal part of the process. "If it seems to tarry," the Lord told Habakkuk, "wait for it; it will surely come" (2:3). Dealing with problems in the Lord's time is an essential part of the process of implementing a vision.

Two years after we introduced the vision, a middle-aged couple spoke to me: "We want you to know," they said, "we thought 'the vision' was one of those schemes that we'd have for a season. We had actually put it out of our minds. But now we see that everything has fallen into place, and we're excited by what the Lord is doing among us."

Measuring progress

One danger when you're seeking to move forward is that slow progress can appear to be no progress. Failing to see movement led me to frustration and impatience when, in fact, we were moving in the right direction. Now, when I look over the past three-and-a-half short years, I am amazed to realize just how many things have happened.

One big change has been in the leadership team. We've gained trust in one another and learned to listen to each other's differing viewpoints. We have found personal acceptance even when our ideas are not always accepted. And we've developed a unity of spirit about where we are and what steps we're to take. These changes have occurred even though our leadership team includes both young and old members and has both traditional and contemporary views.

Not long ago, a lady in her sixties said to me, "Roger, I've been coming to this church for many years. This used to be a white church, but now it's a black church." Florence felt a spontaneity, a sense of rhythm, and congregational participation that made her, a West Indian, feel at home—even though we're still two-thirds white, and quite British. It's clear that we've all gained some flexibility and tolerance, necessary if we want to continue catching God's vision for our historic church.

13

Pulling Weeds From Your Field of Dreams

It's not a matter of throwing out visions; it is a matter of extracting our ego from them.

—David Hansen

In western Montana, spotted knapweed, a weed imported from France, plagues some of our best agricultural areas and is moving swiftly into wilderness areas. Only sheep will eat it. Cattle, deer, and elk won't touch it. A meadow of knapweed won't support a cow. A hillside of it will not feed elk. An infestation of knapweed can destroy a hay or grain field.

Beekeepers imported the plant for its purple blossoms that produce copious nectar even during drought years. The weed is unbelievably hardy, thriving in the driest of weather. It competes unfairly with natural flora; it grows over three feet tall so it shades shorter grasses. Even if you clip it, knapweed will blossom at two inches off the ground.

Its most pernicious characteristic, however, is that knapweed is allelopathic. Knapweed roots secrete a toxic substance that stunts and even kills the plants in its vicinity.

Toxic weeds thrive in visions for ministry, too. It is just as true of spiritual tilth as it is of good dirt: "It will produce thorns and thistles for you" (Genesis 3:18). A fertile spiritual imagination is just as good at growing weeds as a crop. I've noticed at least three weeds that can flourish in my pastoral visions.

The dream weed

I love being somewhere long enough to watch kids grow up. I
love preaching through whole books of the Bible. I love watching a
church grow and change over time. I love presiding at funerals for
people I've called on and loved for a long time.

But I really dislike receiving phone calls, back to back, one from
Euodia telling me that we should have vacation Bible school in June
because that's the only time we can get any teachers, and one from
Syntyche saying that we should have VBS in August because three
years ago at a Christian educcation meeting, didn't we decide to always hold VBS in August to promote Sunday school?

What gripes me is that I know the real problem: these two don't
like each other and are playing a game to see with whom I will side.

In such moments sprouts the dream weed, a mental flash, a phan-
tasm from a subconscious reservoir of restlessness. It speaks to our
disgust with the mess of the ministry. It shows us a place of benefits
without blahs. It may be another church, another career, or just winning the lottery—my kingdom for a day without human foolishness!
And, of course, it can all be had in a moment, enjoyed in rush-hour
traffic, or in the middle of a fight at a council meeting.

The dream weed is only a dream away: "I gotta get outta here!"

I'm not naysaying daydreaming. Daydreaming can be an ally of
ministry. Put to good use, the ability to live through experiences mentally is great for running through sermons, thinking through pastoral
calls, and imagining what might be possible. God gave us the ability
to "see" things in our minds.

However, I know this: the mental ability we use for daydreams,
which God uses for visions, can be marshaled by our frustrations, our
doubts, our anger, our self-pity, and our boredom. When these emotions control our mental scenery, our field of vision fills with dream
weeds.

The dream weed is my weed of choice; I know it best. No other
weed is this much fun. At Dream Weed University, I've gotten any
number of Ph.D.s, been a professor at every seminary in the country,
and published hundreds of books and articles.

I've pastored big churches, the mythical kind where all you have
to do is hang around with a totally cool staff who do the down-and-
dirty work with all the struggling people. I've had offices where I

didn't have to answer the phone, and where three receptionists stood between me and Mr. McBlab, the parishioner with the personality disorder of critiquophilia.

Pulling the dream weed

How do you subdue such weeds? The best way is through confession and repentance. Confession is simply recognizing a false vision for what it is and speaking to God about it: "Here it is again, Lord; the old dream weed is back." Repentance is simply returning to prayer for the right thing: for people, for the church, for stamina and joy.

Other strategies help. Dream weeds are intolerant of contact with anything specific. Jesus tells us to wash one another's feet. There's nothing dreamy about that.

So I call a grump. I go out and bless a curmudgeon. I immerse myself in the details of church work. I fix the leaky toilet in the men's room. I pick up the popcorn off the floor from the Wednesday night program. We have a custodian for that. But sometimes I need to do it.

Every Sunday morning before people arrive, I sweep the outside walks as a form of metaphoric prayer. God talks to us in parables and metaphors, so I return the favor. I talk to him in a metaphor: "Lord, as I sweep this morning, help me commit myself to washing the feet of this church." Then I take the broom and go up and down the concrete walks, brushing away the gravel, dirt, and bird droppings. I'm sweeping away daydreams. As I sweep I am parabolically committing myself, before God, to care for this particular church and these particular people.

With the dream weed gone, I find a re-appreciation for my church. With my field of vision cleared, I can see that God has truly been in this place, and that he calls me to work here.

The greed weed

My fifteen-year-old son and I were hunting white-tailed deer on a local cattle ranch.

Evan was sitting quietly on a knoll overlooking a hayfield, waiting for game to appear. I sneaked around a section of cottonwood trees, willows, and brambles adjacent to the hayfield and walked through it, hoping to flush a nice buck into the field.

I didn't disturb an animal, but I got covered with burrs. I don't remember seeing the burr-bearing weeds, but when I emerged, my hunter's-orange sweat shirt was covered with spiky burrs the size of Ping-Pong balls. Sharp-pointed foxtails coated my socks; they lost no time working through the cotton into the flesh of my ankle.

Rambling through a river bottom, praying for my congregation, I hope to flush out a vision for our corporate life. I never stumble upon a burning bush. I see cottonwood trees and a red-tailed hawk. I hear wind, rushing water, and a Clark's nutcracker.

Visions come like Elijah's still small voice—gentle-whisper visions, unobtrusive projections upon my imagination. They present themselves with the utmost modesty. They don't demand faith; they inspire it. I don't propel them; they propel me. I don't need to flush them out; they flush themselves out in me and in my congregation.

When I pray for a parishioner, often I "see" the person in my mind. As I pray for people, often I see them not as they are, but as they could be. I see possibilities for them. I see what their life might become under the lordship of Christ. These little visions don't intrude or demand; they suggest and propose. They are the working capital of my pastoral calling.

Such visions are good, but opportunism clings to them like burrs. In the middle of "seeing" the building made new, the pews full, and our Sunday school bursting at the seams, I also see a mental image of a new fly rod that I could purchase with the raise I'd get if my ministry thrived. It sickens me.

When my spiritual imagination is at its best, I am also at my worst. Hedonism works its way into the fabric of my visions like foxtails into socks.

Pulling the greed weed

Too often greed sprouts are treated like playthings, harmless plants. They are not harmless. Greed was the sin of Hophni and Phinehas, the sons of Eli. They looked with "greedy eye" at the sacrifices and offerings of the people of Israel, fattening themselves on the choicest parts of the offerings. (See 1 Samuel 2:29.) Their sins brought down the house of Eli and ended their own lives.

Calling on a ninety-six-year-old blind woman who lives in a tar-paper shack doesn't present a conflict of interest. But put the same woman in a richly decorated home three times bigger than she needs, and visions of discipleship can become stuck with burrs and foxtail visions of big donations.

If the power of ministry is the love of God working in and through us, what happens to our power for ministry when we cast a greedy eye on the sacrifices and offerings? We stop seeing the person; all we see is her money.

Before I make a pastoral call on people with financial resources, I pray through my motivations vigorously and relentlessly. I have to pull the greed weeds.

When my mental landscape is congested with greed weeds, I try resetting my timetable for the things I want. Greed has a crude intolerance for delayed gratification. Greed wants it now. I want a new fly rod (they aren't cheap). So I reset my goal for getting a new fly rod by a year. We want to put new windows in the church. Not this year. We must wait. A new computer! Wait. A nice fat raise? Let the little ones build up over time.

Patience pulls greed weeds, and a patient heart is an inhospitable environment for greed weeds. Funny thing is, once the greed weeds are cleared away, love appears. The fruit of the Spirit grows best in a well-cleared field of vision.

The hero weed

An elderly lady stuffed a note into my hand as she greeted me in line after church. She winked at me. Five years later, serving a different church, I have that note taped to the window in front of my office desk. It reads: "There is no limit to the good you can do, if you don't care who gets the credit."

I don't keep that note for sentimental reasons. It's there because, like most of us, I like being a hero. I like getting credit when things go right. Maybe my sagacious friend knew it.

When we desire hero status in our churches we become allelopathic to the people who serve with us. Like that toxic weed from France, we may come off as sweet as honey, but we stunt the growth of those around us. The poison of our pride places a limit on the good that we can do, and the good that those around us can do.

My visions are saturated with my face. It is repelling and embarrassing, but I must admit it: I can take a wonderful vision and muddy it with a mental image of my getting credit.

What a glorious vision to see a little country church on the brink of closing its doors come to life! What a sad splotch of spilled ink to see myself in front of packed pews basking in the glory of being the one the people came to hear.

It's repulsive. But I can't seem to eradicate the problem. Is the answer throwing out vision? If a vision is spoiled by an ego spill, must the picture be thrown out? Can any part of a vision in which I project myself as the hero ever be from God?

Pulling the hero weed

It's not a matter of throwing out visions. It is a matter of extracting our ego from them. What pulls the hero weed is private prayer.

A parishioner was going through an especially acrimonious divorce. Of course, there were darling children involved. Of course, the couple fought over everything, including the Jimi Hendrix albums. I prayed for all parties involved, but one of them attended church regularly, so I felt for him a special pastoral responsibility.

I wanted to save the day. I felt like it was my job to go in and make a difference. I knew well how my pastoral capital would increase if I had a profound impact on this person's life and he shared it with people. I could "see" their accolades. I became more concerned with the glory of being a good pastor than being filled with love and pity for my suffering friend. That's hard to admit.

A couple of times I decided to give an afternoon of prayer to the guy. I can't sit still and pray, so I walk. Well, when I took a long walk and prayed for him, I saw myself staying away from him. The vision was odd, unusual. My impression, though vague, was that my whole responsibility was to pray and stay away. Over and over I asked, "Is this right? Am I just supposed to stay away?"

I didn't hear a voice; I just saw myself staying away. "But what if I get called on the carpet for not reaching out to him? Staying away makes me look uncaring." Fear entered in. Ultimately I obeyed the quieter picture of my staying away and just praying for the person.

My interest piqued when, after his divorce, his church attendance picked up. A year after the dust had settled, I visited the gentleman.

We talked about his divorce. As he began, a deep confidence filled his eyes. The bitterness was gone. I knew he'd lived through hell. He recalled the difficult times. He did not dismiss the pain. But he went on to tell me that whenever he was at his lowest point, for some inexplicable reason, God had always shown up.

"When I was all used up and had nothing left, God was just there. He comforted me in my very darkest hours. God has been so good to me!"

This man, who few would have mistaken for a mystic, had learned to pray. He could hardly contain himself.

I could hardly contain *myself*. I wanted desperately to shout out "I prayed for you! I prayed for you!" Thankfully I held my tongue and smiled.

Private prayer is therapy for allelopaths.

A cleared field of vision

As we pull the dream weeds, greed weeds, and hero weeds, we find a cleared field ready to produce a crop. True vision for ministry can grow.

In my mind, I can still see nails protruding from badly weathered siding. If you pounded them in, they popped back out. The eighty-year-old wood wasn't worth another coat of white paint. The sanctuary was so poorly insulated that the water in the Christmas tree stand froze every December. Of course, the water pipes froze every winter too. The windows were cracked. The ceiling tiles bore yellow-veined stains from the leaky roof. The concrete steps and sidewalks were decomposing.

I did not pray for the renovation of the sanctuary. Frozen pipes and peeling paint were the least of our problems. But as I walked through the woods praying for the church, in my mind I saw not a broken-down church building but a clean, white, renovated sanctuary. I did not realize it then, but "seeing" the renewed sanctuary was a vision. It was so modest a spiritual phenomenon that I barely took it into account.

These little visions never came as announcements, prophecies, or revelations. At no time did I feel a message had come from God to oversee the renewal of the sanctuary. I never thought that seeing a pretty building in my mind constituted a vision. But that gentle, unobtrusive Spirit-whisper became a focus for my ministry at that church.

So I never announced to the church council, "I have had a vision: Our sanctuary is going to be made brand new, and we need to start working on it right away." Fixing up the place never became an intentional goal, but, for whatever reason, at council we began to talk about the building. We never talked about my vision or anybody else's vision; we just started working away at fixing up the building.

Over nine years, little project by little project, the church was made new. We got a new roof. We applied new siding, insulated the walls, installed new exterior doors and double-paned windows. We added handicapped access. We poured concrete sidewalks and steps and painted the sanctuary walls and ceiling. We relandscaped the front yard, planted a new sign, and even insulated the crawl space under the building so the pipes wouldn't freeze.

The sanctuary is now the brilliant white building I saw in my vision. Actually, it is prettier than I thought it would be. The fulfillment exceeded the vision in beauty.

No aspect of church life is too spiritual or too material for visions. We need visions for deeper spirituality and more functional buildings, greater passion for God, steadier finances, and more effective Christian education. Seeing these ahead of time (even if not recognized as visions from God) constitutes the pastor's spiritual field of vision. We simply need to clear that field of its weeds.

PART 3

Strategizing

14

Haphazardly Intent

Pastoring in the twentieth century requires two things:
one, to be a pastor, and two, to run a church.
They aren't the same thing.

—Eugene H. Peterson

One of the worst years I ever had was in my early days at Christ Our King Church in Bel Air, Maryland. Our building was finished, and I realized I wasn't being a pastor. I was so locked in to running the church programs I didn't have time to be a pastor.

So I went to the session one night to resign. "I'm not doing what I came here to do," I said. "I'm unhappy, and I'm never at home." The precipitating event was when one of my kids said, "You haven't spent an evening at home for thirty-two days." She had kept track! I was obsessive and compulsive about my administrative duties, and I didn't see any way to get out of the pressures that were making me that way. So I just said, "I quit."

The elders wanted to know what was wrong.

"Well," I said, "I'm out all the time, I'm doing all this administrative work, serving on all these committees, and running all these errands. I want to preach, I want to lead the worship, I want to spend time with people in their homes. That's what I came here to do. I want to be your spiritual leader; I don't want to run your church."

They thought for a moment and then said, "Let *us* run the church."

After we talked it through the rest of the evening, I finally said, "Okay."

I'll never forget what happened because of that talk. Two weeks later the stewardship committee met, and I walked into the meeting uninvited. The chairman of the group looked at me and asked, "What's the matter? Don't you trust us?"

I admitted, "I guess I don't, but I'll try." I turned around, walked out, and haven't been back since. It took a year or so to deprogram myself. I do moderate the session, and I tell other committees that if they want me to come for a twenty-minute consultation on a specific problem I'll be happy to do that. But I haven't been to a committee meeting now, except in that capacity, for twelve years.

There's a line in a poem about a dog going along the road with haphazard intent. My pastoral life is now like that. There's a sense of haphazardness to it because I don't want to get locked into systems where I have to say, "No, I'm too busy to do that; I can't see you because I have this schedule." But the haphazardness is not careless; there is purpose to it. I like to keep a freedom in which I can be responsive to what's going on with my people.

For example, I've never done visitation systematically. Sometimes I'll read about someone who goes through the whole church list in a year and sticks to a rigid schedule. I've never done that. I do home visitation based on a sense of need, when I know there's something special going on in someone's life. Birth, death, loss of job, relocation, or trouble in the home are good indicators to me for a visit. I go and talk with people, listen to their problems, find out where they are, and pray with them. That's the advantage of pastoral work—it can respond to all the little nuances of community life and participate in them.

Scriptural success model

Because of their different gifts, it's all right for pastors to sharply differ in how they run churches.

I was Bill Wiseman's associate pastor in White Plains, New York. He has personal integrity and is highly skilled in all areas of pastoral work. He did more than any other person to enable me to be a pastor, especially in the administrative and managerial aspects. He runs a tight ship; things like structure and efficiency are very important to him. However, our styles of ministry contrast markedly. He now has a church of 5,000 members in Tulsa, Oklahoma, and he would go crazy running a church the way I do.

Later on, I realized my gifts were not in administration. What I really wanted to do was spend most of my time in personal ministry to my congregation. This is how the Lord has spoken to me through the Scriptures, and in our society if pastors shape their pastoral role informed by something other than the Scriptures, they can quickly feel useless.

A hundred years ago, pastors had a clear sense of continuity with past traditions. They knew they were doing work that had integrity; their life had recognized value and wholeness. Today, that's simply not true; we're fragmented into doing different things.

In the pulpit you *do* have that sense of continuity. When I'm preaching, I know I'm doing work that has continuity going back to Isaiah. I prepare sermons somewhat the way Augustine and Wesley prepared sermons. I'm working from of the same Scriptures as they did, so I don't feel third rate when I'm in the pulpit.

During the week, however, I do feel looked down upon—when I go to the hospital to visit, for example, I'm a barely tolerated nuisance. The doctor, nurse, and pastor are a part of the healing team, but people don't look at you that way. I'm an amateur, they're the experts. And, in a sense, that's true. In the modern hospital it's a different kind of healing center than anything the church has experienced, and we don't fit there—we're outsiders.

Other factors contribute to this feeling of uselessness, too. When you have serious problems with running your church, what do you do? You call up someone to come out and show you how to run a duplicating machine, or you take a course in church management. And who teaches you? Someone from the business community.

All through the week it seems we're intimidated by experts who are teaching us how to do our work—but they don't know what our work is. They're trying to make us respectable members of a kind of suborganization they're running, and as a consequence, we develop a self-image that's healthy only on Sunday. I think pastoral work should be done well, but I think it has to be done from the inside, from its own base. That base, of course, must be the Bible; that's why I immerse myself in biblical materials.

I've written five books on the Old Testament—Song of Songs, Ruth, Lamentations, Ecclesiastes, and Esther. They deal with facets of pastoral work. Song of Songs gives a model for directing prayer; Ruth is a story about visiting and counseling; Lamentations deals with grief and suffering; Ecclesiastes is an inquiry into values, the naysaying sermon; and Esther is the story of community building.

These aren't the only areas of pastoral work, but they are five important resources that provide for my pastoral ministry a great sense of continuity with traditional biblical principles. Today's pastor has to go back to similar scriptural truths. Nothing else will suffice. Modern success models can't match the effectiveness and self-worth provided by Scripture.

Strategic inefficiency

In the process of this study of Scripture, I found I really like being a pastor; pastoral work is my vocation. Through the whole process, I discovered what God has called me to do and the gifts he has given me in order to do it. In my younger years, I often found myself doing things that were not my ministry. I finally learned to say, "No, I'm not going to do that anymore." I say no often. I probably disappoint many people, mostly those in the community and in my denomination. They have expectations of me that I don't fulfill.

To work successfully this way requires mutual trust among church leaders, myself, and everyone in our congregation. The elders don't always do it the way I want them to, but when I decided I wasn't going to run the church, I also had to decide that if they were going to run it, they would have to do it their way, not mine. They listen to my preaching, are part of the same spiritual community, and know the values being created and developed; so I trust them to run the church in the best way they know how.

Sometimes I do get impatient, though, because it's not the most efficient way to run a church; a lot of things don't get done. We have had some leaders who weren't fully motivated. A congregation elects elders and deacons, and sometimes chooses them for the wrong reasons. Some are only marginally interested in the life of the church, so they have neither the insight nor the motivation to be productive. I can either give them the freedom to fail, or else step in and train people to be exactly what I want them to be. I've chosen to let them alone. My first priority is pastoral ministry, and so some other good things, such as making the administration of the church more efficient, must be left to others.

Community to me means a group of people who have to learn how to care for each other, and in one sense, an efficient organization mitigates against community—it won't tolerate you if you make mistakes. This is not the situation in the church. We have inefficiency on our church office staff, but efficiency is not nearly as important as being patient with people and drawing them into a mutual sense of ministry. It's the way we operate; everything doesn't have to be out today. If work is planned well enough, there's room for things to wait.

We had a woman who was working in a volunteer capacity coordinating several closely related programs. When she started, she was excited about it and did a good job. But as time went on, she took on a number of other things and began doing her administrative job indifferently. As her pastor, I was dealing with her on some family problems, and I felt it was important that I not criticize her administrative efforts at this time or ask her to resign. So I didn't do anything.

Matters became worse. I received many phone calls and listened to many complaints. I responded that I would like to improve the situation, but I couldn't promise anything. I kept on being a pastor to her, feeling that to keep from compromising my ministry to her, I had to let the programs suffer some poor administration that year.

Now, many pastors wouldn't have permitted that, and for their ministry styles it might have been correct for them to step in and administratively handle the situation. I'm not against that kind of efficiency, but I need to do what I'm good at. I have to pay the price of being good at certain things but not at everything.

We don't have anyone who is a full-time staff person. We have a man who has been a pastor working with us only on Sundays as a youth pastor. We also pay our choir director and organist; and we have a sexton who works about twelve to fifteen hours a week. There is no paid secretarial staff—only volunteers.

Sometimes I need people to simply answer the phone for me or telephone for me. I'll say, "Why don't you call so-and-so? She's lonely and bored; see if she can come in one day and help us." Sometimes that's just the thing needed to draw people back into a sense of ministry and community. They arrange for my home visitation from a list I give them. It's important, and they know it's important.

Price of essentials

While I'm patient with some inefficiency, I don't let the essentials slide. For several years I felt as though I was losing momentum. I quit doing many things I used to be enthusiastic about. I felt my life becoming more inward. My deepest interest is in spiritual direction, and since our community includes many psychiatrists and counselors, I quit counseling so I could spend more time alone in study and prayer.

But then I found large gaps had begun to form in my congregation's life. I had underestimated the community's needs, and I really wasn't providing community leadership. I felt my people deserved more from their pastor than what they were getting. I thought maybe I belonged in a church with a staff that could be assigned the tasks of parish programs, and I could study more and maintain a ministry of personal spiritual direction and of preaching.

I talked with a friend about this for three days. He listened thoughtfully and then said, "I don't think you need to leave, you just need somebody to be a director of parish life." The minute he said that, I thought of Judy. She's a woman of about thirty-five who came to me last spring saying she was in a transitional stage, wondering where the next challenge was for her. She had organized programs for the community, had done a superb job of administrating them, and now she was relatively idle.

When I asked her if she would be director of parish life, a big grin appeared on her face. She said, "Let me tell you a story." Her husband was an elder, and two years ago he was in the session meeting when I shared this problem about my leadership. After that meeting Don had come home and said, "You know what Gene needs? He needs you."

It took me two years to recognize that. And now Judy is at the place in her life where she is ready to assume the role of parish director. She needs to be in ministry and is filling some of the gap left by my withdrawal. I'm free to study more and be more sensitive to spontaneous needs within the congregation. In a sense, I had gone through a period of failure to discover grace.

Even if administration is not a pastor's gift, every pastor has to make sure it gets done. If you can't see to it that it does get done, you are in trouble. Pastoring in the twentieth century requires two things: one, to be a pastor, and two, to run a church. They aren't the same thing.

Every seminary ought to take their pastoral students aside and say, "Look, God has called you to be a pastor, and we want to teach you how to be a pastor. But the fact is that when you go out to get a job, chances are they're not going to hire just a pastor, they're going to hire somebody to run the church. Now, we'll show you how to run a church, and if you master what we're telling you, you can probably do it in ten to twelve hours a week. That's the price you're going to pay to be in the position of pastor."

I make sure I pay that price. I return telephone calls promptly. I answer my mail quickly. I put out a weekly newsletter, which I think is essential. When the parish newsletter comes out once a week, the people sense you are on top of things; they see their names and what's going on. It's good public relations. Every week our one-page newsletter assures the congregation that everything is under control. If you want to keep your job, people have to believe the church is running okay.

Pastor of a community

Those who choose the style of pastoral ministry that I have chosen must come to terms with how to measure effectiveness. Outward signs of ministry success—big numbers—are unimportant to me. If the search committee of a large church approached me and said, "Here's an opportunity to minister to 3,000 people, when your present congregation is only 300. Look at all the people you could be touching," my response would be simple. If you speak to 3,000 people and are not speaking out of your own authenticity, your own place where God has put you, you won't be any more effective as a servant of God. I don't think the number of people who hear you speak means a whole lot. What's important is that you do a good job wherever you are.

Some ministries are not meant to exist in a burgeoning place. There are ministries meant to be small, in small places, with a few people. Growth, certainly, but not always in terms of quantity.

Our church has grown slowly in numbers. My pastoral goals are to deepen and nurture spiritual growth in people, and to build a Christian community—not collect crowds. We could grow faster. If I did certain things we could double our membership. We could organize house-to-house visitation, advertise, bring in special speakers, create programs for the community that would tune in to some of their felt needs, or develop an entertainment-centered musical program. We could do all of those things—but we'd destroy our church.

Although we might get 350 new people that I could preach to on Sunday, I'd have to quit doing what I need to do—pray, read, prepare for worship, visit, give spiritual direction to people, develop leadership in the congregation. I have to work within the limits of my own abilities while I continue maturing in them.

When we first arrived in Bel Air, one of our goals was to develop spiritual community, and I thought it would be pretty easy. We'd get these people into our home, pray together, sing some hymns, and we'd have it. Well, it just didn't happen. It's very difficult to develop community in our country.

Then a young woman in our congregation died of cancer. She was thirty-one years old and had six children. About a month after she died, the father was discharged from his job and then lost his house. We took those kids into our home. Suddenly things started happening. Food would appear on our doorstep; people would call up and take the kids out and entertain them. It was almost as if we came to a place of critical mass. Then it just exploded, and we suddenly had community in the congregation.

It didn't fizzle out either. The hospitality increased, and people took an interest in each other. It seemed almost like a miracle, and it took just one incident to trigger it. All our earlier attempts to create community now bore fruit because of the meeting of a need that wasn't part of our strategy.

It was five years before that first incident happened to trigger community in our church. Only in the last six or seven years have I really felt community taking hold. I can now sense that I am pastor of a community of people, not just a collection of neighbors. That happened because I felt the freedom to respond in pastoral fashion to a need as it arose. It wasn't great planning. It was a pastoral response.

God can produce in us what he wishes when we are true to how he has made us.

15

Beyond the Firehouse Syndrome

If you accept the notion that a church can have a mission
(other than shepherding), then you will take on
a strategy of leveraging your time in the areas
that will bring the greatest payoff.

—Carl F. George

P astors make many decisions every day, but too often they are
handicapped because they almost inevitably think only in mor-
alistic terms: rightness versus wrongness. "What's the *right* thing to
do? What *ought* to be done?"

But there are other modes to consider: effective versus ineffective,
good versus best, safe versus risky.

I'm not dismissing the moral dimension—virtually every decision
has a moral aspect, either in its consequences or in the way the decision will be implemented. And most of us in the ministry carry an
intuitive desire to reach for the godly, to hear the words of God on
a given issue and line up with him rather than against him. But not
all church administration deals with Mount Sinai issues. Many decisions are more mundane and subtle, yet they still require thought.

Time evaluation

Of the range of decisions a pastor faces, one of the toughest ones,
in my judgment, is what to do with one's time on a daily basis. When
I ask a pastor, "Who are you going to call on this week?" and the
pastor says, "Well, I have seven sick people, a couple of appointments from the new-members class . . . and I suppose other people

will call during the week about various things. . . ."—he is basically playing fire fighter. He's waiting for the bell to ring (or the axle to squeak, or the Spirit to move). He doesn't see that there is such a thing as taking intelligent *initiative* in the area of contacts.

This same person may be very conscientious about sermon topics, laying out an annual preaching plan. He may be very intentional about selecting themes and texts. But when it comes to people, he's a shepherd waiting for the lost sheep to show up, listening for a call from the wild.

If you take the notion that a church can have a mission (other than shepherding), then you will take on a strategy of leveraging your time in the areas that will bring the greatest payoff. You'll spend it with the key contacts who have the potential to lead others. You'll seek out those who show the greatest readiness to make a decisive commitment at the next interview.

Shepherding does give a certain sense of worth; you're the rescuer, the one called in when things are desperate. But if a church leader has a vision that goes beyond being well thought of, a vision that includes *harvest*, then some important decisions must be made intentionally.

The pastor must say, "Given my limited resources, the most precious of them being my time, with whom or on what should I be spending it?"

There are two dangers for pastors: spending too much time getting ready for Sunday, and spending too little time. The right balance contributes to an optimum quality of sermon and optimum exposure to people who need to be recruited.

In the average-sized church in America, the pastor is still the key person to make people feel they are entering a church legitimately. Frequently it requires no more than a five-to-fifteen-minute touch to create a favorable disposition toward the church. From there on, lay people can finish the fishing, hauling the prospect into the boat. All the pastor needs to do is set the hook.

When I was a pastor, I noticed a curious thing: a fifteen-minute visit with someone would produce a member, while if I spent forty-five minutes, I'd never see the person again! Apparently they got too much of me (or I got too much of them). They must have assumed the expected level of commitment in our church was just too high, and they were frightened away.

If you go to a new bank, and the president takes the trouble to shake your hand, ask your name, and say they'd all be glad to be of service to you, you are impressed. You don't expect the president also to take your money; that's the tellers' job. In fact, you may not see the president once in the next two years. But it doesn't matter. You've been favorably disposed to bank there.

The average visitor does not expect nearly as much of the minister as the average member does. That seems counterintuitive; you'd think outsiders would be clamoring for as much attention as insiders. But in most cases it isn't true. In fact, if non-members are given that much exposure, pastors can actually thwart their coming to the church.

Multiplied options

The biggest problem I see is in decision-makers not taking the trouble to multiply their options before deciding. Church leaders tend to construe each problem as black or white, either/or, right or wrong, when, in fact, they need to unravel it a bit. They might see four or five different ways to proceed if they did.

Dave Luecke, a vice-president at Fuller Seminary and a former professor of administrative science, says the English language has a helpful convention along this line in the words *better* and *best*. If I look at a problem and come up with an option, I can say, "I have a good solution." But I cannot say, "I have a better solution," until I have looked at two possibilities. And I cannot claim "I have the best solution," until I have checked out at least three.

Here are some questions to help discover other options:

"What are the decisions I could make, and what will be the outcomes? Are they significant to my long-term ministry? Which decisions ought to be deferred?"

"What are my options? Is this really a yes/no? Or are there options A, B, and C to be considered?"

"Who should be involved in the decision-making process in order for implementation to be effective?"

"How do I know when I have enough information? When is going for more research just a way of delaying the decision? Is it time to bite the bullet?"

The best solution is one that has been weighed and selected from an array of potential outcomes, including whether I should do any-thing at all. In the last thirty or forty years, doctors have been learning that in a lot of cases they shouldn't do anything. They can give the patient sugar pills and send him home. The body will take care of itself, given time.

But there are times when decisions have to be made. For example, say a pastor gets word from someone that a teenager in the youth group has been seen drinking. If that pastor feels it is critical to rep-resent God's opinion accurately, he may come out with guns blazing, hitting every target in sight with: *God is against teenage drinking!*

If, however, he sees this as a human behavior with certain causes, he can more accurately decide where to apply the medicine. *What is this kid fleeing from? What's he trying to identify with? What hungers, what fears are just beneath the surface? Who are the significant oth-ers in his life, and how many of them do I have input to?* Once he studies the context, the parents, the peer group, and the teenager himself, he may find that the cure belongs nowhere near the symp-tom. Only after determining the appropriate assignable cause can a good decision be made on how to respond.

The person who reported the incident probably expects the pas-tor to take out the whip of fury and go after the offender. But if it were that easy, why hasn't somebody already done that?

The pastor might even probe to see whether the reporter is a causal person in the teenager's life. "Who else have you discussed this with? Were they concerned? Are they making any plans? Are you making any plans? You know this teenager; you care enough about him to bring the matter to me. What do you think God may be calling *you* to do?" You see, if the pastor treats this as a fire call, reaches for his hat, and runs out the door with sirens blazing, he may be over-come with smoke. How much better to say to the caller, "I'm sort of the coach here, and I'm deeply concerned about this, as you are. Let's get down on our knees right now and pray until we have some insight on what each of us is supposed to do next in this matter."

Pastors can never forget that people are always testing them. Some of these reports are brought simply to see what the pastor will do about it. The teenager in question may *not* have been the one drinking; it may have been the reporter himself or herself, who wants to know what the pastor will do. And the way he responds will deter-mine whether or not he is granted any further franchise for ministry.

When a pastor hears about a sheep who has become entangled, the goal is to unsnare him. You may mutter under your breath about the sheep's stupidity, but berating him for being entangled does not produce deliverance. Beating the thorn bush doesn't help, either. The only effective action is to disengage the sheep from the snare.

Choice wisdom

After exploring the options, the key, of course, is to choose the best one. That takes wisdom. And not every pastor has that gift. If a pastor does not have a wisdom gift, he would do very well to find someone who does and talk it over. In many of the cases I've counseled, the pastor's wife has the gift her husband lacks in a critical area. The only question is whether he's willing to consult her.

In other cases, key laypersons have such a gift and are discreet enough to be talked to about a problem. The resource is right there in the flock, if pastors have the wisdom to see it. But who does? The person who lacks wisdom may also lack the wisdom to find it. And some leaders may struggle with ego; they don't want to defer, because they hold the power to decide. They forget that even if they defer or delegate, they still have the power to *review*. They can decide:

- that a decision doesn't need to be made
- to make a decision alone
- to make a decision *with* the help of someone else's input and counsel
- that someone else needs to make this decision.

These last two involve the difference between *knowing your mind* and *having your mind made up*. When you know your mind, you know generally where you are on certain elements of an upcoming decision, but you don't know exactly how it ought to come down or what your part should be. When you've made up your mind, you've closed the door to further input.

On certain issues, it's all right to make up your mind—for example, the role your spouse prefers in a congregation. You know her preferences in advance, so that when criticism comes, you can respond without flinching.

But in other matters, such as whether or not to build a new parking lot, you're far better off simply knowing your mind and then remaining open to other angles, weighing the options. You know you intend to minister to more people, and the current space is inadequate, so *something* has to be done, but as you begin, you haven't locked into "We must put fifty more parking spaces where the playing field is now."

In some ways it is best if the pastor arrives at a new action *last* rather than first, after developing broad congregational support. Some decisions need a lot of process attached to them because they are so hard to undo.

I sat with one pastor who was trying to decide how to proceed with planting a daughter church. The problem was, not all the proponents' attitudes regarding the new mission were wholesome. We spent an hour talking and praying together about how to facilitate the dreams and wishes of these people in an affirming, legitimizing way.

We finally came down to "What are the next steps?" At that point, he called in a wise and sensitive staff member, and we tossed it around for another half hour. We explored what actions would keep from hardening attitudes or making people feel fearful. Because of the staff member's input, we wound up with a much different, more seasoned set of action steps than if the senior pastor had written them alone or with me.

This man knew when to stop thinking about the decision himself and call for help. He showed his exceeding wisdom. After I left, the two of them took the plan to a larger group of key laypersons for comment and refinement before proceeding further. The result was a successful launch.

Pulpit decision-making

A leader is a person with the willingness to cast the vision and then call for it to be manifested in behavior. Who will cast the ideal? The leader. That is the one thing he has going over everyone else: He knows where the group is headed.

Effective leaders understand both the nature of power and the nature of giftedness. They behave in a way that enables people's gifts to be brought on-line. Some notions of democracy are so egalitarian that everybody is the same little brick as everyone else. This fails to recognize people's gifts. In any given group, the Holy Spirit does not give everyone equal ability to lead. If that is not recognized, there are going to be problems.

Someone has said the chief officer of any group has more ability to discourage something from happening than to make something happen, and that is true of pastors as well. By our *in*attention we can allow almost anything to die if we don't want it to prosper. It takes a very strong layperson to come forward and minister month after month, year after year, without encouragement or recognition. The pastor holds the power to bless or wither virtually any part of the church by what he chooses to stroke.

Pastors have the incredible power of the pulpit to cast vision. Each week they get one or more opportunities to set the tone for the entire congregation.

I sat with a group of ministers who were worried about growth in their denomination. I didn't have much time to work with them, so I said, "What do you think? Can you grow?"

"Well, I hope so," said one man, "but I don't know. I preached at one of our conferences recently and said I thought maybe we were dead if we didn't do something pretty soon."

"That sounds like an interesting sermon," I said. "Do you have a copy of it?"

He found a copy, and I took it back to my hotel room. There I spread out the eight pages and began a content analysis. In college I studied a little bit of theater, and so I took this sermon apart just like I would a play, noting the various episodes, the climax, the proclimaxes, the anticlimaxes, and so forth. I circled every illustration and examined it for vividness and emotion. The greatest emotional power, as dramatists know, lies in the themes of life and blood; these move an audience profoundly.

This speaker used one illustration from his childhood about the time his father took him fishing. The first time the boy put his hook in the water, he didn't get a fish but instead a snapping turtle. He excitedly reeled it in.

The father was perturbed, however; he seized his filet knife, grabbed the turtle, and proceeded to saw off its head. He threw the body up on the bank behind and then said, "Now, son, let's get back to fishing."

The preacher went on: "But in a little while, I looked back—and lo and behold, the turtle had righted itself and was walking back down the bank—headless. I said, 'Dad! Dad! The turtle's coming down the bank!'

"And my father said, 'Aw, son, don't worry about him. He's dead, he just doesn't know it yet.' "

This was the speaker's analogy for the denomination! His audience included a lot of small-town and country people, farmers, weekend fishermen. *Talk about impact!* A Jungian psychologist would go wild just thinking about it. In that one illustration, he planted despair and hopelessness more firmly than any straight-on assertion ever could.

That pastor didn't know it, but he had used a flame thrower on his audience. He didn't realize what he had done. Illustrations command the imaginations of the people; there is no greater force. With negative imagery pastors can suggest withdrawal; with positive imagery they can suggest victory. Most don't realize they are artists, painting on the inner canvas of the listeners' minds the scenes that will dominate the life of the whole church.

The power of the pulpit is a major factor in decision-shaping. With it we can school people either *not* to attempt great things for God or to attempt them. We can preset their attitudes in the mold either of "we can't" or "we can."

We simply have to think about what we're doing and make intelligent, God-honoring choices.

16

Why I Don't Set Goals

*People and institutions begin to corrode when fleshly zeal
is tied to spiritual goals.*

—Jack Hayford

What are your primary goals for the immediate and long-range future?" The question came from the audience at one of our annual pastors' seminars.

"I have none," I replied.

Dubious stares and blank looks everywhere. I continued, "We never set goals—that is, in the sense of numerical targets, fund-raising drives, or enlargement campaigns. Our one goal is to build big people. Every effort goes into developing each believer in the threefold ministry of worship, fellowship, and stewardship of the gospel."

And I was telling the truth. From the time I came to the Van Nuys church fifteen years ago, I virtually abandoned the church methodology I had used the previous thirteen years. I knew the quotes ("Aim at nothing, and you'll hit it," "No vision, no victories," "Plan your work, then work your plan") and I knew the ropes (zeal, promotion, enlistment, persuasion, training, projecting, enthusing, inspiring, recruiting, educating, etc., etc.). The quotes held an obvious element of wisdom, and the plain work of developing goals and generating means and personnel to fulfill them is a very practical way to get jobs done—*naturally* speaking.

But it was at that juncture—the *natural*—that something inside me began to creak under the weight of the years.

Conviction growth

While pastoring in Indiana and then working for several years at my denomination's headquarters and also at its largest college, I had seen spiritually oriented human enterprise at its finest. I had also seen it bear a certain amount of fruit.

However, God brought me to this church with the conviction that there was a better, simpler way to do things. I didn't know what that way was, however. So the congregation of eighteen members and I began fumbling, trying to apply New Testament priorities in ministry without surrendering either to mysticism or fanaticism.

A primary principle evolved: I would stay away from the pressure to *perform* (something I was well acquainted with from the past). I began to discover the joy of (1) finding direction through prayer and (2) watching the fruit of obedience as people grew—and the church did, too. Individual health became apparent in the larger group, and we began to see more progress this way than I had ever achieved through promotional precision and evangelistic programs.

We did not set out to prove a point or challenge a system. We only decided that the New Testament church seemed simpler and far more fruitful than most of what I had been able to produce. When we investigated why, we found that the Holy Spirit was the director of its life and program.

The goals learning curve

I was in prayer one day about the church's finances at a time when the monthly offerings totaled around $1,000. I felt no complaint, but I knew there was reason to request more cash flow, if for nothing else than refurbishing the building; it certainly needed it. I started to ask God for "more money," when suddenly it came to my mind that I didn't know how much to ask for.

I stopped short, meditating. *Hmmm. If I don't know how much to request, how can I pray specifically?*

On the other hand, God obviously knew at that juncture exactly what our church ought to be doing. So I decided to ask him to teach me. Then it would be easy to ask in faith, since the amount was his idea.

"Lord, how much should I be asking you for for the general budget each month?" I'd never phrased it that way before, and I knew it would sound clumsy to many, but the risk was small.

"Two thousand dollars a month."

That was the answer—and I won't be offended if anyone accuses me of imagining the number. "Sure," someone may say, "you just thought up the figure, or your subconscious suggested it." I'll only say that I have been surprised often enough by such promptings to know, at this point in my life, that they don't spring from within. The numbers have often been far different from what I would have ventured.

So I began praying, "Lord, I ask for your blessing and increase of church income toward the $2,000 per month I felt you called me to expect." It was my version of "Give us this month our monthly income," and I prayed it two or three times a week.

After four months, without any special appeals, the monthly income stood at $1,700. I began to sense a strong need to ask for the *next* figure before the present "goal" had been reached. One day I stopped in the middle of my praying. My usual request for $2,000 didn't seem right. No voice spoke, but I sensed an inquiry inside:

"Why haven't you asked the Father lately for a new amount?"

I did—and immediately felt an inner sense of freedom to pray for $3,000 a month. Later I realized that the key to my liberty was my choosing to become as a child. I was not setting goals; I was simply asking questions of my Father. I refused to intellectualize the promptings, nor did I try to psychoanalyze myself. I simply believed.

I seek to walk in the same simplicity today, even though the monthly amount is now comprised of six figures, and the church's annual total runs into the millions of dollars. I rest knowing that we have not come to be a congregation of more than forty-five hundred through human kingdom-building or financial goal-setting, but rather by responding to the Holy Spirit's step-by-step direction.

This does not mean we escape the practical duties of responsible management. All monies are carefully accounted for and reported to the penny. We leaders project an annual budget each fiscal year and adhere to it. But we do not proclaim that budget to the congregation or flaunt it to others as an attainment. Neither do we burden one another with it as a challenge to fulfill. We simply plot it on the basis of the track record and then wait in prayer for God to fulfill or adjust it.

Whenever he prompts us to expect greater income, we pray accordingly. Whenever we sense a need to cut back, we do so without feeling guilty. Since the "goal" is not something we set, we don't have to defend it. It is rather a case of God's purpose being clarified as time goes by.

I have given an economic example, not because I feel it is more important than any other area, but because it is probably as good an indicator as any of general spiritual health. I am not surrendering to "prosperity-ism" in that statement; I am simply pointing out a fact that can be demonstrated in the Third World as well as the First. Life in the church manifests itself in giving, and giving begets new life.

The principle

The general advantage of goal-setting, as I understand it, is that it enables both the pursuit of ideals and the measurement of progress. I would not criticize either ideals or progress, for the Word of God endorses both.

The problem arises, however, when we take this philosophy into church life. Without realizing it, our goals become numerical: so many workers trained, classes conducted, decisions registered, dollars given, missions begun, results tabulated. That is the way goals are verified.

It is hard to write about this, because in no way would I devalue any of the above ministries. But given enough time, something sinister often invades, and the goals begin to haunt their makers. If we reach the goal, we conclude that "God is blessing." The next assumption is "God is in this program," and before long we are serving the program instead of the Lord himself. People and institutions begin to corrode when fleshly zeal is tied to spiritual goals. We pastors have a propensity for launching our crusades with righteous intent and then fueling them with carnal energy.

For example, religious organizations frequently arrive at deep financial difficulty by doing nothing worse than concluding that "blessing" is *carte blanche* to pursuing bigger and better projects. Again, let me say that I'm not against growth or large finance in the kingdom of God. But the mindset that employs goal-setting as the key to growth is in real jeopardy of setting time bombs for itself.

What if a goal isn't reached? We could discard it as fruitless—but we seldom do, because built into the definition of our goal is that it is "for God's glory." So the goal must be pursued by all means, even by promotional means frighteningly parallel to Madison Avenue. Why? Because "they work."

The implications

I do not mean to be an obscurantist who denies the worth of contemporary technology or media. I am fully aware I risk sounding like a childish iconoclast.

Nor do I propose leadership by whim of a pastor who claims the Lord spoke to him. In fact, I am quite in favor of strategizing. I *do*, for example, appreciate the modern computer analyses of world missionary efforts and the consequent focus on pockets of hidden peoples yet unevangelized. I *do* think that analyzing a congregation's growth (or nongrowth) rate may effectively disturb the status quo and explode people out of the rut of passivity. I *do* believe dreams and visions are worth formulating into strategies for action.

But goal-setting must be approached in the light of some primary questions:

1. Is this goal a direct result of a God-given directive, not just a desire to "be like the other nations"? Has the Holy Spirit spoken to the leadership, and has this sense of direction been submitted to elders and deacons? Have they confirmed it? Is the congregation generally positive toward the vision?

2. Does this goal sacrifice any principles or people on the altar of exigency? In God's order, there is never a situation so desperate that it must grind people to powder or press a financial appeal at the cost of integrity, exploitative tactics, or world-styled salesmanship.

The plan

In the past four years, The Church On the Way has completed and paid for a major building program and now has another $5 million development underway. We are not approaching the task with reckless abandon. But our desire is to "birth a plan" rather than "plan a birth." The conception of vision, gestation of plans, and carrying to delivery are all pursued in an unabashed spirit of prayer and absolute dependence upon the Holy Spirit to *lead*—to correct, to time, to inspire faith, to release resources, to stir response.

Surely many readers of this chapter who set goals think much the same way as I have described. But I am suspicious of the practice of erecting targets, however noble the intent. Much of my early ministry was the fruit of setting goals and then pursuing them with all my promotional zeal. Naturally, I prayed. But things tended to stay on the natural level.

My intention is not really to debunk goal-setting but to confront the tendency to dissolve into naturalism—to pursue holy goals by merely human means. "No goals," in my mind, does not mean the absence of direction, strategy, or planning. It does mean:

- We will not undertake anything without a clear sense of the Holy Spirit's direction, confirmed by eldership.
- We will not utilize any means of promotion or fund-raising that depends on human genius or style to be effective.
- We will not pursue anything that overlooks the priorities of *worship, relationship*, and *ministry*.

At the same time:

- We *will* pray much, often, and always.
- We *will* think—trusting God's Spirit to give clarity, coherence, and conviction to us all.
- We *will* believe, knowing that "without faith it is impossible to please God" (Hebrews 11:6). As we do so, he will grow his purpose in us.

The following translation of Philippians 3:13–14 (my own) expresses and summarizes my perspective: "Brethren, I do not count myself as having attained any goal, but I do this one thing: Leaving what is past, I reach ardently for what is ahead—in quest of that goal which is God's high calling to Christlikeness."

17

Identifying Priorities

*The pressure to succeed by secular standards, to measure
success by visible accomplishments rather than by
biblical guidelines, is subtle and often insidious.*

—Ted W. Engstrom

Consider the pastor with a priority.

At eight-thirty on Tuesday morning he's at his desk, re-
freshed, motivated, and abounding with energy to tackle what he
considers his most pressing problem. His church sits at the edge of a
growing medical complex in a southern city with a large ratio of re-
tirees. The potential—yea, the need—for ministering to these people
weighs on him. Very little has been done.

Now he sees some light. One gifted leader has volunteered to get
involved. A businessman on the board has hinted he would give
heavily to support such a ministry. The board itself has endorsed the
idea, and dozens of church members have signed "I'm interested in
helping" cards. One person added an enthusiastic note to the card.

So with yellow pad in hand, our hero considers his priorities for
the week:

1. Call the businessman; have lunch soon. Too bad! He just left
for two weeks in Hawaii.

2. Call the board chairman; light a fire under him. The board
chairman must wear asbestos pants. He wants to know if it can wait
until next week.

*3. Drop by and see the volunteer at her office. She runs a small
accounting firm.* Oh, no! This is the first week of April. She's probably working right through lunch hours and into the evenings.

4. Sound out the woman who scribbled the note on the card. Well, so much for that. She had almost forgotten she wrote the note. Compulsive type, probably, who wrote it in a fit of enthusiasm. But she's already up to her earrings in community club work.

Frustrated, the pastor turns reluctantly to another task. Well, at least he can work on next Sunday's sermon. He doesn't depend on anyone else for that.

The people problem

The problem will return, however, to plague him, just as it does every other church leader. It's the gap between what we think should be done first and what we can actually do. It's the pull between priorities and our ability to move the resources needed to attack the priorities.

We know what's important—but without the right people in the right place at the right time, we can't get very far.

Now I think I hear a few solemn counselors of Job dismissing the problem with "We must wait for God's timing" or, "You must always put people first." Those answers are much too simplistic. For the pastor who has already waited on God to confirm a set of goals and priorities, this is a multifaceted problem.

For one thing, the church, from a human perspective, is a volunteer organization, and pastors must understand how to work with volunteers. An entire genre of literature has developed on this topic, and as you read it, it's easy to conclude that if you follow the rules, you'll get as much from volunteers as from paid staff. Not true! Some volunteers are highly committed, but in most cases they have at least one other major commitment—earning a living—that cannot be shelved.

Bill Templeton, pastor of Northside Baptist Church in Charlottesville, Virginia, says flatly, "It always takes longer with volunteers." Templeton's organizational skills plus his highly motivated style turn on a lot of laypeople. "Yet," he says, "I'm a realist. I allow volunteers more time than I'd like and certainly more than if I were doing it myself, so I'm not disappointed."

Templeton must have heard of Murphy's Law, which says that if anything can go wrong, it will. A contemporary sage has formulated O'Toole's Comment on Murphy's Law: "Murphy was an optimist." My own corollary to Murphy's Law is that the more people involved in a program, the greater the probability that something will go wrong. People get sick, they forget, have accidents, take on too much, lose interest, have second thoughts, and fail. These are the joys and the drawbacks of working with people.

There is no quick solution to the problem of making things happen via volunteers. But if you continually find yourself frustrated because people aren't available when you need them, step back and ask why. Are the people working? On vacation? Involved with other projects? Forgetful? Uninterested?

Keep a log of the various reasons/explanations/excuses/alibis for a month; then tally them up. It may tell a lot about your own management style and leadership ability. Are you expecting too much? Are you unreasonable in your time demands? Or do people need more personal seed-planting, probing, and encouraging?

George Lambrides, a pastor in Davison, Michigan, says, "Rather than pursuing my own burning desires these days, I go around planting seed thoughts. I've found that anything of any magnitude has to grow out of someone's gifts. And someone else besides me has to own the idea."

The chances are that when you analyze your frustrations, you'll find yourself stymied a *smaller* percentage of the time than you thought. A colleague of mine, Ed Dayton, has postulated Dayton's Law: "At least 50 percent of the things you plan will go right. Rejoice!" (Baseball hitters should do so well.)

Divine delay

I've always set goals in my work, and once a decision is made to do something, I want to see it done. I might have mellowed a little with age, but I'm still inclined to mobilize all the resources I have and push full speed ahead. My enthusiasm translates into a desire to see results. So when I hear a manager excuse failure by saying it wasn't God's timing, I tend to scowl.

Yet I've had to admit more than once that what I thought was the right time to solve a problem or reach a goal was not God's timing. He *does* make us wait sometimes. The pastor in our first example may have to wait a little longer to begin a ministry in the medical complex. Meanwhile, the delay may provide valuable gestation time. While he's waiting for the people to move into place, he can do some good old-fashioned thinking about it.

Unfortunately, we often skip this phase of problem solving. In our world of instant answers, we move directly from bright idea to action plan with little time between.

Priority questions

To have to revise our project list doesn't necessarily mean we made a mistake in the first place. We make decisions on the basis of the information we have at the time. We constantly need to update. Accidents, new information, unforeseen opportunities—even the weather—sometimes force us to reevaluate what we attempt first.

We can't do any of this, however, unless we have a clear basis on which to function. Over the years I've set three broad levels of priorities that have often helped me make day-by-day decisions.

The bottom level, which is the foundation for everything else, is my personal commitment to Jesus Christ. Knowing Jesus, becoming like him, worshiping him—these are first and most important.

Second, I'm committed to the church, my brothers and sisters in Christ. Observers in New Testament times were astounded at the way Christians showed love for one another. This is the mark of the Christian, by which my behavior and attitudes are to be evaluated.

My third priority is the work God has given me. It rises directly from my commitment to Christ and his church.

Usually, if I appear to have a conflict, a clash between what I think I should do first and what I'm actually able to do because of the people involved, I need to examine these levels to see if my priorities are in the right order. This forces me to put people before programs. If I find myself frustrated in driving toward a goal, I need to check and see if I have put level three before level two. Have I put the work of Christ ahead of the body of Christ? That's very easy for any of us to do, especially in light of the fact that our families are part of the body.

Here are four red flags to keep us out of the ditch of misplaced priorities.

1. *Are my motives pure?* Why do I want to accomplish a particular task or promote a program? Will it make me look good? Will it move me up a rung or give me a little more leverage?

We may frown at the idea that we could be less than sincere, but motivations are complex. We all struggle daily against the desire for recognition and power. The same program, for example, that will comfort the sick may also score points for the pastor. This is where our human reasoning often fails us, and we need to ask the Spirit of God to search our hearts. This is a time to pray as David did, "Search me, O God, and know my heart . . . and see if there be any hurtful way in me" (Psalm 139:23–24, NASB).

2. Do the goals of the program fit my theology? *Time* magazine told about a church in Florida that runs a bar in its parish hall. The pastor believes it brings people together in a good setting and contributes to the life of the church. That's an extreme example, and most of us would fault the practice. But the issues are often more subtle, and while we'll always have well-meaning people who will think up off-the-wall programs, we must test all proposals through the grid of our theology. If we don't—and find ourselves stymied along the way to implementation—perhaps we have skipped this important question.

3. Will the program enhance the lives of the participants? A ministry to the medical complex might change the lives of many patients, but it may also jeopardize the workers. We have to ask whether this or that program will put novice Christians in leadership roles, tempt the weak with celebrity status, or pull mothers and fathers away from their children one more night of the week.

These are tough questions, but they provide the checks we need to avoid putting level three before level two.

4. Have we been seduced by our culture? Do we have a numbers orientation? Are we prone to think bigger is automatically better? Has society's worship of size, success, speed, production, promotion, and glamour crept into our evaluation of church programs?

The pressure to succeed by secular standards, to measure success by visible accomplishments rather than by biblical guidelines, is subtle and often insidious. But in the light of eternity, our effectiveness is based on our being members of the mystical body called the church and the love we have for one another.

18

First Things First

There are some things that every church—
to be a church—must do well.

—Howard Hendricks

S ome time ago I visited a church that has an unusual strength in
fellowship. I was so profoundly impressed I asked the pastor,
"How in the world do you attract this many friendly couples to one
church?"

He said, "It's very simple. You can't get in and out of this church
without somebody inviting you to lunch." Even though it's massive,
it's the friendliest church on planet Earth, with a fellowship virus that
has spread to everyone. Objectively, I wouldn't say it was the greatest
preaching center in the area, but it's developed this one strength to
an inspiring level.

At the beginning of any new ministry year a church must evaluate
its last performance. I would use three questions:

1. What are we doing well? What are our strengths? If you don't
capitalize on your strengths, you tend to minister on a basis of weaknesses.

2. What are we doing that needs to be improved? You may be doing many things reasonably well, but how much can you improve
them? We are embarrassed by our weaknesses and we excuse them
rather than find ways to overcome them.

3. What are we not doing that we should be doing? Many churches
tend to do what any other human organization can do, instead of
what the church alone can do. In planning a new church year, church
leaders must be aware of the unique contribution the church makes

to the community—the spiritual contribution.

Yet a church can go overboard in emphasizing its strengths and neglect the many other necessary ministries that make up a church. There are some things that every church—to be a church—must do well. Chapter 2 of Acts gives the heart of a New Testament church. In this context four essential disciplines stand out: instruction, worship, service, and fellowship. Now, the context of the paragraph at the end of Acts 2 is evangelism. It begins with people being added to the church daily, and it ends the same way. If the church ever loses its evangelistic thrust in the process of teaching, worshiping, servicing, and fellowshiping, these disciplines will degenerate into ends, rather than means to an end.

Here are some thoughts on these four disciplines of the church, which every board should evaluate as it plans for the future.

Instruction

The pastor-teacher's role is defined in Ephesians 4:11. His primary task is to be an equipper of the saints for their work of ministry. He's committed to a ministry of multiplication, not addition. He's not doing the work of ten men, he's equipping ten men to do the work.

Many of our board members aren't involved in spiritual ministry; they're involved in activities that others in the congregation can do. If a Christian leader is going to make a spiritual impact, he must surround himself with a group of people into whose lives he's pouring his own—which, by the way, is a tremendous blessing to him. That's when he starts growing, when he becomes personally responsible for somebody else's spiritual growth.

We have the idea that instruction has to take place within four walls. That might be one of the greatest barriers to learning. For example, I can teach for hours in a classroom, walk down to the snack shop, sit down with a student, and get involved in a conversation that will change his life. That doesn't mean I should abandon classroom teaching, but some of my most effective teaching has been done in my office, over at the snack shop, and out of my home. You can impress people at a distance; you can only impact them up close. The general principle is: The closer the personal relationship, the greater the potential for impact.

True discipleship is a commitment, a lifestyle. It has to be as high a priority to the pastor as preaching, but not to the exclusion of preaching. I often think of the Savior's words: "This you ought to have done and not to have left the other undone." Don't stop preaching and do start discipling.

One question I ask a pastor—I love to do it, particularly when I'm leaving—is, "When I come back, I am going to ask you to show me the core of people into whose lives you are building. Who will be here when you are gone?" The answer comes through effective preaching and discipling.

For instance, the Lord Jesus sent his disciples out after he had carefully instructed them about how to minister. When they came back they were higher than a kite. The text says they rehearsed everything that had happened. And he was excited with them. On another occasion they went out on their own, and they struck out. Jesus bailed them out, performed the miracle they had blown, and the text says, "The disciples took him aside and privately asked, 'What happened?' He said, 'This kind comes out by prayer only.' " Prayer? What in the world does prayer have to do with it? They had cast out demons before and they had done it successfully. Now they were learning they had been spending too much time using their gift and not enough time developing the spiritual resources needed to maximize their gift.

Instruction can begin right in the retreat room. I'd start a Bible study that revolves around passages such as Acts 2, Ephesians 4, and Matthew 28, and get people involved in a discovery process.

I'll never forget one time when I was studying a passage of Scripture with a group of men, and one of them said, "Hey, hold it! I've got the picture! Jesus Christ never became blind to his objective. He was always on target!" I said, "Okay, why don't we come up with our objective?" The next time we met they all came with their lists. We lined them up and I said, "Okay, you prioritize them." For the first time, some of them began to focus the gospel on their daily lives. One man very quietly said, "It's hard for me to believe this, but something that's number two on my priority list is number twenty-two in my life." The impact upon his life of that confession was twice as great because *he* had discovered it, not because I said, "Look, Tom, it would be a good idea for you to get a list of objectives and prioritize them." Some of the best sessions I have ever had with a church board have come through this kind of discovery.

In our retreats and board meetings, we need to spend more time praying, studying, and sharing.

I was meeting with a church board one night when it really got heavy. Finally the pastor broke down; I mean he broke down and wept like a baby. In between sobs he said, "Men, I just can't carry this load." Then one member said, "What in the world are we holding you responsible for? This isn't your burden, this is ours." That launched a discussion that went until midnight about our ministry responsibilities as lay leaders.

Worship

I had an elder who would have failed an audition for a choir, but during the hymns he would stand down in front of me with a hymnbook open, mouthing the words. One day I asked him, "Mr. McFadden, what are you doing?" He said, "I'm worshiping." I asked, "You mean you're repeating the words?" He replied, "That's right. Remember, Pastor, you have not worshiped until you've told God your personal response, and these hymns are my response."

Worship is a personal response to a divine revelation. You haven't worshiped until you've responded.

Developing a higher level of worship among the people must start with the board. The board sets the pattern; they are the behavioral model given in Titus and Timothy. Unfortunately, we don't worship very often in our board meetings. When I was being trained, professors would say, "Look, men, one of the problems you'll face in your ministry is board meetings, spelled b-o-r-e-d. It's a grim scene, but that's part of the price you have to pay."

This doesn't need to be true. Board meetings can be a time of worship and celebration. I worked with a board where the members knew each other, loved each other, and confided in each other. As we faced difficult and complex issues, it was not uncommon for someone to say, "Pastor, I don't think we have enough wisdom for this problem right now. Why don't we pray?" We would bow our heads and pray around the room. More times than not, we would find the insights and wisdom we were seeking. Worship must start with the elders.

In addition, Sunday morning worship can be jeopardized by inadequate planning. One way this happens is by allowing worship to be set in concrete. I happen to have the crazy idea that preaching should precede rather than follow the worship service. Preaching should be followed by sharing, application, prayer, and other worship responses, and that requires careful planning and training.

We should prepare our people for change. Individually, we are predestined to be changed, conformed to the image of Jesus Christ. Corporately, the church should be the most revolutionary agency on earth. Too often, though, people come unglued because the service didn't start with the *Gloria Patri*, or the Lord's Prayer was in the wrong place. Board members, who are the opinion shapers, must set the worship pace and say to the people: "This is what we are going to do and this is why we are going to do it."

The use of response in corporate worship can enhance authentic worship. Worship becomes more meaningful when we realize that all of us face the same tempter and the same struggles, and that we can look to the same Lord and each other for help and support.

Service

Service must be seen in a broad context. It's easy to see it only in terms of our local church—what are we doing at Fourth and Main on Sunday morning in Sunday school. I see service as what goes on in the office or factory Monday through Friday. The average layperson has the idea that his or her vocation is a penalty. That's what he or she does five days a week in order to "serve the Lord" on Sunday. Actually, what takes place on Sunday should equip someone for the service to be performed all week.

We also need to recognize that within the church many of our people are overworked and undertrained. I find more and more people who do not enjoy church work, they endure it. When the focus is ministry activity to the exclusion of the individual's spiritual life, then burnout is inevitable. A typical example is the person who pulls back and says, "I don't want to get involved." This is one reason why a lot of people like to go to a big church and get lost in the crowd. I think we're asking people to minister when we've never sufficiently ministered to them. You can't minister out of a spiritual vacuum.

My goal for a local church would be to help every member serve Christ in at least one way, outside as well as inside the church. The average layperson isn't serving in that way because he's not trained to do it; but once he's properly trained, it's amazing how he will begin to enjoy it and become comfortable with it. When a person serves within the borders of his spiritual gifts he will enjoy the work of the Lord.

How you enlist a person usually determines how he or she will serve. A moratorium should be declared on at least three ways of enlisting people. One is the public announcement read on Sunday morning: "Beloved, next Tuesday we are going visiting. Please show up. Last week nobody showed up. Won't you please come this week?" Usually, no one will come the following week except the two people you should never send visiting!

Another one is the last-minute conscription; it's the situation where the Sunday school superintendent slips in during the adult class opening exercises, taps the person on the end of the row, and sentences him to the junior department for life. The moral of which is, "Don't sit on the end of the row."

The third scene is a desperate C.E. director who approaches a sincere, good-hearted person and says, "We've been all over the building looking for someone to take the high school class and we can't find anybody who wants to take it. We've lost six people in the last seven months, and now we're coming to you. Will you take it?" If this good-hearted Christian says, "Well, I don't have much time," the C.E. director usually responds, "That's all right. It won't take very much time."

A better way to recruit is to get people involved right away— when they join the church. People need to know we're not operating the Church of the Sacred Rest.

I saw a church go from about 34 percent participation, which is very high, to 93 percent. They committed themselves to the idea that everyone in the church was going to have a responsibility. No exceptions. They matched person with job and began to develop a realistic training program, which was hands-on. They learned to teach, for example, by teaching. I like the idea of apprenticeship.

I also love the idea of long-term commitment. I would like to meet more people who have been teaching sixth-grade boys for ten years, love it, and are still working on becoming the best sixth-grade teacher in the world. Single-year appointments destroy continuity. Since there is no continuity of ministry, there is little development toward the mastery of a skill. Single-year appointments also assume people will burn out in a year. It's almost a Pygmalion effect. If you assume it, it will happen. On the other hand, if you develop workers with the idea of long-term commitments, you'll train some real experts.

The greatest nursery teacher I know is a person who has been teaching for thirty-eight years. If there is anything to be known about teaching nursery children, she knows it. Even more exciting, she's trained another twenty-five or thirty people in her skills. I've heard her say, "I'm no good with adults; they bother me, they threaten me." But she loves little kids, and they love her.

To evaluate the way your church works with its laity, I recommend asking two questions:

1. *How are current members functioning?*
2. *What potential resources do new people represent?*

You work on it correctively by recruiting people who are already members but not serving. You work on it preventively by recruiting new people who are just coming into the church.

For people who already have become spectators, many churches have used a questionnaire very effectively—a means by which people can indicate the service areas that interest them. There is one warning I give to churches using surveys: Follow through! I recommend a committee examine the data, match the jobs with available people, and—this is the key—go to the prospect personally and say, "The committee has spent a lot of time thinking and praying about this matter, and we feel that God would have us approach you about the possibility of working in such-and-such a position" (that is, if you have as a committee thought and prayed about the position and the appointee before approaching him/her).

We enlisted a neurosurgeon to serve in our college department in this manner. Three of us made an appointment and went to see him. When he saw us he said, "Good grief, what is this?"

"Well," we said, "we have a challenge for you." Before we could continue, he called his nurse and told her not to disturb him for any reason. We described the task as clearly as we could, and then very straightforwardly told him, "Doc, it will take everything you have and then some, but we think you're our man." That night he couldn't sleep. His wife asked, "What's the matter?" He replied, "I have to make an important decision." "What, are we going to leave Dallas?" "No." "Are you going to sell the practice?" "No, I'm struggling with the fact that three Spirit-led men came to my office and said, 'We feel that God would have us approach you about the possibility of taking the college class.' How can I view that lightly?"

And most of all, laypeople need simple encouragement to continue their service. I was walking through town with a well-known pastor when we met one of his members. Calling her by name he said, "I was going over the Sunday school reports and I saw the names of the kids you led to Christ this year. I want you to know that you are engaged in a significant ministry."

That's how to build up lay leaders.

Fellowship

The tendency of leadership is to stifle fellowship—which means, "to share in common"—by gravitating toward vertical rather than horizontal relationships; professor and student, teacher and disciple, pastor and parishioner. We need more horizontal relationships that are developed around commitment to the same goals. Regardless of our station in life, all of us are in the process of learning and maturing.

Also, the average layperson doesn't think that his vocation has spiritual importance. Most physicians, salespersons, and business managers think their "secular" tasks are unrelated to the body of Christ. Our faith commitment to each other should be the great equalizer. Because we are members of the same family, it's very important to me, the pastor, for Jim, an elder in our congregation, to do good work at the local television station. I am going to pray for him and support him in his work.

One day I was at Dick Halverson's church and he said, "Howie, how would you like to make a call with me?" We went out to a junior high school where one of Dick's members was the principal. He was expecting us and had some sandwiches brought up from the cafeteria. After lunch, we studied the Word and spent some time praying together. Just before we left Dick said, "Let's take a walk." So the three of us walked all the way around the block. After we had returned to the front door, Dick said, "Okay, let's pray and claim this place as your center of ministry."

Dick was as concerned about this man's ministry as he was about his own. He sought to help equip him to function as a Christian leader in society. That's how you develop fellowship.

The dynamics of fellowship in the New Testament, though, had a lot to do with the times. They operated in a context of persecution. Interestingly, in our times, the greatest Christian fellowship you see around the world is in persecuted areas.

I was in India some time ago, where we conducted a pastors' conference outside one of the communist-controlled states where it is against the law to preach the gospel. Three pastors who had just been released from prison for preaching came to the meeting. I said, "What's it like in your state?" They said, "Just like the Book of Acts. The more they persecute us, the more we flourish. We're conducting four or five services every Sunday to accommodate the people."

They told me about one church where the leaders met with the pastor and said, "Pastor, we have a problem; there are some people coming to church more than they should. From now on let's tell the people, 'If you come this Sunday, you must stay home next Sunday.' "

I've watched this phenomenon over and over again. My son attended Harvard, and the thing that really hit me was watching how his ministry and that of his friends took off the moment they were nailed to the wall for what they were doing.

I keep asking my friends, "How can we launch a persecution in Dallas?"

The persecution against Jesus Christ always started when he became involved with people and changed their lives. Satan is for any program that doesn't change people. But once you start overhauling the lives of people, watch out.

Which brings me back to the four disciplines. If I'm right that God has called us to make the church a center for instruction, worship, service, and fellowship, all in the context of evangelism, you can expect powerful things to happen. You will impact the community. You won't have to stir up trouble; it will come to you. When the Holy Spirit begins to convict, convince, and rebuke, hang on, for resistance is on the way. And not just outside resistance, but internal resistance as well. You'll know when you're on target because that's when opposition always comes.

When you are doing what Jesus Christ has called you to do, you can count on two things: You will possess spiritual power because you have the presence of Christ, and you'll experience opposition because the devil does not concentrate on secondary targets. He never majors on the minors.

Even in our planning, it's critical to remember what Paul said in Ephesians: "We wrestle not against flesh and blood."

19

Managing to Minister

All nonprofits have one essential product:
a changed human being.

—Peter F. Drucker

M any people are surprised to find out that for thirty-five years I have been working with nonprofit institutions—hospitals, schools, charitable organizations. They ask, "What do you do for them? Advise them on fund-raising?"

I reply, "No, I don't know a thing about fund-raising. I teach them management."

Thirty years ago, many nonprofits were contemptuous not only of the word *management* but even of the concept. They said, "We don't need management. We don't have a bottom line." But now they all know that nonprofits need *better* management precisely because they don't have the discipline of the conventional bottom line to measure effectiveness.

Better management for nonprofits, such as churches, begins with several keys.

Clarify your aim

Although nonprofits don't have a conventional bottom line, they do need to know their aim. All nonprofits have one essential product: a changed human being. This is a different approach from business. In business, your goal is not to change the customer; it's not to ed-ucate the customer; it's to *satisfy* the customer. Whenever a business forgets that, it's in trouble. When General Motors tried to tell us what cars we ought to drive, we began to drive Toyotas.

But nonprofits aim for change. Hospitals seek to change sick patients into healthy ones. Schools aim to change students into educated individuals. The church has a difficult problem in that the books are not kept on this side. (So far even Congress hasn't been able to force an audit of those accounts.) But I would say the church's aim is to make a difference in the way the parishioner lives, to change the parishioner's values into God's values.

I've been teaching now for almost sixty years. If I have had any success, it was the rare instances when I said something that really made a difference to a student. Those results are not easy to quantify. They don't happen every day, not even every week, and maybe not even every month. But if a year goes by without it happening, I think I wasted a year, basically, as a teacher. In ministry, I surely would ask myself whether we make a difference, both in the way people live and above all in the vision of people.

It is essential for a local church to develop a unified, clear vision, and yet in nonprofits, you're almost always dealing with a number of constituencies, each of which wants something different emphasized.

When you look at churches, the mission is clear. It comes straight out of the Gospels. Basically, you are to bring the gospel to all of mankind. Very clear. Very simple. Maybe the simplest mission. I'm not saying it's the easiest, but it's the simplest.

But in all nonprofit institutions the various constituencies see the specifics in sharply different ways. School boards and teachers and parents and students all see different purposes for the school system. Fifty years ago, the vision was clearer: the school's purpose was to see that students learn. The school focused on skills—the ability to read, to do the multiplication table. In recent years, various constituencies began arguing about what *learning* means. It was broadened beyond skills to include traits (development of character, personality, social tasks), and as a result, the unifying focal point was lost. With so many goals to accomplish, you can't function as effectively.

Maintain the common mission

Despite the conflicting visions any nonprofit faces, it has to be held together somehow. This is the pastor's challenge with the church—to maintain the common mission. And if you don't, well—one of the basic weaknesses of the mainline liberal church is that it hasn't maintained the common vision. The leaders see the church as dedicated to social causes outside the church. But the congregation doesn't see it that way. The result is confusion and ineffectiveness.

To arrive at a common vision for a particular local church you have to know when to say no. That's particularly difficult for a church. But you have to admit some things are not your responsibility.

If you go to the American Lung Association and say, "Haven't you seen those frightening statistics that 97 percent of all Americans have ingrown toenails? Why don't you help cure ingrown toenails?" they'll tell you, essentially, "Our interest stops above the neck and below the navel." And even there, they are not interested in the heart or the esophagus. If it doesn't have anything to do with the respiratory system, I'm sorry, but you'll have to go elsewhere.

Often people feel the church exists to take care of problems. And it's terribly hard for the church to say no. Yet the effective ones say no. They know what their mission is, and they make no apologies for sticking to that.

I made myself terribly unpopular by saying recently, "I know the homeless have needs, and their plight bothers me too, but should your church really be in the shelter business?" It's one thing to encourage trained laypeople to go into the community and perform various services; it's another to see these functions as part of the church's mission.

On the other hand, I'm not consistent. I have friends in a major Catholic archdiocese who run the only schools in which local inner-city kids really learn. The public schools there are notoriously bad. And 94 percent of those kids are not Catholics and probably never will be. The archdiocese is strapped for money, and the parishes are screaming, "We need money to repair the church roof, and you put all our money into those schools for non-Catholics." Yet I've been encouraging them to keep the schools open because I think that maybe this comes before repairing the roof.

Two factors made the difference for me in this situation: The need is there (without those schools, the outlook for those kids is pretty grim), but equally important, the church has proven its competence.

The church has demonstrated its effectiveness in teaching young people.

Saying no is tough, but it's what makes for effective ministry in other areas. So beyond merely recognizing a need, the key question is "Can we make a real difference? Can we minister competently?"

Need and competence are preeminent, but we must also look to see if anyone else is already doing the job. There are many groups taking care of alcoholics. I'm not saying there's anything wrong with churches ministering to them, but to be blunt, that's not a way most churches can make a unique contribution. And the homeless? As I looked at what this particular church was doing with the homeless, it struck me as no different from what several other organizations were offering. And the results in changed lives were zero or pretty close to it. At times we all have to say, "The need is there, but this ministry is not for us."

The church is the only organization that is not entirely concerned with the kingdom of this earth. All the others are totally focused on this side. We're the only one with another dimension. And for that reason, many good concerns around here are not our primary focus. Any organization can do only a certain number of things. The greatest danger for a successful organization is to take on things that don't fit its personality.

Another danger for an organization is to be internally driven. The organization must not do just what it wants to do, but it needs to be "market driven"—adjusting to the needs of the customers. That applies not only to business but to churches. The church needs to be market driven. But it also needs to understand its purpose. The two things have to mesh.

If you're only internally driven, you quickly become bureaucratic. You lose touch with people and lose your effectiveness. If you're only market driven, you quickly become mercenary and totally opportunistic.

You need both. There's nothing wrong with the Girl Scouts, but the church is not the Girl Scouts. There's nothing wrong with the country club, but we aren't a country club. We are a church. And we have certain things we value that are not of value to anybody else. That's where we should focus.

Know thy strengths

The key question for a leader implementing direction in an organization is *What can I do in this organization that nobody else can do?*

Several questions emerge from that: *What did the good Lord ordain me for? What are my strengths? What am I good at? Where have I seen results?*

Few of us ask these questions because few of us even know how we perform. *What am I good at?* We don't usually ask that question. We've been trained to notice our weaknesses, not our strengths.

Schools, of necessity, are remedial institutions. When teachers meet with parents, rarely do they say, "Your Johnny should do more writing. He's so talented in writing." No, more likely you'll hear, "Johnny needs more work on his math. He's a bit weak in that area." As a result, few of us really know our strengths. The great teachers, and great leaders, recognize strengths and focus on them.

There are two simple ways to get an accurate reading about strengths and unique abilities. One is absolutely reliable but takes a little time. The other is about 65 percent reliable but immediate. The 65 percent reliable approach is to ask your secretary. (It's not 100 percent reliable because the really good secretaries won't tell you. That's the secret of their control—they know and you don't!) The absolutely reliable method is to think through what your key activities are, and every time you do something in a key activity, write down what you expect to happen. Nine months later look at what really happened. Within a year or two, you find out what your strengths are.

This method, of course, has a great link to church history. Historians continue to puzzle over one of the great mysteries: how to explain the sixteenth century. In 1560, two institutions dominated Europe, neither of which had existed twenty-five years earlier. The North was dominated by the Calvinist movement, the South by the Jesuit order.

In 1534, Loyola gathered the nucleus of his new order and took the vows of poverty, chastity, and obedience. In 1536, Calvin arrived in Geneva. Twenty-five years later, Europe had been changed. Nothing in the history of the world, not even the rise of Islam, can compare with the rapid growth and effectiveness of these institutions.

How do you explain it? Both were, by 1560, large institutions, each involving thousands of ordinary people, most of them working alone. Many worked under great pressure and danger, yet there were practically no defections. Very few bad apples. What was the secret?

Now we understand it. Both Calvin and Loyola taught a similar spiritual discipline: that whenever one does anything in a key activity (they were usually spiritual activities, but not entirely), one writes it down and so keeps track of what happens. This feedback, whether it's a Calvinist examination of conscience, or the Jesuit spiritual exercise, is the way you quickly find out what you're good at. And you find out what your bad habits are that inhibit the full yield.

Monitor your intentions, actions, and the results. Also monitor whether the results were the expected results. For instance, I may discover that when I put a person in charge of a particular ministry my batting average is very high. I see by this that when it comes to people decisions, I do well.

On the other hand, I may find that when I start a new program it usually flounders. And when I ask what I did wrong, very often I can identify the bad habit. It may be impatience: I insert myself in the activity and discourage the people delegated to lead it. If you pull up a radish every two weeks to see how it's growing, it will not grow. Or, it may be the other way: I wait too long. I don't build in checkpoints early enough. This timing can be readjusted.

Or, I may recognize that I haven't tested the idea. Again and again I see people who don't pilot, who go from the good idea straight into full-fledged operations. It's always good to pilot. Start small, for example, on a small-group ministry or a community outreach program before launching a major church-wide emphasis.

Know thy organization

No matter what your personal strengths are, you have to know each key task for your organization and make sure someone is doing each one.

Growing churches can get into trouble in two ways. For instance, the pastor may be very good at preaching and pretty good at training, but there are two other major tasks in any organization: managing money, and managing people. Let's say the pastor is not good at money matters—raising it, and planning its most effective use. In fact, his interest in preaching, not investing money, was one reason he chose seminary in the first place. And let's say the pastor is not gifted in direct human contact but basically an intellectual and a communicator.

The temptation is to make one of two mistakes, either of which will kill or cripple the church. The pastor can assume, though not consciously, that what he does well and what he likes to do are the only things that matter. The other tasks just don't get adequate attention. That's the lesser mistake, because at least two important things still get done well.

The mistake that really kills the church is when the pastor is conscientious and says, "I know money is important. I know people contacts are important," and he forces himself to do them. As a result he spends inordinate amounts of time on these things, does them poorly, and slights the things he is good at, and thus does them poorly, too. Within a few years, you have an ungodly mess on your hands.

The secret to ensuring the key areas are adequately covered is to sit down with your associates and board members individually—not in a group—and say, "Think through the major activities of this church. What things have to be done if this church is going to be effective?"

After you sit with those seven to nine people, look at the lists you've compiled. In most cases, you won't have complete congruence, but there's such substantial overlap that it's really unanimous. There are usually few exceptions. But take the exceptions seriously— they may simply indicate that somebody misunderstands, but they may also represent a major opportunity or blind spot in the group's thinking.

Then call a meeting of the group, share the list, and say, "The next step is for each of you to look at all the other people in this room. Put down the strengths of each person. Not your own. What is Joe good at? What is Mary's strength?" Collect the lists and compare them privately.

Again, it's amazing how much agreement there usually is. But any dissent is important. Because if six of us see Joe as being good with people, and three do not, we need to refine the question. It becomes, *What do we mean by being good with people? How do we want people to be treated?* You may need a recruiter, a trainer, a disciplinarian, or an encourager. Joe may be gracious, an excellent quality, but he can't say no. Some people are *pleasant*; others are *good with people*. Those aren't necessarily the same. So at times you have to be more precise about strengths.

Likewise, being "good with money" usually needs to be defined. Jack may be great keeping the books, but he has a tendency to forget the church doesn't exist for the sake of finances. Now, you need someone to sound the alert when the books don't balance. He should be able to say, "We don't have the money given the current budget," but he should not be the one to say, "This is the wrong thing to do." The bookkeeper should be the hair shirt, not the policy maker, because he judges by different criteria.

After you've evaluated strengths and key activities, then you begin matching them up, making sure each activity is covered, and you're beginning to build an effective team.

Pay attention to personnel

Part of the leader's job is to set the spirit of the organization. That doesn't mean simply to lay out policy and plans, but to exemplify them, to pay personal attention to the areas where the vision is being worked out.

When you look at well-run organizations, you see that the top people sit in on personnel decisions, even at fairly low levels. That's where the key difference is made. In corporations, it can really annoy the personnel department when suddenly the big boss appears for a meeting to discuss the promotions to general supervisor.

Alfred P. Sloan, the man who built General Motors, sat in on personnel decisions down to lower middle management. Not every time, but enough so that you were not surprised when, for instance, he would show up unannounced in Tarrytown, New York, and say, "I happened to be in the neighborhood, and I understand you're meeting to decide who is going to be master mechanic here." Simply by sitting in, he focused attention on the task, and better decisions were made.

The key, I think, is the commitment to be available to people when they are receptive. There was an episode in the life of Martin Luther when he was in deep despair. He went to his Augustinian prior, who said, "Brother Martin, it is a sin to be in despair."

For Martin, that was the important thing for the prior to say. What would have become of that young monk without that moment? The prior intellectually was surely his inferior, and probably spiritually, too, but he said the right word. He was available and used the moment of opportunity. It did not answer any of Martin's spiritual and theological questions, but it totally changed him. It was an example of effective ministry.

When we manage ministry well, we make it possible to be at the right place, at the right time, fully available to those who need us most.

PART 4

Decision-Making

20

What's Behind Your Decisions?

*The most obvious and frequently the most influential
reference point is precedent. What did we do last year?*

—Lyle E. Schaller

On this second Tuesday evening in June, the big agenda item before the governing board at Trinity Church is the proposed schedule for the coming program year (August 1 through July 31). The first date that raises any questions is December 24.

"I see the proposed schedule calls for three Christmas Eve services. Is that the same as this past December?" questions one board member.

"Yes, it is," replies the pastor. "This is identical with last year's three services at five, seven, and nine on Christmas Eve."

That answer appears to satisfy everyone except Sandy Evans, who asks, "Why don't we add a fourth service to reach some of the people we missed last year? Maybe we could have two concurrent services at seven, or perhaps we should add an eleven o'clock service?"

This glimpse into one board meeting raises a question about the reference points used in decision making. It is important to understand what criteria board members use to make decisions.

Power of the past

The most obvious and frequently the most influential reference point is precedent. What did we do last year? Did anyone complain about that? If not, the past can legitimize the future.

For example, the pastor may explain to the board, "I plan to take two weeks of vacation in early January and the other two weeks in August." When a new board member questions that, the pastor replies, "That's the schedule I've followed every year since I came here seven years ago." Everyone appears satisfied.

In many communities someone should ask, "My impression is that July, August, and early September are the peak church-shopping months for newcomers to this community. Do you think it's wise for our minister to be out of the pulpit for two Sundays when our number-one goal is to grow? Would it be possible to move those two weeks in the summer to June?"

The usual answer is, "No, the number-one criterion in scheduling vacations is the convenience of the staff; number two is local tradition."

A parallel example of the power of the past can be seen in the aging congregation that has decided to focus on reaching younger generations. In March the pastor explains to the governing board, "As you all know, I plan to be on vacation the last half of June and the first half of July. Do you have any suggestions on who should fill the pulpit the four Sundays I will be gone?"

"Why don't we ask Dr. Harrison?" urges one. "He was our pastor from 1967 to 1975. He retired two years ago, and he and his wife live only forty miles from here."

"That's a great idea!" agrees the oldest member on the board. "A lot of us old-timers would be glad to see him again, and I'll bet he and his wife would be delighted to come back. Maybe we should ask him to preach on two Sundays?"

"I'll support that," declares another member, "and maybe we could ask Reverend Olson, who followed Dr. Harrison. I'm sure he would enjoy returning."

Within five minutes it is agreed to ask three retired ministers to share those four Sundays. No one questions whether that emphasis on yesteryear will create a favorable impression on first-time visitors born after 1960.

Real-estate reality

Consider a second example of how different criteria affect a board's decisions.

"When I came three years ago as your new pastor, we were averaging about 85 in worship," reflected the thirty-four-year-old pastor of Central Church. "For the past nine Sundays in September and October, we've averaged 163, almost double three years ago. I am convinced the time has come to add a second service to the Sunday morning schedule. I believe if we revised the schedule to offer worship at 8:30, Sunday school at 9:30, and worship at 10:45, we could be averaging well over 200 a year from now."

"I admire your enthusiasm and your optimism," began a veteran leader, "but that would take us back to where we were before you came. This building was designed to seat nearly five hundred, including the choir. When we had fewer than a hundred, we rattled around in here like peas in a bushel basket, and the congregational singing was almost inaudible. We've finally got decent-sized crowds now. I don't think we should go to two services until we're forced to. When we get up to about 400 in church, that will be the time to talk about adding a second service."

"Before we make a hasty decision," cautioned another board member, "I think we should talk about the people we might reach if we added an early service to the schedule."

"My hope would be to broaden our appeal," explained the pastor. "We could build one service around the pipe organ and traditional church music and the other around contemporary Christian music with an instrumental group."

Which should control this decision regarding schedule? The plans of the building committee of 1923 who designed this building? Or a desire to reach a more varied constituency?

Money mandate

"After talking with five different fund-raising organizations and calling two dozen pastors from reference lists," the committee chair announced, "We recommend hiring the Smith & Brown firm to help us raise $800,000 for our building fund."

"I have only one question," interrupted Harold Jackson. "What proportion of the churches they have worked with have met or exceeded their goal? We need someone who can help us meet our goal!"

"I have two different questions," added Tracy Green. "First, which firm does the best job of enhancing the spiritual life of the congregation? Second, which one leaves the most satisfied group of parishioners behind when the campaign is over, and which one creates a bunch of people who feel they have been pressured?"

What are the criteria to use in selecting a fund-raising agency? Its effectiveness in meeting financial goals? Or the atmosphere the agency creates?

Two sets of questions

These examples show how the questions asked by board members can influence the decision-making process.

The point can be further illustrated by two sets of questions that may be criteria for board members.

Set A

 1. What did we do last year?
 2. What will our older members think?
 3. Is it consistent with our local traditions?
 4. Is it compatible with the design of our building?
 5. What does our pastor prefer?
 6. Can we get a majority of our members to support this?
 7. Will it be asking too much of our people?
 8. How much will it cost?
 9. We tried it in the church I was in before, and it didn't work. What makes you think it will work here?
10. Will it place too much of a burden on our pastor?
11. Can we secure the necessary approval from our denominational headquarters?
12. Will it require adding another staff person to the payroll?

Set B

 1. How will it improve the quality of our ministry?
 2. How will it expand our capability to reach the younger generations?
 3. How would a first-time visitor respond to this?
 4. How will it enrich the spiritual journeys of our members?
 5. How will it strengthen our ministry with single-parent families?
 6. How will it enhance our teaching ministries?
 7. Will it really challenge the commitment level of our people?
 8. Are you suggesting we try to do yesterday again, only better?

9. Which change should we introduce first and which one should come later?
10. How will the leaders in the year 2020 evaluate our response to this issue?
11. How will it enrich our ministries to families with young children?
12. How will this glorify God?

Who chooses the criteria?

Who decides on the criteria that will guide the decision-making process?

In smaller congregations the answer often is a mix of (a) local traditions and precedents, (b) respected and influential veteran leaders, (c) the real estate, and (d) comparative dollar costs.

In larger congregations the criteria frequently originate in (a) the senior minister and/or program staff, or (b) books, workshops, and visiting experts.

In middle-sized congregations the criteria are more likely to be articulated by the pastor and/or board members.

Regardless of how your criteria are chosen, it is important to answer these questions:

Which criteria are used by our board? Which criteria would improve the governance system in our congregation?

21

Secrets to Making Great Decisions

*We need to follow a decision through the valleys until we
get back to high ground.*

—Fred Smith

I worked with a vice-president of a major corporation who was a great decision maker.

"You make such good decisions. What's your secret?" I asked.

"First, I decide if I have a choice," he told me. "If not, I don't waste my time deciding."

That advice has often saved me from mulling over a fact of life that can't be changed. When I genuinely have a choice in a difficult leadership decision, I rely on ten helpful questions.

1. *What are my options?* J. C. Cain, a distinguished doctor of Mayo Clinic, once told me, "A great diagnostician knows the most symptoms. Any practicing doctor can diagnose the common illnesses. At Mayo, we specialize in knowing and thus seeing what's not obvious." Similarly, those who know the most options see what's not obvious and make a better decision.

Robert McNamara, former president of Ford Motor Company, once asked an executive who brought a decision to him: "What did you decide *not* to do?" He wanted to know that the person had thought of more than one option before making the decision.

The secret in developing options is to do our thinking early. If we wait until the last minute, we don't have time to make the best decision. I've become so option-driven that my son, Fred, gave me an engraved sign that reads: BUT ON THE OTHER HAND. Increased options increase our chances of being right.

2. *Is this mutually beneficial?* Maxey Jarman, who built Genesco into the world's third largest apparel company, was one of my mentors. He acquired many businesses as he built the corporation, and he would say, "Don't drive a bargain so hard that the other person becomes a loser." That creates a wedge in the relationship and generates retaliation.

Some decisions are difficult to make mutual. Several times, I've had to let an employee go. I agree with the chairman of a bank who called such moments "throw-up time." No effective executive I know enjoys firing people.

Yet many times, looking back, both the employee and I have seen it was the best thing that could have happened. Roger Hull, who was chairman of Mutual of New York, once said to me, "I've lived long enough to have people whom I fired come back and thank me for their termination." (I don't want to paint this too rosy; the hurt of being let go can last a long time.)

Harvard University commissioned a thirty-year study of successful CEOs. One common trait among them: altruism. I define altruism as this: "I give before I receive." That attitude makes for mutually beneficial and better decisions.

3. *What's the risk?* Once in New York City, I looked out my hotel window and saw several teenagers walking an eighteen-inch ledge, thirty stories up, with no railing to grab. I couldn't look. These students hadn't calculated the risk and the reward.

This principle of calculating the risks is seen in the verse, "What good will it be for a man if he gains the whole world, yet forfeits his soul?" The benefits of temporary gain are offset by permanent loss.

I've heard some Christians confess things in a small group that they should have kept to themselves. I think they got a short-term reward—they felt better—but in the long run, their confession proved disastrous to relationships. The risk was too high.

To accurately assess the risk, we must know when enough is enough. A twenty-seven-year-old man I know, worth $3.5 million, recently ran across a business deal that promised to convert his present net worth into $25 million. He asked my advice.

"What can $25 million do for your family," I said, "that $3.5 million can't? It's too risky. You'll be jeopardizing your wife and children's security."

He gambled and lost. Fighting bankruptcy, he and his wife are laden with debt during the years they should be enjoying their small children.

Money isn't the only thing we need to say "enough" to. What about prestige, ministry, power?

4. Is it timely? I once asked a successful executive in California what traits he wanted in his leaders.

"The trait I value most," he said, "is a sense of timing."

As Kenny Rogers sings in "The Gambler," "You gotta know when to hold 'em, know when to fold 'em."

When making decisions, more leaders are late than early. I think that's due to a natural fear of making decisions. Whether starting a program or buying a stock, most of us tend to procrastinate.

Timing is an intuitive matter, so some leaders are better than others in sensing the right time. (This is a place where I ask for help.) But we can all develop our sense of timing by cultivating what a friend calls "disciplined imagination." That means taking the present facts and extending them into the future—what will be their relationship in the future?

Many problems in American industry can be traced to poor timing, which comes from not extending present facts into the future. We have a hard time creating even five-year plans for our organizations. Recently an acquaintance traveled to Japan to study that country's business practices—they're making 100-year business plans!

5. Do I have staying power? When we make a decision, we need to follow it through the valleys until we get back to high ground. We need to make sure we have the emotional resolve to carry out our decisions even if they prove harder than we expect.

For example, some parents do not have the staying power to back up their decisions. This teaches their children to scream when they're small and rebel when they're older, knowing their parents will not stand their ground. I feel for the parents, because it takes a great deal of emotional stamina to say no to a child. But it's better never to make a policy you will not enforce.

Murphy's Law works often enough in life that we had better develop staying power. In business deals, for example, I have learned I need at least 50 percent more money than anticipated and 200 percent more time. In making a decision, we need to anticipate a possible downturn and not presume on the future.

A young man from a well-known ministry once approached me

for financial support. "I've recently purchased a van on faith for our ministry," he said. "Would you contribute to pay off the loan?"

"Did the car dealer know you didn't have the money?"

"Uh, no."

"Then you didn't buy it on your faith," I said. "You bought it on his. I recommend returning the van."

6. *What are the long-term ramifications?* Every action has a reaction. We are free to act, but we are not free from the consequences of our action.

Some Christian leaders make poor decisions because they fail to look at the long-term ramifications. Not long ago, I had the opportunity to speak with ten well-educated pastors.

"How can we get our churches to adopt our vision and programs?" they asked.

"Did you found the church?" I replied.

"No."

"Are you going to stay there if you land a better opportunity?"

"No."

"Then maybe the church isn't yours to change," I said. "That's short-term thinking. A long-term strategy would say, 'How can I help our church create a ministry that will continue after I'm gone?' "

A leader's job is to become dispensable, equipping others to do his work. A litmus test of leaders may be how well the organization can run without them.

The late Ray Stedman once invited me to take a trip to Africa with his eleven pastoral staff members.

"Who's going to run the church while you're gone?" I asked.

"The same ones who run it when we're here," he replied. "The church doesn't depend on us."

That stayed with me. In my family life, I would like to make decisions so that when I die, not a single person will need me but all will love me. I don't want to make decisions that make me indispensable.

7. *Have I built in escape hatches?* Not all decisions can include correction points, or escape hatches. When you realize you have no possibility for correcting the decision, act carefully.

But often we can build escape hatches into our decisions. In contracts, for example, I like to stipulate an evaluation of the agreement at some specific future date.

Once I was involved with a company whose president's contract did not cover unsatisfactory performance. When it became clear their decision to hire this person was a mistake, the company had no escape hatch. They fired him but were required to make good on his salary.

A friend of mine in the banking industry once said, "Never delay a failure with your money. Get out of a failure as fast as you can." His comment reminds me to build into major decisions the opportunity to get out.

8. *Have I asked for advice—after doing my homework?* Arrogance sometimes keeps us from asking for help. In one business meeting, I needed help, so I called someone and asked for his advice. An executive overheard me and said, "I could never do that."

"Why?"

"I can't admit I don't know."

"My ignorance," I said, "is my greatest asset."

I get by with a lot of help from my friends. But I try to have the integrity of not asking for their advice until after I have done my homework.

When I ask for advice, I use three criteria:

- Will this person take my question seriously? If I'm serious enough to ask for advice, I want people to tell me what they honestly think, not just what they think I want to hear.

- Is my question in this person's area of expertise? Theologians are great, but they're not the people to ask about cancer.

- Does the person have time to think through my questions? I can't call someone five minutes before a major decision and expect thoughtful advice. If my decision is important enough to ask for outside help, then it's important enough to give my outside help enough time to make a good call.

Last year a young man told me, "We have a baby who's ill. The doctor is keeping her on an expensive medical machine. I'm not sure my child needs the constant technological care she's receiving at the hospital, and the bills are mounting.

"You know a lot of people, Fred," he continued. "Could you call someone to see if we're being ripped off by this doctor?"

I called my friend at Mayo Clinic, who took my request seriously. He found an expert—a co-writer of a medical journal article about this child's symptoms. That physician saw the baby and said it didn't need all the high-priced medical equipment. The original doctor had been dishonest. The situation showed the reward of asking for advice.

9. *Have I validated the decision in prayer?* When Theodore Hesburgh was president of Notre Dame, David Rockefeller asked him to join the board of directors of Chase Manhattan Bank. Father Hesburgh laughed. "I'm a priest," he said. "I don't even have a checking account."

"You are trained to know right from wrong?" asked Rockefeller. "Yes."

"That's why we need you on our board," Rockefeller said. "We understand banking and finance. We need your help when difficult questions of right and wrong come."

To be right, we need more than facts: we need the truth. The Pharisees were experts in facts but missed the truth.

Christians have an advantage in making decisions: we have the help of the Holy Spirit when we really want to do the right thing.

I have never found a foolproof way of discovering God's will for the future. Looking back, I see his hand clearly, but looking forward requires faith, and faith is what pleases him.

By validating a decision in prayer, I mean talking to the Lord exactly as I would to a business partner about all the details. I am actually praying to see if my mood, motives, and method are correct. I ask the Lord to let me remain in neutral—willing to go any way—until after I've talked with him and been honest about what I should do.

I follow the saying, "When in serious doubt, don't." When making a decision, I hope not to violate scriptural principles knowingly. For example, I believe greed violates scriptural principle, and often this belief has protected me.

A friend who was knowledgeable in the silver market once suggested I get in at $35 an ounce; the price was rising fast. When I felt my greed meter going up, I talked it over with my wife, Mary Alice, and we decided against investing. That decision proved not only morally right but financially wise when the silver market collapsed.

I'm also suspicious of any decision that stirs my pride. If I'm asked to join a board, I try to define any uniqueness I would bring. If I find none, I refuse, no matter how prestigious the invitation. If I do have a uniqueness to contribute, then it's my responsibility, not an honor.

10. *Am I afraid to pull the trigger?* One person who gave the Lyman Beecher lectures at Yale remarked, "Some people, if they saw a sign, THIS WAY TO HEAVEN, and another sign, THIS WAY TO A DISCUSSION ON HEAVEN, would take the discussion." Some people like to wear out a decision just talking about it.

Others stall on decisions out of fear they won't be liked. We can't make good decisions on that basis. One question I've added to my evaluation of people is "What will this person do to be liked?" Peer pressure and false humility both cripple effectiveness.

When Maxey Jarman retired, I asked what he had learned. He said, "Not many people will make a decision. Many can, but few will."

To shoot a rifle, you have to pull the trigger. To make a decision, you have to act.

22

Dangerous Decisions

Risks must be taken; confrontations must be made.

—Terry Muck

In *A Word From the Wise*, I. D. Thomas tells the story of a Georgia farmer living in a dilapidated shack. He hadn't planted anything, so nothing needed to be cultivated. The farmer just sat, ragged and barefoot, surrounded by the evidence of his laziness.

A stranger stopped for a drink of water and asked, "How's your cotton doing?"

"Ain't got none," replied the farmer.

"Didn't you plant any?"

"Nope. 'Fraid of boll weevils."

"Well," continued the visitor, "how's your corn?"

"Didn't plant none. 'Fraid there wasn't gonna be no rain."

"How are your potatoes?"

"Ain't got none. Scared of potato bugs."

"Really? What did you plant?"

"Nothin' " was the reply. "I just played it safe."

The church leader who never takes risks quickly finds: no risks, no returns.

The Bible supplies many instances of this Law of Risklessness. Proverbs predicts the non-rewards the sluggard can expect. Jesus' parable of the talents rests on the futility of trying to avoid all risk. The risks of not taking risks are the riskiest of all. One study showed that leaders who made few or no major decisions per year, regardless of the type—theological verdicts, institutional judgments, interpersonal choices—were the most likely to have been dismissed from a church at some time in their ministry. Conversely, leaders who were willing to take a stand—even when that seemed perilous—usually found secure footing.

One pastor recounts a budget skirmish: "The board had talked over the budget, and we had made the changes we thought necessary. When the budget was presented to the church for ratification, one board member, who had been through the whole budgeting process and voted for our budget, stood and said, 'I don't see why we have so much money going to outreach. We've never had money for local outreach before. I think we should pay the pianist instead.'

"I thought, *You're a former pastor! You have to know better.*

"I had to make a quick decision whether or not to say anything. I don't like getting into an argument in front of the church, but I couldn't stay silent, so I gave a few reasons for the outreach program. Then I said that paying the pianist was going inward instead of outward. This was the first time in our church's history that we'd had some extra money to put into outreach, and I thought it important to do so.

"I didn't know how the church would react. They had been through some hard times, and most had the idea it's best not to rock the boat. In this case, I had one key element going for me. The pianist this board member wanted to pay was his wife. Even people who didn't want to rock the boat could see the self-interest. His idea was voted down.

"Afterward many people came to me and said, 'I don't think his idea was good. Thanks for taking a stand.' Only one person objected."

Taking a risk, paradoxically, may be less hazardous than doing nothing at all.

Reluctant risk taker

This doesn't mean risk taking is something one merely decides to do and does. Even those outgoing souls who thrive on the thrill of risk sometimes have to force themselves to act—and will readily admit to the continual need to sharpen their skills.

For some, though, risk taking seems next to impossible. They would sooner tame a lion than confront a parishioner. For them, it is not a question of wanting to take a risk; it is a question of going against the natural inclinations of their personalities to resist conflict at all costs.

Such resistance is not to be taken lightly—nor demeaned. The third-century Turks tell a fable about a soft-wax candle that was lamenting the fact that the slightest touch injured it. The candle felt cheated by this apparent personality flaw. How the candle admired the rock-hard bricks, impervious to dents and nicks. Seeing that bricks started out as soft clay and only grew hard from heat, the candle had an idea. To acquire the brick's hardness and durability, the candle leaped into the fire. It quickly melted and was consumed. The moral? It is useless to malign the "disadvantages" inherent in our personalities.

Psychologist Frank Farley, in *Psychology Today*, identified a cluster of characteristics that make up the "Type T personality," high-profile people who are risk takers and daring adventurers. The roster of Type T's includes such people as DNA researcher Sir Francis Crick and aviator Amelia Earhart. Type T's prefer uncertainty to certainty, complexity to simplicity, and novelty to familiarity. They prefer to work in flexible structures and tend to be stifled by the nine-to-five mentality.

At the opposite end of the personality spectrum are Type t (little t) personalities, people who avoid risks. People at this end of the personality spectrum are rarely public figures. Farley thinks big T's and little t's are determined largely through genetics, though very early experiences may play a role.

Little t's don't relish decisions, even when the groundwork has been laid and the time appears right. Witness a little-t pastor in action:

"Recently our board considered putting ceiling fans in the sanctuary. We talked about the advantages and the disadvantages. I was for the fans because they're economical. They blow the warm air back down in the winter; in the summer they create a breeze, so we don't have to run our air conditioner as often.

"Some on the board, however, didn't want to risk destroying the appearance of the sanctuary. We have a beautiful cathedral ceiling, and who knows for sure what hanging fans would do to the look.

"After all the discussion, we took a vote. The tally was five votes for the fans, three opposed. A split vote is unusual for our board, but the people who voted against the fans accepted it calmly, saying in effect, 'We voted against it, but that's the decision of the board, and we'll support the decision. Let's get it done.'

"But I haven't purchased the fans. My head tells me they will save money—the facts support that. My head also tells me the fans will be accepted by the congregation. But my gut tells me not to do it, that it's not that necessary. I've thought about why I'm dragging my feet. If it had been an eight-to-nothing vote, I think I'd still feel uneasy. And I can't quite say why. Something is just telling me not to do it. It's a very real feeling, though not quantifiable.

"Actually, I'm causing more trouble for myself. Since the committee voted for the fans, I'm supposed to buy them. If I don't, I'll have to explain why I haven't and then get them to agree *not* to do it. But I just don't feel right about it."

This pastor simply does not have the temperament of a Nathan Hale, the Revolutionary War spy who, when about to be hanged, said he only regretted he had but one life to give for his country. Some church leaders (Hale himself probably would have been a minister had not the American Revolution broken out) have the bravado and gusto of a Hale. Others don't, and struggle with what to do.

Although big T's take to risk taking more easily, Farley notes that little t's *can* develop the necessary skills. But they need to use the skills in ways congruent with their personalities. They are more likely to learn confrontational techniques through analytical descriptions—by the book, perhaps—than through actual experiences (which they may be too timid ever to initiate). People with little-t temperaments can be taught to take risks; it simply is more difficult for them.

Even people with insecure personalities are risk takers of a sort, although they normally choose risks of a different category. Psychologist John Atkinson showed that two motivations drive people to take risks. One is the motivation to achieve; the other is the motivation to avoid failure. Those motivated to achieve generally take regular, consistent, intermediate risks. Those motivated to avoid failure go to one extreme or another. They either play it unusually safe, trying to avoid risk altogether, or they make extremely risky moves. The person who sinks his life savings into a speculative stock venture after a lifetime of passbook savings is typical of the avoid-failure personality.

Another reason some of us are reluctant risk takers is outlined by Nathan Kogan and Michael Wallach in their book *Risk Taking*. They found that people with intuitive personalities tend to see the big picture better. They scan long-range implications of success or failure more quickly than others, and thus tend to take risks and force confrontations earlier. Those who have a more rationalistic orientation, on the other hand, tend to focus on the immediate and overlook the need for risk taking or confrontation until too late. Intuitively, Kogan and Wallach see the optimal personality to be a balance between the two.

A third polarity has been drawn between the perfectionistic personality and the nonperfectionistic personality. Perfectionists are generally motivated by the fear of making mistakes. They are unusually cautious and averse to risk taking. Those with the nonperfectionistic personality, on the other hand, are more willing to put things up for grabs. David D. Burns, in his book *Feeling Good*, says, "Show me a man who can't stand to be wrong, and I'll show you a man who's afraid to take risks and who has given up the capacity for growth. I probably make three mistakes in every therapy session."

None of the personality experts who study risk taking discount the possibility of people who are predisposed to not taking chances learning to do so. All would agree that training and experience have a great deal to do with a person's risk-taking skill. Those who trade futures on the Chicago Board of Trade, for example, learn to take risks; their living depends on it. Training for such a position involves gaining a good grasp of the statistical probabilities of various situations—and learning to analyze one's intuitions.

Tactics: short-range

Few church leaders are trained in risk taking, although decision-making courses are becoming more common in seminaries. Still, they are far down the priority pole in divinity training. Most pastors then, regardless of personality, develop risk-taking skills on the job. Here are some tactics to further pastoral skills and help determine what risks can and cannot be handled.

Take a reading of the emotional climate of the risk-taking situation. Focus particularly on your emotional situation by asking these questions:

- Am I ever a little irrational? Is this one of those times? How do I know? What can I do about it?

- Am I afraid? If yes, of what? If not, why not?
- Am I ready to act? Will I ever be ready to act? What is holding me back?

It's equally productive to determine the emotional involvement you have in this particular project. Helpful questions to consider:

- What feeling am I trying to express by taking this risk?
- Will people think better or worse of me if I succeed?
- Do I care what opinion people have of me? What opinion of me would I like people to assume?

Convince yourself of the need to act. Sometimes action needs to be immediate. Make sure you consciously decide to act promptly or else have good, valid reasons for delay. Remember stories like the following:

"One of the elders, a pillar of the church who had been around seemingly forever, became angry over a church financial decision. The board decided to allocate some money to a project Bradley didn't like. It was obvious to everyone as he left the board meeting that he was very upset. I knew I needed to talk to him immediately, but I believed it was usually good policy to let things cool a little. In this case it wasn't. The next morning I had Bradley's resignation as an elder on my desk.

"I prayed over that letter, and the next day I went to his house. We spent the afternoon together, and by the end of the visit, although we still disagreed on the financial matter, he had withdrawn his resignation. We saw that in Christ we can have differences and still have fellowship.

"I will be forever grateful to God for leading me to work it out quickly with Bradley. Over the next sixteen months, we became dear friends. We shared intimate times; he became a confidant for me.

"Bradley was a farmer. He had a small front-loading tractor, and one day he was carrying a load of stones in the front hopper. He went up a small grade—probably not more than two feet high—but it was enough to cause the load to shift, and it rolled that tractor over on top of him. He was killed instantly.

"I went out to the house. The medics had laid him under a blanket, still in the yard. His wife was in the kitchen. There was nothing I could do except put my arms around her and cry with her.

"Later I thought, *What if I hadn't talked with him when he wanted to resign?* I would have regretted it forever. As it is, I can rejoice in the friendship God gave us."

Tactics: long-range

In addition, there are some long-term strategies:

Define your style. Ellen Siegelman, in her book *Personal Risk,* has developed an informal self-test that measures risk-taking style. She defines three categories: anxious risk takers, balanced risk takers, and careless risk takers. According to her, knowing your style can help you prepare for a risk. For example, an anxious risk taker needs to push himself to make the decision. A careless risk taker, on the other hand, needs to slow down and do more research before taking action.

Develop an assertion message. Michael Baer, a former pastor in Texas, suggests a technique he learned from Robert Bolton's *People Skills.* Professional managers use a simple, brief formula to teach employees basic confrontational technique. It provides a framework for saying what needs to be said without sending the wrong messages. Essentially it is made up of three parts:

"When you (insert the other person's behavior), I feel (explain how it makes you feel) because (give a specific negative effect of their behavior)."

1. The formula gives a nonemotional description of the behavior you want to see changed. For example, you might say, "When you come late to board meetings . . ." Keep it specific and do not exaggerate by saying things like "When you are always late for board meetings . . ." Few people are always late.

2. State your *feelings* about the behavior. For example, you might say, "When you come late to the board meetings, I feel angry." This lets the other person know you care.

3. Finally, point out the results of the undesirable behavior. You might say, "When you come late to the board meetings, I feel angry because it causes all of us to get home late."

The formula is not a panacea but a beginning toward confronting others in situations with potential risk. By mastering the technique, some of your reluctance to confront may be dispelled.

Costs and benefits

In our survey, pastors who said they made no tough decisions during a year were more likely to be fired than pastors who could identify such decisions. Pastors willing to face decisions last longer.

Yet longevity is not the only indicator of fallout from making or not making difficult decisions. There are other, less obvious factors. To identify those, one survey asked a series of questions about the toll risky decisions take on the leaders' personal well-being, their ministry effectiveness, and their families.

The good news from the survey results is that when a tough decision is over, most of the pastors who stay (85 percent) and even most of those who leave (81 percent) see benefits from the process they have been through.

Surprisingly, tough decisions cost pastors who stayed more *personal* pain than those who were forced to leave. Seventy-five percent of the pastors who stayed after a tough decision said the process took a toll on their physical/mental/emotional health compared to only 63 percent of the pastors who were fired. The fired pastors did perceive the cost to their children to be more expensive. But even here the reported difference was small. Ministry decision making takes a toll on everyone in the pastor's family, no matter what the outcome of the decision.

Ministerial effectiveness, as perceived by the pastor involved, always suffers. Both fired and nonfired pastors recognized that a church in pain cannot serve as well as a church in good health.

What can you handle?

No one loves risky decisions. For some the fear of consequences is worse than for others. Risks must be taken; confrontations must be made. There will be personal and ministry costs, as well as benefits.

Once these truths are accepted and weighed, it is perhaps helpful to go through one final checklist of questions to help determine *Just what can I handle personally?*

Will taking this risk make me satisfied if I am successful? How do I know? What else would satisfy me? Do I need to risk for that?

Do I allow myself to feel hurt, sad, angry, anxious, or joyous?

Am I aware of my moods and how they influence my actions? Do

I recognize my feelings? Can I take a rejection in this case? If I am rejected, how will I act?

What are the limits to the amount of emotion I can show without adversely affecting the body of Christ?

The ultimate reason many of us are scared to make a necessary but risky decision is fear of the consequences. What will happen if we make the wrong decision? It's helpful to consider the stories of fellow pastors who saw a risk go bad—yet found healing and productive ministry on the other side. One pastor's wife, whose husband had lost a battle with an elder, told how they were forced to leave the church:

"I felt a sense of betrayal, a sense that grew on me. After we announced our resignation, we continued to serve from the end of August through December. I read negative feelings into a lot of what people did. If they didn't say anything, I thought they were thinking bad thoughts about us. I became suspicious and withdrawn. It could have gotten pretty bad, but the Lord provided insight for me in a dream.

"One night I fell asleep crying out to God, and I dreamed of dried cornstalks in my garden. Ordinarily in the fall I cut those stalks into pieces. In my dream, the Lord gave me a choice: I could cut up the stalks and leave them on the ground, or I could till them into the soil, nourishing it for next year.

"I saw clearly that those cornstalks were like my anger. I could leave the pieces lying on the ground to pick up and throw at anyone who came near me. Or I could plow them under and use this experience to help me grow in the future. I learned that painful experiences could be something nourishing to me and others through me—if I let them. Or I could keep those pieces of pain and anger in my life and allow the resentment to remain. I remember making a deliberate choice that night: 'Lord, I want this painful time to nourish my life, but you're going to have to help me because I'm too angry to do it myself.'

"God has indeed helped that process. The pain was real, and I wouldn't want to go through it again. But God does help make everything work together for good."

23

Why Deciding Is Only Half the Battle

*The steps necessary after the initial decision is made
are as important as the decision itself.*

—John Vawter

There really was no choice. After four years of growth, despite enlarging the parking lot, our problem was becoming more severe.

Street parking was already jammed. Purchase of adjacent land wasn't feasible. The only alternative, concluded the long-range planning committee, was to pave part of the church ball field, which hadn't been used in three years and was covered with weeds two feet high.

The elders voted unanimously to recommend the proposal at the next congregational meeting. It seemed such an obvious decision that we quickly moved on to the next item of business.

At the congregational meeting, however, person after person raised strong objections:

"Buy more property."

"We built that for the kids."

"Are you certain we need more parking?"

When the vote was taken, the motion failed to carry. I was more stunned than disappointed. I was amazed at the vociferous reaction over a minor issue. And why weren't the people more concerned about our continued growth?

As I evaluated the meeting with the chairman of the elder board and long-range planning committee, I realized we had made a fundamental mistake in our decision-making process: we had made a decision without adequately preparing to follow through. We had not informed the congregation prior to the meeting that the vote was going to be taken. We had not considered how to prepare the congregation for the vote, nor had we marshaled the evidence to support the paving of the ball field.

Simply making a decision is meaningless unless it is carried out effectively. Later on, when clearly shown the implications of our decision, the congregation voted overwhelmingly to pave the field.

Unfortunately, this incident didn't cure me of my penchant to neglect the second half of the decision-making process. I had to learn the hard way.

Recently we completed a new worship center. In our old facility, we had been filled to capacity with double services and two Sunday schools. Now, since everyone could fit, I announced we could return to one worship service. It seemed a simple decision, so I made it . . . and nearly had revolution on my hands. If lynching wasn't outlawed in Minnesota, my staff members might have tried it.

I hadn't thought through how the decision would affect the Christian education department, which had grown so much with double sessions that even the new facility couldn't handle everything at once. But I had announced one worship service, and therefore one C.E. session.

After much negotiation and analysis, we finally agreed that we'd likely grow enough this year to be in double worship services again next September. So we settled on a less-than-ideal C.E. program for a year in order to have everyone together in worship. One worship service, I'm convinced, was the right decision. But I went at it all wrong. I didn't think through the follow-through, and thus I was responsible for a lot of grief. In retrospect, the decision needed to be discussed with my colleagues, those affected by the decision, before everything was set in cement.

Since then, I've become more aware of the steps necessary *after* the initial decision is made. In many cases these are as important as the decision itself.

Resistance preparation

Any decision-making process should include asking these questions:

- Who might this decision affect, and should their advice be sought

before a final decision is made?
- What will be the impact when they hear the decision?
- What kind of resentment will have to be lived with if this decision is made? Is it worth the price?

My staff members felt betrayed when I announced we would have one Sunday school. I should have consulted them before making the final decision. On the other hand, if you wait until everyone is happy before making a decision, you can bring the church to a standstill. It is a fine line to walk.

I once heard that every institution is made up of 10 percent innovators, 40 percent maintainers, and 50 percent inhibitors. The percentages may exaggerate the point, but the principle holds: you must weigh, not count, the critics. Some will always complain and resist change if they haven't made the suggestion themselves. We must be ready and prepared for resistance.

Are there certain people who should *not* be consulted in advance? I have made it a practice not to ask the advice of the chronic complainers and those who appear to resist all change. Nor do I seek out those who appear consistently carnal. I refuse to mollify (here you see my personality style coming through) those who never seem to have a good word to say about anything.

Disagreement, however, is not the same as carnality. It is foolish not to listen to dissenters and use their insights when implementing a decision. After all, no one person, including the pastor, has a corner on truth and wisdom.

Who's responsible?

Decisions frequently go to waste because no one is given responsibility to carry them out. Board members agree to act on something, but no one is assigned to make sure it's done. Sometimes too many subjects are discussed at once, and just as discussion on one item winds down, someone introduces the next agenda item or raises a question off the subject. Assignments are overlooked, and no action is taken.

We're improving on this, thanks to our chairman, who is a strong proponent of making as few decisions as possible but making certain the ones we do make are effective. He runs a tight ship, making sure one subject is completely finished and assignments are made before a new topic is raised.

We've also discovered the assignments must be specific. Usually this means *one* person must be given responsibility, not a group.

When we were adding the new worship center, we also decided to renovate three portions of our old facility—the kitchen, the old worship center, and the balcony. Since this renovation was not part of the building contractor's contract, we decided to do the work ourselves and assigned three individuals to research the costs if we used volunteer labor. Unfortunately, we did not assign one person to oversee the whole project. Consequently, blueprints were lost, communication broke down, time spent on research was wasted, and ten months later we were no further ahead than when we began.

The fault was not with the three volunteers. The problem was caused by not authorizing someone to be in charge of the project. No one was ultimately responsible, and therefore the job wasn't completed.

Sometimes the opposite problem occurs: too many people feel responsible, which leads to confusion and tension. In this situation, not only responsibility but *authority* must be spelled out.

For instance, one of our secretaries has the responsibility for the maintenance of our building and grounds, authorizing repairs, directing the custodian, and paying the necessary bills. Although she is accountable directly to me, because of her newness on the job and her conscientiousness some people in the church began telling her what to do. Trying to keep everyone happy, she was intimidated until I made clear that she reports only to me, and *she* is the one in the best position to decide and follow through on maintenance problems.

Wise assignments

When responsibilities are assigned, they must (1) be given to responsible people, and (2) be defined clearly.

Responsibility to carry out decisions is sometimes given to people without considering their capabilities. It is naive to assume that everyone in the church is equally able to follow through.

"One of our elders is a detail person," said a pastor friend. "He loves data, and although he's good at one-on-one, he has a hard time getting groups of people motivated. Thus, we are careful not to assign him to personnel tasks, but we do give him responsibility in areas demanding paperwork. On the other hand, another elder does poorly with details, but he's a great motivator and recruiter. We assign him the people tasks."

Too often decisions turn sour not because they were wrong but because they were assigned to the wrong person. Thus, part of the responsibility of the pastor and/or board chairman is to know people well and know what they can handle.

Sometimes even capable people fail to follow through because they weren't given clear enough directions and parameters. Do they have the authority to act or only inform? What are the deadlines? Is there a budget at their disposal?

Several years ago, we were trying to discover ways to maintain our building more effectively and be more energy-efficient. We asked one woman to research several churches in the city to see how they handled these problems.

When her report came in, it detailed administrative systems of the churches surveyed but said nothing about building, grounds, or energy conservation. It was a classic case of poor parameters. The report and the researcher's time were wasted.

Supervisor assignment

In addition to assigning the specific responsibility, someone else needs to be responsible to make sure the assignee is on target and on schedule.

Often in church circles, we act as if everyone is a "nice guy," and therefore we don't need to supervise assignments as we would in any non-church situation. Consequently, decisions are sometimes carried out poorly or not at all.

One of our elders, a genius at long-range planning, has helped me with this. As I was preparing my section of the church's five-year plan, he called almost every week to ask how everything was coming along and if there was anything he could do to help. He knew this was a new area for me, and ultimately he was responsible to the board for the plan. Thus, he wasn't taking anything for granted and was making certain I was getting the report done the way it needed to be done. I did not take this as a put-down of my pastoral office or personal abilities; I perceived it as good leadership on his part.

Another way we're working on this is to have my secretary take minutes at all elder meetings. She knows what assignments have been given to each elder and what needs to be done before the next meeting. Everyone knows she'll be calling before we meet again to give gentle reminders of their assignments and the respective deadlines.

Organizations and churches can get careless and allow details to be overlooked. Assigning someone to keep track of the implementation of decisions is the best prevention.

I remember sitting on the district board of our denomination when we decided to subsidize a mission church for one year. The decision was made with the understanding that the church would be required to show significant growth and development within that year or the subsidy would be discontinued. Exactly one year later, without any discussion, we were voting to continue that subsidy when a board member said, "Wait a minute. Wasn't this subsidy only for one year, pending a progress report?" He was exactly right. No report had been made, and without it, no continuing subsidy should have been considered. We informed the church that the reports would have to be submitted before we could authorize further funds.

Only the board member's memory kept us from being careless administrators. Assigning someone to monitor the project would have been better.

Admitting mistakes

A sometimes-overlooked reason why decisions are not carried out is because they were poor decisions in the first place. Often we don't see the flaws in a decision until we try to implement it.

For example, in the midst of discussing our evangelism efforts, I decided we needed some kind of outreach in the local park. I immediately assigned an assistant pastor to work on it. Later, he came to me and said he didn't think the timing was right and that he didn't see how it fit into our overall strategy. Rethinking it, I realized he was right, and we decided not to pursue the idea further.

Backing down from a poor decision is wiser than trying to prove yourself right when the follow-through falls apart.

Standing alone

Often, especially in the initial stages of implementing a decision, the pastor will have to stand (and sometimes act) alone. Learning to live with resistance and criticism is part of the pastoral task.

My predecessor was more of a topical preacher than I am; my style is more exegetical. My first series on Ephesians took fifty sermons, and I was criticized for that. I have been criticized for not being sufficiently committed to our denomination—although I serve on our district board and have been asked to serve on various committees. I have been criticized for my tight control of what appears in the bulletin. Regardless of the issue or decision, there will be criticism. I am learning to accept criticism without continually second- and third-guessing myself.

Occasionally it's also necessary to stare down the critics. A colleague in another church was criticized because he allowed guitar music in a worship service—in spite of the fact that the kids in the growing and healthy high school ministry appreciated it. The critics thought worship music should be confined to organ and eighteenth-century melodies. The pastor held firm, however, saying, "We are a family, and we will endeavor to have a bit of music for everyone's tastes. Each of us needs to be patient when our tastes are not being satisfied."

Finally, at times you must act alone to implement a necessary decision. In some circumstances, the pastor has to function as a shepherd and enforce tough decisions unilaterally.

Another pastor friend is in a church with a detailed and involved process for removing deacons from the board. One deacon, however, was disruptive, given to anger at board meetings. His presence was so counterproductive the pastor felt he couldn't wait for the "system" to work. He felt he needed to take immediate steps to correct the situation, to confront the sin involved that was affecting the whole group.

In a spirit of gentle correction, the pastor met with the deacon and said, "I love you, Ed, but I also need to protect the unity and effectiveness of the board. Your anger is inappropriate and is sabotaging the church's ministry. I think you need to either stop your outbursts or resign." The man admitted to his anger and opted to resign because the board was more pressure than he could handle.

I'm not a proponent of violating guidelines. However, there are those rare occasions when decisions must be acted upon immediately. The pastor must invoke the "War Powers Act" because waiting for an "act of Congress" would prove disastrous. Obviously this must not be done impetuously but with a genuine sense of God's guidance—and an explanation to the board.

Unenviable but inevitable

As one National Football League season was beginning, Dallas Cowboys coach Tom Landry made the decision to bench starting quarterback Danny White and replace him with Gary Hogeboom. Landry, a successful coach for many years, said the decision was so unpleasant he wished he were "on a lake fishing with Bud Grant instead of making decisions like this!" (Grant had just retired as head coach of the Minnesota Vikings.)

The significance of Landry's sentiment was not lost on me. Landry was a veteran coach, a brilliant football mind, a strong leader. And yet he still struggled with decisions.

The same will be true of our decisions in ministry. That is why we need to know ourselves and whether or not we are capable of making the difficult choices necessary to develop and protect the parts of the body with which we have been entrusted. We need receptivity to God's signals and willingness to obey those signals, which allow us to make wise decisions—and make them in such a way that we can follow through on them.

24

Calling Plays the Players Can Run

The key is progress, not perfection.

—Kennon Callahan

One congregation I visited recently was scared and scarred by events of the past. Although they had no explicit objectives, it was clear their main purpose was what I call "protecting their place on the face of the cliff."

In mountain climbing, sometimes climbers find themselves on the face of a cliff where they can't find a handhold or foothold ahead or behind. In that predicament many people freeze. They cling for dear life. They fear any move could mean the abyss below.

This church was frozen on the face of the cliff. They couldn't find anything in their history that would save them. They couldn't see anything hopeful ahead. They became preoccupied with maintenance, membership, and money.

To help a church like that, the one thing I do *not* do is shout instructions from the safety of the ledge above. I join them on the face of the cliff and gently coach them: "We're going to start with the left hand, and we're going to move it four inches up and one inch over, and we're going to hold there. Now we're going to try the left foot." You coach a congregation in that predicament gently and wisely forward, one step at a time.

Most churches are not frozen on the cliff, but they do suffer from an uncertainty about what to do next. About half the churches I help are stable and growing churches that want to improve their mission and outreach. The other half are churches in some form of crisis—stable and declining, or dying. Usually some event has precipitated the call, and they want someone to share some wisdom and research, to help them gain a sense of direction.

What these churches have in common is that they sense the challenge of planning for both the short- and long-term. There are many things churches ought to do, many problems with which to deal, many needs in the world. How do we choose which to address? How do we plan for the future?

Finding do-ables

The art of organizational planning is to match the plays and the players. The wise coach never sends in plays the players cannot run. I try to help churches match their objectives and their team.

Consultants, pastors, and key leaders are tempted sometimes to ask congregations to achieve some imposed goal. A given church's gifts, strengths, and competencies may be to deliver corporate, dynamic worship. But some leader may insist, "What we should be doing is starting new small groups."

Small groups may be created eventually, but the art of helping a church move ahead is to build the key major objectives on the strengths a congregation presently has. The church that denies its strengths denies God's gifts. The church that claims its strengths claims God's gifts. I urge congregations to discover the strengths God has given them, so they can build on those. That, in turn, leads them to discover and nurture yet new strengths.

As leaders plan, I think it's better to use the term *objectives*, rather than *priorities*. Priorities can be vague. Objectives are specific and measurable, concrete and achievable. We can know and celebrate when we have achieved them, and we can confess when we have not.

Every church has objectives. The key questions are: Do they *know* what their objectives are? And do these objectives help them do what God calls them to do?

Many churches I meet with don't have explicit objectives—at least not at the beginning. But as I look closer, I discover they have implicit and informal objectives, usually the result of a variety of elements: congregational values, customs, habits, and traditions; the decision-making process; the communication system. Implicit objectives guide a church just as surely as explicit ones do.

But having explicit objectives doesn't solve all of a church's problems. One church I consulted had excellent leaders and an excellent pastor. The pastor's strengths lay in developing and maintaining competent programs and activities. In every church he had served, he had built strong programs.

Yet this church longed for a pastor who would be a good shepherd, practice pastoral care, and train laypeople to visit. They also wanted more dynamic worship and preaching. The pastor kept saying, "What we should be emphasizing are our church's programs and activities." The congregation kept saying, "We do that well enough. What we want is a good shepherd and a good preacher."

Churches get themselves into such predicaments in three primary ways.

First, the pastor and key leaders get caught up in the "should syndrome." They decide the congregation should, must, ought to do this or that. They pursue objectives without considering whether they match the congregation's strengths.

Second, pastors and key leaders are tempted to universalize programs: if an idea worked well in one church, they assume it will work in theirs. When they try to transplant the idea, though, it often creates a mismatch, because their church doesn't have the gifts or strengths to effectively use the idea.

Third, people sometimes grasp for a straw in the wind, some idea or program that will transform the church, what I call "a short-term, quick-closure, highly visible, immediate-satisfaction achievement." Whether this fits the strengths of the congregation is hardly considered in the hurry to find a quick fix.

When I find a church whose objectives don't match their competencies, I approach them like I did the young player on one of the baseball teams I once coached. He had pleaded all season, "Let me pitch, let me pitch." So near the end of the season, I started him as pitcher. One of the hardest things I ever had to do was walk to the mound in the first inning. We were nine runs behind, with the bases loaded and no outs.

"Good friend, this is my fault," I began. "You are our best shortstop. Please, now, play shortstop. Sam is coming in as our pitcher, and between your fielding, the rest of the team's fielding, and Sam's pitching, we'll get out of this inning and beyond this game."

The temptation in working with churches is to think that someone—the pastor, the board, or the church itself—is simply incompetent. I begin with the assumption that there's no such thing as an incompetent person or church; there is sometimes a mismatch of competencies. I try to help the pastor and church work in areas in which they're competent and to "build forward" on these strengths.

Progress not perfection

More often than not, churches have too many objectives. Ironically, such churches accomplish little. It works like this:

Generally, leaders and pastors have a deep desire to please. In addition, somewhere along the way they begin to think they have to have something for everyone. Many people feel the church should be like a supermarket.

On top of that, and more problematic, they bring to planning a latent "compulsion toward perfectionism." Combined with a desire to please, that compulsion drives them to suggest ideas, goals, programs, and activities that the church "should" be committed to. On a Saturday retreat, a planning group will wallpaper three walls with newsprint of all the things everybody can think of to do. A ninety-seven page document of the priorities and objectives is created. They end up with too many goals, set too high, to be accomplished too soon.

That creates the desire to postpone. They sense that with these expectations, they're likely to fail. So they postpone action in order to postpone failure. That, in turn, creates depression. And that leads to dependency: "If only the denomination . . . If only the culture . . . If only the pastor . . . If only the members . . . *then* we would be a great church." I sometimes say to churches, tongue-in-cheek, that it takes considerable ingenuity, creativity, imagination, drive, energy, and determination to create a stable and declining congregation.

But I have seen churches break that pattern many, many times. The key is progress, not perfection. The three good friends are progress, pace, and prayer. It sometimes takes a church twenty years to get itself into a predicament. It may take more than two years to move beyond it! It can take a professional football organization five years to build a winning team. If it takes five years in something as simple as professional football, it may take at least five years in the complex matter of God's mission for a church.

When a church focuses on progress, not perfection, it sets a few objectives that are realistic and achievable. That creates action, not postponement: "Yes, we can achieve that." That action creates satisfaction not depression: "Our lives do count for God's mission." And satisfaction creates not dependency but growth and development, not in numbers in the church but in the congregation's sense that they are maturing in God's mission.

Front-line care

It's also helpful to think more clearly about some of the analogies we propose for the church. For instance, supermarkets, even the largest of them, don't offer something for everybody. They don't sell cars or manufacture parachutes. They don't even sell every kind of food available. The best supermarkets have specific objectives.

A better analogy is this: a local congregation is like a M.A.S.H. tent, delivering competent "missional care" at the front lines of peoples' hurts and hopes. It has a specific purpose. It doesn't try to do everything.

Four principles help churches focus their objectives.

Find the objectives that build the competence and confidence of the congregation. Coaching basketball years ago, I learned one key to success is to help each player find his best shot. In practice I encouraged each player to work on that shot, so that seven out of ten times as the ball left his hand, he would have both the confidence and the competence that the ball would go in. That created a spillover effect. When the player got the ball in another part of the court, he brought with him the confidence that the ball would go in from there, too. That confidence often produced a new competence.

Each congregation can find the areas in which they are already competent. I suggest they study the following twelve central characteristics of church life, and identify their best strengths:

Relational Characteristics
1. Specific, Concrete Missional Objectives
2. Pastoral/Lay Visitation in Community
3. Corporate, Dynamic Worship
4. Significant Relational Groups

5. Strong Leadership Resources
6. Solid, Participatory Decision-Making

Functional Characteristics
7. Several Competent Programs and Activities
8. Open Accessibility
9. High Visibility
10. Adequate Parking, Land, and Landscaping
11. Adequate Space and Facilities
12. Solid Financial Resources

Expand a strength first. Take a current strength that is, on a scale of one to ten, an eight. Advance and improve that to a nine or a ten. Build on your strengths. Do better what you do best.

That means, naturally, you will want to be at peace about some weaknesses, at least for the time being. One church I was helping concluded after an evaluation, "Our pastoral and lay visitation in the community is, on a scale of one to ten, a low two."

"It's an excellent two!" I said. They were a little puzzled. I continued. "Good friends, it's among your best weaknesses." By that I meant they could be up front about not investing immediate resources in a current weakness.

We can refuse to let our compulsive perfectionism sidetrack us. With honesty and candor we can say, "A-ha! This is an excellent two. That's where it ought to remain."

De-emphasize the negative. The four questions I encourage churches to give up for Lent are

- *What are our problems?*
- *What are our needs?*
- *What are our concerns?*
- *What are our weaknesses and shortcomings?*

Those four questions I call "The Four Horsemen of the Apocalypse" or "The Four Assassins of Hope."

I help lots of churches with their problems and concerns, but when you begin with your weaknesses, you're in the weakest position to tackle them. When you first improve your strengths, you are then in the strongest position to work effectively on your weaknesses.

Add complementary objectives. One church I was helping said, "We have two objectives. We plan to become the church in the county known for using only classical music in worship; that will make us distinctive. Second, we plan to reach young couples with small children."

"You have two excellent objectives," I replied. "One of them heads you in one direction, and the other heads you in almost the opposite direction. I happen to know the results of radio marketing surveys of this community. Young couples here listen to two kinds of music: soft FM and country western.

"Now if you had told me, 'We plan to launch the best preschool program in the community, and we plan to reach young couples with small children,' you'd have complementary objectives. They reinforce and help each other. If you had told me, 'We plan to sing only classical music in our worship services, and we plan to have the best preaching in the country,' you would have complementary objectives."

I also said to them, "If you plan to sing only classical music, be sure to have the best preaching in the country. It will help greatly." (I say that as one raised on classical music. I also know the world is a mission field.)

As they begin the planning process, churches ought to think of themselves as a mission. The purpose of planning is action in mission. We live on one of the richest mission fields on the planet. I encourage churches to determine their future based on mission rather than growth, based on strengths rather than size. We do mission for the sake of mission, not for the sake of gaining more members. The ultimate goal of planning is to help people with their lives and destinies, whether or not they ever join this particular congregation. We're not trying to grow an institution; we're trying to grow a mission, no matter our size.

Even a small congregation—a small mission outpost—can decide to be an excellent small congregation. The key is to discover the central characteristics and a few key objectives that God calls this congregation to achieve.

Better-planning principles

The biggest misconception people have about long-range planning is that the job is to figure out what the congregation should be doing three years from now. No. We plan long range to know what to achieve today, this week, this month. The reason we look three years ahead is to know what to accomplish now.

It's like planning a wedding. People set the date for the wedding, and then they work backward. Once they have the long-term objective in place, they can determine when to order invitations, hire a photographer, rent a reception hall. Once they set the date, they know what to do this week, this month, next month, and the next month. People who set the date tend to get married. Those who never set the date for the wedding hardly ever get married.

I encourage churches to look at least three years ahead, and to do so developmentally.

An ineffective way to plan is in three-year blocks. In the fall of 1991, the church looks at 1992, 1993, and 1994 and determines a three-year plan. Then with a sort of driven determination, it sticks to that plan for three years. Then at the end of 1994, it creates another three-year plan.

In a developmental approach, long-range planning advances continually over three years. In the fall of 1991, for example, a church would determine objectives for 1992, 1993, and 1994. Toward the end of 1992, it would do two things. First, advance and improve the objectives for 1993 and 1994. They might delete some things, improve others. Second, add the new third year, incorporating objectives for 1995. Thus, they always look three years ahead—flexibly and dynamically.

Developmental planning looks more like a fast break down the basketball court than a neat, tidy plan where every detail is in place and stationary. A church shouldn't take much time at it each year. Planning is more like a time-out in a basketball game. The Callahan principle of planning is that "Planning expands to fill the time available. Therefore, limit the amount of time you invest in planning."

Churches invest best in six planning sessions totaling nine to twelve hours to discover their long-range plan. It takes even less time to keep it moving. The art is wisdom more than time.

Churches can accomplish much in a short time by following a few planning principles.

One is the twenty/eighty principle. Twenty percent of what a group does delivers 80 percent of its results. Eighty percent of what a group does delivers 20 percent of its results. We're not trying to create a ninety-seven page long-range planning document. The best long-range plans are three pages long, five pages long, or even one page long! It takes no wisdom to list many, many goals. What takes wisdom, and what makes a difference, is finding the 20 percent that produces 80 percent of the results.

A second planning principle: Work smarter, not harder. The myth in the church is "If we were only more committed and worked harder, things would get better." The truth is that when people work harder they get "tireder," but things don't automatically get better. When a church headed in the wrong direction works harder, it gets there quicker and faster.

A third planning principle: Plan less to achieve more; plan more and you will achieve less. That relates closely to another principle: The purpose of planning is action, not planning.

The importance of both these principles is illustrated by a church I visited some time ago. As I stepped off the plane, the pastor and the chairman of the long-range planning committee met me. As we were waiting on my luggage, they gave me three notebooks thick with data, which they had invested two years in gathering. They asked me if I would look at them before the 7:30 breakfast the next morning.

Data and I are old friends. By 2:30 A.M. I had worked my way through the three notebooks. When the pastor and committee chairman joined me for breakfast, they asked, "What do you think?"

"Good friends," I said, "the day for analysis is over. The day for action has arrived. The day for data is done. The day for decision has come."

They were facing a tough decision. If they had a bar graph to determine the level of certainty for a decision, it would have read 65 percent in this case. They'd spent two years and gathered three notebooks of data because they believed the more data they gathered the more they could raise the level of certainty—perhaps to 85 or 90 percent. There are a lot of decisions we have to make in life that have a 65-percent level of certainty.

I said to them, "I can show you how to gather four more notebooks of data that you haven't even thought of. It will take two years. Then you will have spent four years and gathered seven excellent notebooks of data. But the day for decision will have passed you by. And even with seven notebooks of data, the level of certainty for the decision is still going to be about 65 percent. So let us decide."

A church should involve as many people as possible in its long-range planning. The classic mistake is to appoint a fifteen-person planning committee to spend two years developing a plan. Then they have the problem of convincing the congregation of the committee's conclusions. That top-down approach does not work.

I encourage churches to create a five- to eight-person steering committee for long-range planning. Their task is to lead as many people as possible in the congregation through the planning process so that planning comes from the grassroots. The rule of thumb is to involve at least 20 percent of the average worship attendance. That figure might be higher in a small, rural parish and lower in a large parish. The point is to achieve a critical mass. Involve enough people so that members know the plan is theirs.

In putting together the steering committee, you invite people who have the capacity to look at the whole not the parts, the long range not the annual, who prefer to plan less, not more. You look for people who have the capacity to share leadership. Members of this steering committee serve as study, planning, and action leaders. They lead as many people in the congregation as possible through a study, looking at the twelve central characteristics of effective churches.

After the study comes the planning. The planning sessions are done in teams of two. If you have forty people participating, they are grouped into twenty teams of two. The point is, no person works alone; each person has a chance to check his or her ideas with another person. These teams are charged with coming up with one or two excellent suggestions they know will help the whole. Then these teams report back to the larger group.

Then, perhaps, fifteen possible key objectives are offered in total. Each team picks eight out of the fifteen that they feel the church could most likely achieve, given the church's strengths, gifts, and competencies. What I often find is that the group quickly forms a consensus on two to four key objectives. So they choose these objectives. The other eleven were excellent ideas, but these four are the "20 percenters."

I encourage churches to develop a mission budget, organized around the central characteristics and key objectives the church plans to expand and add in the coming one to three years. You might have a section on "corporate, dynamic worship" and another on "pastoral/lay visitation in the community." Staff salaries are allocated to the various central characteristics in proportion to the time invested there.

Regrettably, organizational budgets are often structured in terms of the committees in the church. They focus more on which committee controls what money than on the key objectives to be accomplished in the coming year. In a mission budget, the focus is on the specific key objectives decisive for the year ahead. The important point: the budget is based on mission objectives to help people with their lives, not on committees and control.

The pastor's role in long-range planning is not to be the prime keeper of the vision; nor is his or her role to be the enabler of the congregation with regard to its vision. The task is to discover together the mission to which God is calling a particular group. Were a pastor to think that he or she is the prime keeper of the vision, that would deny the priesthood of all believers. Nor is it helpful for the pastor simply to enable the congregation to develop its goals. Enablers tend to focus on the process but tend not to share with the group their best wisdom.

For me, the pastor is leader and coach. As leader, the pastor leads, sharing his or her own best wisdom and judgment. Thus the congregation is not bereft of the pastor's best thinking. In addition, the pastor coaches the congregation's best wisdom forward, so that they together discover excellent ideas and new suggestions. The long-range planning steering committee also serves with the pastor as leaders and coaches. The pastor should not have to carry the leader and coach roles alone.

Motivational bridge

As a leisure activity, long-range planning probably isn't the activity of choice for most church members. To motivate the congregation to participate in planning, we need to understand the five motivational resources that draw people to a church, encourage them to be workers and leaders, and help them to contribute their time and money. The five resources are compassion, community, challenge, reasonability, and commitment.

All five are present in every person; and two of the five are generally predominant at a given point in a person's life. Among the key leaders, challenge and commitment are the strongest motivators. They're committed to the church, and they rise to the challenge of seeing it thrive. Among grassroots members, the best motivators are compassion and community. They want to help people, and they want to belong.

What we have in many churches, then, is a motivational gap. Often the same few people do everything in a church because the key leaders, motivated by commitment and challenge, send out messages on the radio frequencies of commitment and challenge. But the grassroots listen on the radio frequencies of compassion and community. That's a motivational gap.

I help a lot of dying churches in which the only people left are key leaders committed to the challenge of keeping the doors open. When I ask those key leaders what drew them to the church in the first place, they usually talk about a compassionate pastor and the sense of family and community. But in the thirty years that have come and gone, weighted down by the institutional baggage of trying to keep the venture afloat, they have "nurtured forward" the motivations of commitment and challenge. They say to me, "Dr. Callahan, what we need in this church is people with more commitment."

"You just told me that compassion and community are what drew you to this church," I reply. "Now if compassion and community drew you who knew church culture to the church, how do you expect to draw unchurched people by means of commitment and challenge?"

Then I gently add, "It was not said of the early Christians, 'Look how committed they are to one another' but 'Look how they love one another.' What we need is people with more compassion, not more commitment."

I'll often invite the key leaders to a "bridging" challenge: "From today forward, I invite you to commit yourselves to the challenge of doing whatever you do out of what drew you here in those early years, namely compassion and community." You'd be amazed at how many key leaders rise to the challenge and make that commitment. Consequently, we create a motivational match between key leaders and grassroots, pastor and unchurched.

Pastors can reflect this in their preaching by centering less on commitment and challenge and more on compassion and community. Note I said "more." All five motivators are present in each individual, so it's appropriate to address each of the five from time to time. But the bulk of preaching is best not focused on "The Challenge of Our Future," filled with scoldings like "If we will only deepen our commitment . . ."

Nor is it wise for preaching to center on institutional objectives: "We need more teachers, money, members." People cannot be scolded into Christian service. They can be won with compassion and community.

I'm talking, of course, about a compassion that is rich, full, tough, and helpful; not a syrupy, sentimental understanding of compassion. People are not interested in superficial forms of community. They can find those lots of places. They're looking for roots, place, and belonging.

Effective leadership begins with the confidence that hope is stronger than memory: the open tomb is stronger than the bloodied cross. Easter is stronger than Good Friday because resurrection is stronger than crucifixion. Effective church leadership is built on the confidence that we are the Easter people.

Confidence is crucial. If we plan and organize our churches in a way that builds confidence, we will find that the results are strength and fruitfulness.

25

Investing in Small-Church Futures

*A vision is owned only to the degree that it corresponds
with people's unspoken sense of purpose.*

—John Koessler

Several years ago, I purchased ten shares of IBM stock at $116 per
share. It seemed like a great opportunity. We were in the middle
of a bull market, and the price of the stock had fallen from an all-
time high of $175.

Over the next few years, however, I watched in dismay as the
price of my shares inched lower and lower. Soon their value had been
cut by more than half. So when I heard that Louis V. Gerstner, the
former chief of RJR Nabisco, had become CEO of Big Blue, I was
keenly interested in his vision for the company.

Imagine my surprise when Gerstner stated, "The last thing that
IBM needs right now is a vision."

When asked to explain, he said, "A vision is often what somebody
turns to when it gets hard doing what's required, namely, good, solid
blocking and tackling. Remember, the Wizard of Oz was a vision."

As pastor of a congregation of seventy-five, I have sometimes
wondered if the last thing my church needs is vision. The blocking
and tackling alone are overwhelming.

But as we have worked to formulate a long-range vision, I have
learned much about vision in the small church, both the difficulties
and the benefits. In the small church, talk of church vision may seem
as out of place as Robert's Rules of Order at the family dinner table.
There are several reasons for this.

Limited resources. One week before we completed the grueling process of formulating a vision for Valley Chapel for the year 2000, the church's Sunday school superintendent and financial secretary resigned. The superintendent was relocating to another community, and the financial secretary had begun a new job, making it impossible for her to continue. Since the Sunday school superintendent also taught the eighth-grade class, we also needed a new teacher.

Suddenly our grand design for the next century didn't seem all that important. I worried about getting through the next quarter. When a small church is struggling with limited resources, the only vision it may be able to muster is the will to see beyond the next utility payment!

Family orientation. The small church, writes Anthony G. Pappas, is "a single cell of caring people. It does not exist to do, as the mid-sized-program church does. It exists to be. Its essence is not in its administrative structure, charismatic leadership, and long-range plans, as is the case in the large church."

At the beginning of our vision formulation process, I outlined the project to one member. Her face fell. "If you expected me to say that I like the idea," she said, "I'm afraid I can't."

I was surprised and disappointed. I considered her one of our more progressive members. If she hated the idea, what would everyone else think?

"As a teacher," she explained, "I see this sort of thing all the time. It always turns out to be some administrator's idea of what we should be doing."

She feared that by focusing on the vision, we would no longer focus on the needs of our own people: "Maybe it's time we started concentrating more on ourselves," she offered.

Short-term pastors. Many small churches have learned to be wary of the "pastor's big ideas." When I had been pastor of Valley Chapel for seven years, an elder complimented me on a suggestion I'd made. "You almost always have good ideas," he said, beaming.

His remark amazed me (I'd thought all my ideas were good ones!). Not long before, he had often questioned my ideas. Now, apparently, he had come to trust my judgment, but it had taken years.

The average tenure of the small-church pastor is somewhere between four and five years. Each new pastor brings a different vision. It may seem to church members that their pastors stay just long enough to stir up trouble, then leave the congregation to clean up the mess.

For small churches with a long history, this natural skepticism is augmented by a tendency to focus on the past rather than on the future. "Since the heart of the small church is neither pastor- nor paper-oriented," writes Doran McCarty, author of *Leading the Small Church*, "the vision of the small church often comes from its heritage. Through the generations the members have committed themselves to values and family (in this case, the family is the church family). Their vision is personal, not organizational."

During one Sunday school class, we watched a video by futurist Joel Arthur Barker. The video began by describing the natural reluctance people have toward change. As soon as the word "change" had been uttered, a voice piped up from the back of the room: "Change? We don't need to change. We're fine just the way we are."

Three key questions

Despite the above obstacles, I felt that our church would benefit from a ministry vision. During the previous eight years, the congregation had grown, and its programs had nearly doubled. This burst of expansion culminated in the completion of our new church building. Afterward I felt the church had the right to take a well-deserved rest.

In time, however, that rest began to feel more like apathy. I became convinced we needed a new challenge. *I* certainly did. As we sought God's ministry vision for our church, we asked ourselves three basic questions: *Who are we? Where do we live?* and *What is God calling us to do?*

Who are we? The reason a church needs to be self-aware is practical: Once a vision has been formulated, the congregation must implement it. The church's members may be its missionaries, but they are also its primary consumers. Members will own a vision statement only to the degree that it corresponds with their own unspoken sense of purpose.

We began the vision-formulation process by taking a good look at ourselves: What are we currently doing? Is it something we enjoy? Do we wish we were doing something different?

To find the answers, I created a questionnaire the church members filled out during Sunday school. I could have hired someone to do this, but formulating my own survey enabled me to tailor the questions to specific interests. I used a simple software program to translate the data into graphs that enabled me to visualize the survey results (rather than drown in a sea of percentages).

I hoped the questionnaire's results would point to an overriding passion—the one thing we like to do more than anything else. It seemed to me that, if we could match that one area with a primary need in the community, we would have our ministry vision.

The questionnaire did reveal a number of clear trends. Generally speaking, people wanted to continue doing what we were already doing. Our primary strength was children's ministry. People felt we should have more small groups, but they didn't necessarily want to attend them. They were committed to their families but not much interested in discipleship. They wanted to hear more music in the worship services. They didn't want to teach adults or be placed in positions of leadership.

The survey didn't tell me anything I didn't already know. But it confirmed our strengths—our children's ministry, for example—and revealed a few holes in our ministry infrastructure—developing and discipling leaders.

Where do we live? Answering this second question forced us to look at two features of our ministry environment: demographics and lifestyle.

At first, a demographic analysis seemed daunting, especially since I had nearly flunked statistics in college! During a visit to the local library, however, I discovered *The Sourcebook of Zip Code Demographics* (CACI Marketing Systems, 1991) that summarizes results from the most recent census, listing the data by ZIP code. I simply had to find the category that interested me, whether age, population, income, or marital status, and look under the ZIP code of the community I was researching.

I used the same software that had worked so well with the survey. The program translated this data into graphs, and before long I had visual aids that gave me a clear demographic picture of the communities surrounding our church.

Lifestyle information was more difficult to gather. I studied back issues of *American Demographics*. I also asked several church members if they would interview their friends, using another questionnaire I had developed. I was pleasantly surprised when several members agreed. Many, though, took a copy of the survey home but never used it.

During a Sunday school class in which the results of the survey were being discussed, one member exclaimed, "You mean people were actually willing to talk about these things with you? I find that amazing!" Others had trouble finding willing participants. One member asked ten co-workers if they would complete the survey. She was turned down by every one.

Some did find willing subjects, however, and their answers proved revealing. Most of those who participated in the survey agreed that their lives had improved in the last ten years. Single mothers, who expressed concerns about finances and their children's adjustment to divorce, were chief among those who disagreed. Everyone listed family as being among the top three spheres of life from which they derive satisfaction, with most ranking it as number one.

Interestingly, a majority of those who were not church attenders also ranked church among the top three priorities in their life. Friendships and family matters, particularly the needs of children, were most important. When asked to describe the kind of church they would most likely attend, the majority identified friendliness as a key factor.

The survey concluded by asking participants to draw a map of their typical day and note the time spent at each location. Most of their time was spent at work, home, or commuting between.

The survey revealed that those our church is attempting to reach feel a hunger for primary relationships but are unable to develop them because of hectic schedules. Family is a primary concern, especially if the family has been touched by divorce.

At the same time, those interviewed often made choices that worked against these priorities. For example, one woman who listed church among her top three priorities also indicated that "quality time with the family" kept her from attending church.

"Sunday is my husband's only day off," she explained. Yet, she went on to say that on most Sundays, her husband left home to hunt and fish.

In short, we discovered our church could address many of the needs felt by our neighbors, especially relational needs and those related to the family. But we also discovered we must take the initiative.

Our neighbors would not come to us on their own.

What is God's call? To answer this question, I formed a Team 2000 that comprised four key laypeople and myself. Our purpose was to draft a vision statement.

I chose team members who were supportive of my ministry and generally positive in their outlook. I included a member of the church's governing board because of our tradition of strong elder rule. I chose another member because he was a fairly recent convert: he could still remember what it was like to visit our church for the first time.

Despite their interest in the project, crafting a vision statement did not come easily. After our third meeting, one member of Team 2000 said he felt frustrated because of the lengthy process. "Somehow I thought the vision would come together in just a couple of weeks," he said. "We don't really seem much further along than when we started."

Then, I used the adult Sunday school class to draw the rest of the congregation into the discussion. We spent several weeks discussing the mission of the church, the results of the congregational survey, and the analysis of our community's demographics. These classes culminated with a panel discussion during which the members of Team 2000 shared the results of their interviews with unchurched friends and neighbors. There we unveiled the vision statement, which included our overarching ministry vision: "In order to create a bridge for sharing the gospel, Valley Chapel will seek to be God's family to the families of our community. We will design our ministries to strengthen healthy families and will seek to be an instrument of healing for hurting families by helping them to become functional.

"To that end, we envision expanding our ministries to include a family ministry center, which will provide Christ-centered educational, counseling, and recreational resources for our area."

How successful were we?

We produced a vision statement, communicated it to the congregation, and had our church departments use it to set goals.

But I wasn't convinced the vision statement was strong enough to produce what John Naisbitt and Patricia Aburdene refer to as alignment: "that unparalleled spirit and enthusiasm that energizes people in companies to make the extra effort to do things right—and to do the right thing."

So at first, I thought the payoff might come not from the vision itself but from the process that generated it. Whether or not we had uncovered God's vision for our church, at least we had learned valuable things about ourselves and our mission.

The process itself did produce a payoff. Our demographic research, for example, forced us to come to terms with this truth: We cannot wait for the unchurched to seek us. We must think more like missionaries.

The process also reminded me of my critical role as pastor. The frustration expressed by many during the process showed that while the members expect to have a say in what happens, they also want to be led.

Now, however, there are signs our new vision is taking root.

Not long after we finished crafting our vision statement and its goals, I received a call from a member. A friend had told him of a used school bus our church could purchase for $1,000.

"John, it's in really good shape," he said, with excitement in his voice. "My friend was planning on buying it himself, but now he is planning to move."

I could hardly believe my ears. Not until the year 2000 were we expecting to meet the new goal of purchasing a vehicle for our Sunday school department. The price was right.

The comment his wife made, however, excited me even more. "I thought the Lord would do something through these goals," she said. "But I never expected him to give me the burden I have now for this ministry."

God had indeed given us a vision.

26

The Launch

Any endeavor that works seems to require a leader.

—Don Cousins

As a whole, ministers are rarely accused of not working hard. But I want to make sure I'm also working smart.

When I look at the marketplace, which I often do as a strategist, I see leaders who are forced to work smart because there's a bottom line telling them if their strategies are working. But in the ministry, the bottom line remains more intangible. It's difficult to evaluate how well we're doing, so we tend to work hard and pray hard and trust God that the "bottom line" will turn out to his liking.

I try to work hard, pray diligently, and trust God. But I don't want to spin my wheels using unproductive strategies. So I've learned to be specific about what it is we're trying to accomplish.

For example, I was once part of a fine church youth group. The Bible was taught week by week. The group served at a state hospital and a children's home. We sponsored activities on Friday, Saturday, and Sunday nights. There was Wednesday night Bible study and Sunday morning Sunday school. But we averaged the same number of kids year after year. We had no end of activity, but it wasn't focused.

Then, through improving the program a little, our attendance shot from thirty to seventy. We began to wonder, *What would happen if we designed the program to meet the needs of the outsiders?*

So we built a program around outreach. The first night 150 showed up. The Christian kids all brought friends whom they'd been afraid to invite to our earlier activities designed for Christians. I brought three myself, and they came back the following week be-

cause it had been such a positive experience. Many such friends became believers. I've continued to be impressed with the way the Son
City ministry impacted high schoolers.

What happened? Did we work harder than other youth ministries?
Not necessarily. We employed a strategy.

Since that time I've had a part in developing and refining various
ministries at Willow Creek Community Church. The following five
steps, we've found, are central to successfully launching a ministry.

1. Build on leadership, not need

Ask most leaders, "On what basis do you start a ministry?" and
the reply is, "We see a need, and we try to meet it."

According to our experience, that's a good answer, but not the
best. We've found need is an insufficient foundation. We start with
leadership. Any endeavor that works seems to require a leader.

It's easy to cite examples. Industry: Where would Chrysler be
without Lee Iacocca? Or IBM had it not been for Tom Watson? Ath-
letics: Mike Ditka and the Chicago Bears. Peter Ueberroth and the Los
Angeles Olympics. Or, better yet, religion: When God decided to start
a nation, he went to Abraham. When God wanted to reach out to the
Gentile world, he knocked Saul off a horse. Everything starts with a
leader.

And yet too often in our churches, what do we do? Well, we have
a need, so let's round up a committee and . . .

Traditionally, as pastors we feel we have three options when con-
fronted with a need. Let's say there's rumbling about the lack of a
junior high program. What can we do?

First, the pastor can run a program personally. In most cases, that
adds an eleventh hat to a person struggling under the weight of ten.
And maybe the pastor has few qualifications or little interest in junior
high ministry.

Second, some pastors can ask a staff member to take on the ministry. But often the CE director ends up doing children's ministry, junior high, high school, college, and singles, and none of them well.
Why? Because it's not humanly possible to do a great job in five different ministries.

A third option is to turn to some well-intentioned parents. That
creates problems of capability and continuity. Are the parents

trained? Well-intentioned parents often just don't know how to direct a program that builds the kids' Christian maturity, and I've found a poor youth program is often worse than none. Also, when their kids graduate, it's amazing how suddenly parents' motivation is gone!

Since none of these traditional options looked promising, we searched for a different approach. In one sense, everything does start with a need, because we wouldn't look for leadership if there weren't a need. But we've made the difficult decision of putting any need on hold until we find qualified leaders who can make that ministry their specialty.

At Willow Creek we went four years without a junior high ministry—no youth meetings, no Sunday school, nothing. Parents came to us asking what we were doing for junior high kids, and we had to gulp and say, "Right now we can't meet your needs, although we're working on it."

We took a lot of heat from parents when there was nothing for their kids, but to do something first-rate takes specialized leaders.

Most people don't do ten things well. They do one or two things well, maybe three if they're extremely gifted. So when we get the right kind of person, gifted in the right areas, doing what he or she does best—and only that—we can expect great results.

We looked high and low for qualified leaders—volunteers or paid staff—who would specialize in junior high ministry. The man who eventually became our key leader had another occupation and at first questioned his call to junior high ministry. But we were confident about his abilities. So we said, "Scott, we know you don't feel led right now to make this change, but would you be willing to put together some one-day events? It would be a good exploration for you, and the parents would like it." He agreed to organize some scattered events.

We could have begun with three or four untried volunteers, but it's a lot harder to undo a weak program than to build a quality program from scratch.

As it turned out, Scott gained a zeal for our junior highers and eventually joined the staff. His ministry with the kids is tremendous. We're convinced it was worth the wait to find the right person and build the ministry properly.

2. Settle on one purpose

Once we've found the key leader, we assemble a think tank—five or six individuals who begin to brainstorm about the ministry. The group typically consists of the person who will lead the ministry, two or three other people who have a passion and a corresponding gift-edness for that ministry, and one or two staff members or strategic-thinking elders. We aim for a mix of people, though each should be adept at thinking analytically about purpose and philosophy.

This think tank may gather once for a day or regularly for several months. As we planned Willow Creek's missions ministry, eight or nine of us met several hours a month for a year, and between meetings participants pursued intensive research.

Our evangelism think tank, on the other hand, met only twice before we began to implement some of the ideas. It all depends on the scope of the ministry.

Our first consideration is determining the primary purpose of the ministry. Just as we like to give our leaders only one responsibility, every program or meeting needs to have only one declared purpose. If we accomplish anything else, we consider it whipped cream.

Take Sunday morning. What are many churches attempting? To equip the believer, to bring the nonbeliever to receive Christ, to encourage fellowship, to foster communication, to worship faithfully, and on and on. Can one gathering accomplish all those tasks? Not really. Why? Because it's difficult to edify believers and evangelize lost people at the same time; they're two different audiences.

So at Willow Creek we decided our single purpose for our Sunday morning service was to reach the unchurched. We make no apology for not doing anything else as long as we accomplish our primary objective. People visit our church and say, "It's not a worship service. As a believer I couldn't live on this."

We say, "You're right, because that's not our purpose. Wednesday night is the service for you."

So the think tank's job is to identify one objective for a ministry. We want each ministry to do one thing well, to meet one need through the leadership of one key person.

We've noticed that when we meet one need thoroughly, we attract the people and resources that enable us to move on and meet another need. For instance, if we do a great job of evangelism, people come to know Christ, they're thankful for what's going on in their lives, and they are willing to give to start other ministries. But if we never do step one right, we won't accumulate the people or resources necessary to go to step two.

A single focus also benefits the workers, because it allows them to gauge their effectiveness. Take our food pantry, whose one purpose is to get food and clothing to people who need them. If we do nothing else but provide those necessities, that's success.

It happens that as a result of our distribution of food, people have heard the gospel and become Christians. We've discovered financial needs and marriages falling apart, and sent people to appropriate counseling. But these are side benefits.

The volunteers measure their effectiveness by one goal: getting food and clothing to people with needs. And since they get thank-you notes and hear people saying, "I don't know what I'd do without you," the fulfillment level skyrockets.

But suppose the workers sensed the unspoken goal of the pantry was to distribute food so that people would become Christians. Then frustration would increase unless many people were coming to Christ. We wouldn't attach that purpose to the pantry without making it clearly the primary purpose and then training the workers so they could be effective witnesses.

3. Determine a philosophy of ministry

The next job for the think tank is to establish a philosophy of ministry. And that's a tough task.

People nearly always want to skip the "why" questions and go on to the "how-to's". But here's where working smart comes in. We first must decide why we choose to accomplish our single task in a particular way. We start with two questions: *What do we know about the target group? What do we know about doing this ministry effectively?*

In thinking through evangelism for Willow Creek, we began by asking, "What do we know about 'Nonchurched Harry'?" Those in the think tank started writing on the board: "Probably will not change his life and worldview in an hour; doesn't know who God is; thinks God is out of it, a rule maker, a killjoy, no fun; is fully occupied without church" and so on.

Then we asked ourselves, "What do we know about effective

evangelism?" We decided it doesn't put pressure on people to change quickly, because that's unrealistic. It usually isn't as effective in a single event as through a continuing process. Effective evangelism helps people systematically process the truth over time, so that they can make a rational decision to which they will want to stay committed. And so on.

Now we were circling in on how evangelism could be most effective at Willow Creek. Suppose I said to you: "I've got a friend I want you to meet. But before you meet him, I ought to tell you he's difficult to get along with. He's very selfish. He tends to talk a lot about himself, and he's a little moody. And, oh yes, bring your wallet, because he probably won't have his, and he may ask you for money to cover his expenses." Would you want to meet him? Probably not.

But suppose I said, "You've got to meet my friend. He's been a true friend for more than ten years and would give me the shirt off his back. He's the most gracious, giving, thoughtful person I've ever met. I could trust this guy with anything. If I were in a jam, I could turn to him, and he'd drop everything to come to my side." Would you like to meet that person? The way you picture my friend makes all the difference.

So what is Nonchurched Harry thinking about God—that he's gracious, loving, kind, forgiving, all-powerful, all-knowing? If he thought that, he'd never refuse God. Nonchurched Harry, however, probably thinks God is a backward, restrictive killjoy. That's why he has chosen to refuse or ignore him.

So as we brainstormed our philosophy of evangelism, we realized we had to design something to change people's concept of God, because if we change their understanding of him, chances are we'll change their response to him. Therefore, in everything we do as a church, every statement we make—whether through a clean, well-designed building or through the music we use on Sunday or the written material we make available—we want to state that God and his followers are *not* backward or second-rate or dull. We designed a Sunday morning service that's fun, that talks about the identity of God, because we believe once people understand who God is, they'd be crazy to refuse him.

All that came from thinking through a philosophy of ministry. People don't do that naturally. We have to sit down and talk through the right questions: What's true about the people we want to reach?

What motivates them? What turns them off? What works? What doesn't work? Are we arranging our ministry to be most effective?

If we come out of that think tank with a clear picture of our target audience and an understanding of what works in ministering to that group, we've accomplished our purpose.

4. Establish a strategy

When we've determined the philosophy of ministry, often we have a long list of ideas and concepts. The next step is to synthesize them into a strategic plan, to set priorities, to think how we're going to make this work.

Again using our evangelism example, we gathered the information we'd brainstormed and came up with four groups of people—two groups of unbelievers and two of believers:

Nonchurched Harrys. Nonchurched Harry doesn't even come to Willow Creek. On Sunday mornings he's popping open a beer in anticipation of the Bears game. He isn't interested in God or church at all.

The seekers. These sensitive people are looking for something, and sometimes they come to church. But they haven't crossed the line yet to become Christians.

The average believers. The word *evangelism* scares this group to death. They know they ought to evangelize, but they have neither the will nor the training to attempt it.

The zealots. These folks have the gift of evangelism. They want to do evangelism. The trick is to use their gift effectively, without turning people off.

If we want to involve all of these people in evangelism, how do we do it? Obviously it will require four different responses. So we began to formulate a purpose for each group:

- To get Nonchurched Harry seeking.
- To turn the seeker into a believer.
- To take the fear out of evangelism for the average believer and to make witnessing a natural part of life.
- To organize the zealots so they aren't randomly alienating people but are wisely deployed for concerted evangelism.

Then we outlined our philosophy for each group: What's true

about this guy drinking beer on Sunday morning? What's true about the seeker? And on down the list. Once we knew what these groups needed, we had to find a way to divide the task into manageable parts.

As we considered our overall strategy, however, one question dominated: *Where can we make the greatest impact with what we can invest initially?* We had to set priorities, because we couldn't attack on all fronts simultaneously. We realized our zealots were vastly outnumbered by our average believers. But if we could turn loose these average masses, we'd make a major impact. So we decided the average believers would be our first target group.

Our strategy to get them involved in evangelism was to take away their fears, build their confidence, and give them the tools to be evangelists. We put together a four-week evangelism seminar on consecutive Monday nights. We gave people help with giving their testimony, answering the ten toughest questions, and presenting the gospel in a clear, concise way. In the last year we've guided about a fourth of our committed people through these seminars.

We experienced a wide spectrum of responses. If zero is complete fear and ten is sharing one's faith, one couple in my small group went from zero to one because of the seminar—not much progress, but some. Others zoomed up to ten. I know of one man who led two people to Christ in two months following his seminar.

Now that we've got the seminars rolling, we're moving on to the zealots. Our strategy is to equip them and put them into organized groups to do evangelism. For example, we've started a class called Foundations that meets each week to handle the tough issues that come up when we confront our culture with the gospel.

This week's issue is reincarnation—will I ever be around again? And we've handled the topics of biblical authority, damnation, suffering, and others. These are subjects we probably won't touch on a Sunday morning, but a solid five to eight percent of our people come out early on Wednesday evenings to discuss them.

We've already begun to reach the seekers through our Sunday morning service designed especially with them in mind. Where we feel the weakest is in our response to Nonchurched Harry. But we decided before doing anything for him we needed to get the other three groups rolling, because those groups are the keys to reaching him.

We do aim our newspaper advertising at the guy who's not coming. We ask ourselves, *What section of the paper is he reading? The church section? No. He's reading the weekend entertainment edition. And what kind of ad appeals to him? A picture of a steeple? No, something more like a movie advertisement, something that looks interesting and addresses his needs.* So we put an enticing, need-oriented ad in among the movie notices. People tell us they first came to Willow Creek because of these ads. So that's one strategy for Nonchurched Harry.

We're also building a sports ministry. We live in a sports-crazed society, but evangelism can happen through sports. If we can intermingle evangelist/athletes with Nonchurched Harrys in our softball or basketball leagues, build relationships, and expose outsiders to the church, we're on our way toward evangelism. They say, *This isn't so bad. Wonder what their church service is like?*

The point is that these are all strategies, ways to wisely deploy our leaders and implement our single purposes and philosophies of ministry.

5. Direct the resources

From this point on, it's a matter of allocating the finances, setting the times, and deploying the people. This is the fun part—actually making ministry happen.

One of the groups we're just beginning to unleash is called "the Defenders." This group contains the hard-core apologists, men and women who have a heart for the intellectual issues and tough questions of faith. They like nothing better than researching thorny issues such as the problem of pain or creation versus evolution. With the mental stimulation of fellow Defenders, the synergism in this group is tremendous.

So now when anyone gets stuck on a difficult question, there is someone to turn to. Our staff directs both questions and questioners to them. People witnessing to their friends have someone to help them with challenging arguments. In fact, the Defenders not only research a problem, they're also quite happy to meet with the questioners.

What a resource we've deployed—a group of Defenders dedicated to leading skeptics to Christ. It's their passion.

It's my passion, too. And as a pastor, working through others, I know it's going to take five steps to reach that goal.

27

Escaping Congregational Doldrums

*Only tough love will resolve some issues that slowly
hemorrhage the life from churches for years, or decades.*

—Bob Moeller

Ancient mariners feared the doldrums. They could die of thirst or
starvation if they were caught in the wrong latitudes for too long
with no wind. Churches are much the same if they're caught without
motivational winds.

I once talked with a church member who had no hope that the
church could continue. "There are no people left to come here," he
sadly explained.

That seemed odd to me. The church was located in one of the
most densely populated areas of a major city. What he was really saying, however, was, "The reason people used to come here no longer
exists, and so no one is coming." On that score he was right. The
problem was not an inadequate supply of people but rather an inability to connect the church's purpose to the people it touched.

The church that once went full steam ahead with a clear and definite sense of mission, the church that once drew members almost
effortlessly through a contagious spiritual life—that church may now
be struggling, thirsting for a reason to exist. But how does that happen?

Here are some often-overlooked causes and cures of congregational doldrums.

Cultural time warp

Some churches that find their sails hanging listlessly have lost
touch with their community's current needs.

I once heard of a well-meaning parishioner who suggested the church lights needed to be on even on Sunday evenings when they weren't having services, as a witness to the community. Apart from the ethical question of possibly creating false appearances, I had trouble understanding the evangelistic value of such a luminous testimony.

Yet in my own parish, I received a phone call from a neighbor upset that the church had no social conscience—we were wasting energy by leaving lights on in the offices all night. I was struck by the changing attitudes even toward church lighting.

What drew people in the 1940s, 1950s, or even the 1970s may have little or no relevance in the 1990s. Sunday school competitions were so popular that school playground fights actually erupted among children from competing churches arguing as to whose was best in the district.

Today parents, when choosing a church, take a close look at the quality of the nursery, the cleanliness and attractiveness of the facility, and the learning options available during the week for their children. If these aren't cared for adequately, you won't see those parents next week.

While the gospel never changes, the cultural attitudes that shape how these truths are presented do change. Our challenge is continually to seek new ways to present the gospel to *this* generation, a challenge that often can breathe new life into a congregation.

One way of doing that is to develop an "outside-in" perspective by looking at a church's programs, facilities, and personnel as an outsider would. Our temptation is to evaluate the needs of our community from an "inside-out" perspective, which is hazardous to the future health and vitality of the church. An outside-in approach can help us avoid becoming painfully out of touch with the needs of the culture.

Unresolved conflict, unaddressed sin

The captain of the *Titanic* refused to believe the ship was in trouble until water was ankle-deep in the mail room. Only then was it apparent the multilayered hull had been pierced, and the unsinkable ship was going to sink. Ships that could have arrived before the great ocean liner went down weren't summoned until it was too late.

Often there has been water in the mail room of a church for some time, but no one has been willing to acknowledge what it means. Perhaps a feud between families in the congregation has been brewing for months, but the pastor doesn't feel his position is secure enough to get involved. Attendance, giving, and visitor trends have all been headed downward for several years, but no one wants to admit the church is hurting. Or, there has been a secret liaison going on between a man and a woman on the music committee, but no one wants to handle the potentially explosive issue.

These and a host of other situations occur in churches in one form or another all the time. But for a variety of reasons—fear, uncertainty of what to do—the problems are left unaddressed.

A pastor friend once learned that money from the benevolent fund was going to make alimony payments for one of the church members. Word of this had filtered out, and many in the congregation felt it was an inappropriate use of the fund. As a result, contributions to the fund dried up. But no one was willing to discuss the issue.

Churches and church leaders unwilling to deal with moral, ethical, or financial misconduct in the church pay an enormous price in the loss of energy and motivation that inevitably occurs.

The corrective, of course, is wise and courageous confrontation of sin and conflict. It's wonderful when revival sweeps a church and the ugly problems seem to resolve themselves in an entirely supernatural fashion. But that's more the exception than the rule. In the midst of unresolved sin or conflict, more often than not, someone has to take on the difficult and thankless task of confrontation before things get noticeably better.

Sometimes it's tough to get people to help with this task. On one occasion, an elder knew he would be involved in confronting a friend. Rather than do that, he slipped his resignation under the pastor's door, stopped coming to church, and was never seen on the premises again. The heat in the kitchen had sent him out for fast food permanently.

Only tough love will resolve some issues that slowly hemorrhage the life from churches for years, or decades.

I grew up in a church that was racially mixed—long before it was acceptable. In fact, it was a source of bitter dispute in those days. Hundreds left because it was feared certain minority groups would take over.

It was not until the last of such opposition left that the new church was born. But from that point onward, a ninety-year-old church took on the zest and enthusiasm of a new church plant. The long and sometimes acrimonious board meetings, the whisper campaigns, and the not-so-veiled threats to take the money and go elsewhere finally ended. When it did, the survivors watched as the church blossomed and was given a new life.

So the principle that some conflict must be escalated in order to resolve it can be true as a church struggles to gain new purpose and direction. It's no one's first choice, but at times it's the only viable option left when a church finds itself adrift because of long-standing conflict or hidden sin.

Unrewarded effort

A friend of mine as a child once painted his entire backyard fence during the heat of the summer. For his efforts his parents didn't give him a dime. Sometimes that also happens in the church. People in the various ministries give and give, year after year, and receive little or no recognition for doing so. The burnout rate in such settings stands alarmingly high.

This is particularly true in settings with an entrepreneurial leadership style. Launch one new ministry, and the attention turns to beginning another. Those in charge of making the program work are left to carry on alone. The excitement of the program fades into dull routine and weekly effort.

While the ministry itself may be effective, the sense of significance is gone because the leaders are wrapped up in new interests. The result: diligent workers are given the impression that their sacrifice of time and energy is no longer important.

I'm well aware that our reward is in heaven, and our workers should seek the praise of God rather than men. But expressing appreciation for a job well done is also part of Christian virtue. When we forget, we end up going through volunteers like aluminum soda cans in a college dorm. And with such a disposable attitude, often motivation and involvement are discarded as well.

But as important as it is to recognize and appreciate people's efforts, the even more significant strategy is to help people discover they can make a difference. There is nothing more discouraging than feeling your work doesn't matter. One of the more cruel punishments inflicted on prisoners during World War II was to assign them to dig holes each day and then to fill them in at quitting time. That devastating psychological tactic cost many an individual his sanity and will to live.

Sadly, some people in church also arrive at the conclusion that their work is meaningless, an exercise in futility. They lose the will to try because they've lost the hope of making a difference.

During one pastorate, I visited a family that had left the church in anger years earlier but was still on the membership list. When I knocked, I was invited in, but it was clear their feelings toward the church were mixed at best. They spoke of how they had been unappreciated at the church and intended never to come back.

Not long afterward, the husband was diagnosed with brain cancer. It was a shock to everyone. He died within three months. I conducted the funeral, and in the follow-up counseling, I suggested to the widow that she get involved in the church's ministry to the poor of our neighborhood.

With some hesitation, she agreed. Each Tuesday morning we handed out clothing to approximately one hundred people. Many were street indigents, bag ladies, and homeless families. Her job was to bring cookies and serve coffee to the people as they searched for clothing.

Although I knew the experience would help, the extent of her transformation amazed me. Her disappointment and hurt melted away week by week as she served coffee and cookies and helped distribute clothes. Instead of the painful memories of how the church had failed her, she was filled with the joy of knowing she was making a difference in people's lives.

The same is true for a church. Years of anger, frustration, and hurt can be healed by helping others with needs. It's hard to feel aimless when you see God at work through what you're doing.

Uncontrollable cures

Perhaps none of these cause a particular church's doldrums. Even when the cause remains unidentified, a number of cures can revive sagging spirits. Some might surprise you.

A churchwide crisis. The noted English satirist Samuel Johnson once said something to the effect that nothing clears your mind as effectively as the prospect of being hanged.

The same may be said of churches. Either an imminent or a present crisis can galvanize members into working as a committed and concerned group of believers once more.

In a church I once served, an elder's son died in his sleep while the man's hospitalized daughter was fighting for her life with a deadly viral disease. After the funeral, the entire church took on a spiritual seriousness that remained evident years later.

Often a lawsuit will accomplish the same mobilization of the troops. Or a building fire. I listened in amazement as a fellow pastor told how he'd planned to preach from Peter on the refining fire of God's work in our lives. The same week their new church building, only days from completion, burned to the ground. You can imagine how seriously the folks listened to his sermon the next Sunday.

The point, however, is that sometimes difficult and adverse circumstances can stir people to action. Adverse circumstances can become the opportunity for the people to search their hearts and recommit themselves to serving Christ in that church.

We obviously can't control such crises, but we can be alert to the ways they affect a church.

A profound spiritual experience in key leaders. I had been given two churches to serve part time as I completed seminary. Each weekend I'd drive 125 miles to a farming community north of the Ohio River.

The smaller church was about to celebrate its centennial. It was a lovely group—kind, hardworking, and faithful to attend the old-frame church with its well-worn pews and slightly out-of-tune piano. But many of the men felt only a cultural obligation to church or attended because their wives coaxed them. In rural life, you don't pry into one another's lives much, and things tend to remain as they have been throughout the years. But this church was about to be stood on its head, and me with it.

I had invited a professor from school to hold a weekend of meetings, which they called a revival. It was actually as predictable as Veterans Day, and all that was meant by the term *revival* was an extra service on Friday and Saturday nights. A Kleenex box was placed dutifully at the altar, just as it was every year for the one or two souls who might respond, but it had been years since anyone did.

The first night when the sermon was over, I thanked the speaker and dismissed the people. Usually such a benediction brought a stampede toward the door. That night no one moved. I got up and assured the people that everyone could leave now, that we were finished for the night. Not a person stirred. I turned in somewhat awkward amazement to the guest speaker.

The old professor and I walked through the pews praying with people as they requested it. Something powerful was at work.

The next night the same thing happened. No one left following the benediction. We prayed with more people. It seemed something much larger than we had ever imagined was stirring.

We were right. A few weeks later, a farmer knocked at our door during supper. He was an ex-marine with a reputation for being tight-fisted and just plain mean. He was crying, holding an old Bible in his hands. Soon it was not uncommon to see many of the hard-shell cases weeping in church on Sunday mornings. The Spirit of God was at work, and no one knew why or how.

For the first time in half a century, the church started to fill up again, and a new education wing was added. I felt much like an observer in a rowboat experiencing the deluge of a tidal wave. The professor confessed that in all the years he had been traveling and speaking, he'd never seen anything like this, either.

Churches can be restored to life and health in short order when the Holy Spirit chooses to act in a powerful way. While we cannot depend on this to be the norm, we cannot rule it out, either. I learned a lesson in that rural church about how big God is and how little I am.

The Spirit's wind

But by far the most important action we can take to bring life back to a drifting congregation is persistent prayer.

Collegians have a term for their fellow students who exhibit study habits above and beyond the call of duty: "Black and Deckers." The term refers to a line of solid-steel tools that often set the industry standard for durability and toughness.

Churches reawakened after years of slumbering apathy and ineffectiveness invariably have been influenced by people that qualify as Black and Deckers in their own right. They have prayed without ceasing for years on end. Intercession differs from the brief invocation mumbled at the beginning of a board meeting or before taking an offering. This type of prayer continues for years and sometimes for decades, not infrequently occurring early in the morning or late at night.

The results may be years in coming. That's why so few people actually exercise this ministry in a given church. The patience, the faith, and the persistence it takes quickly thins out the ranks.

Yet, because God in his sovereignty seems to allot every church a Black and Decker or two—and possibly more—the hope remains for a spiritual breakthrough.

I've known such people of prayer. In general they aren't critical souls; they tend to save their complaints for the Throne of Heaven, where they pour out their concerns. They don't advertise their ministry; it's far too private and important to discuss on a casual basis. Rather, they tend to be discerning individuals who can assess the needs of any given situation with little outside input. Perhaps it's their gift of discernment that makes their prayer so powerful.

In each of my last two churches, after going through times of churchwide difficulty, I later learned that two or three individuals had been praying, in some cases for years, that we would address the problems that were sapping our motivation. Their persistent prayer for renewal was eventually answered.

When all is said and done, it is prayer that changes churches and events. But again, this isn't quick and easy prayer. On the contrary, it is prayer so difficult and so worthwhile that at times it hurts. But the results speak for themselves.

Shortly after the death of Franklin Roosevelt in 1945, a newspaper columnist observed the irony of the late president's influence on the nation. Though he himself never fully recovered the use of his legs after his bout with polio, and though he spent much of his adult life in a wheelchair, it was FDR who taught a crippled nation how to walk again. Thrust into the presidency during the darkest days of the Depression, he inspired hope and vision in a nation immobilized by despair and pessimism.

Pastors, too, even when somewhat infirm themselves, can help congregations crippled by apathy and malaise of spirit not only to walk again but to run. It's not easy, and it requires both the wind of God's Spirit and a crew that keeps the sails trimmed, but it can be done.

PART 5

Reassessing

28

Beyond Meeting Needs

I have never seen strong values come out of a committee.
Values, to be held passionately, require a point person.

—Paul Johnson

I was not yet out of college, only twenty years old and starting a new church. My wife, Darla, and I were newlyweds playing house and, in a way, playing church. Darla would cook up someone's new recipe, and I'd experiment with someone's recipe for church growth.

My recipes usually called for ingredients from marketing: I'd identify people's needs, build programs to meet those needs, and then administrate those programs. The programs worked, people's needs were met, and the new church grew. Since we didn't have any children and were in a rural community, my wife and I could make regular visits to every attending family. People loved the personalized attention they received.

It wasn't long, though, before I realized my methods were restrictive. My passion for meeting people's needs was building a congregation with ever-increasing needs. The church grew because people came to have their needs met. But when I could no longer meet their needs, they could leave just as quickly as they came. I came to see that few in the church had actually adopted my vision—they just appreciated having their needs met.

I began to realize that need-meeting, as a method of church growth, works only to a point.

Woodridge Church, for example, my latest church plant, is in a metropolitan setting. If I introduce programs that meet people's needs and attract visitors, many of the visitors will tell me, "There are fifteen churches within a fifteen-minute driving distance that have better programs than you do." I can't compete with that.

After five years of on-the-job training in my first church, I began preparations to start a new church. I decided need-meeting would not be the basis for my new venture. Instead of focusing on the purpose for the new church, I tried to discover what its passion would be.

Passionate values

Prayerfully I reflected on my experience and identified values I felt had been missing in my pastorate. Programs, strategy, and meeting needs would still be important to me. But the basis for my church-planting ministry would be passion—deeply felt values explained in visionary language.

I've been refining these values in each of the four churches I've started. Here are several values that reflect my passion now.

1. *We will be a contemporary and progressive evangelical church, intentionally committed to discipleship.* Each one of those words communicates a value to which people can give themselves.

Darla and I were once in a music store buying an electronic keyboard. The store manager asked, "Are you starting a group?"

"Yes," I replied, "but probably not the kind of group you're thinking of. We're starting a church."

Before he could change the subject, I pressed on to talk about our being progressive: "This church is going to be contemporary and relevant. People often feel that the church is answering yesterday's questions, but I think real Christianity is on the cutting edge. It's relevant and provides real answers to today's questions. In fact, we don't want this church just to be contemporary, we want it to be progressive—to be moving ahead, not static. I know God is powerful, and his church should make an impact on our city."

Intrigued, he visited the church, accepted Christ, and became a significant part of our new church.

2. *Our worship will be seeker-sensitive.* We have chosen a slightly different tack than seeker-*directed* churches, where everything is done with converting seekers as the goal. The main purpose of weekend services in a seeker-directed church, for example, is to help seekers come to faith.

We don't want to cater solely to seekers, but neither do we want to limit our ministry to believers only. Instead we want to walk the middle ground.

Our goal on Sundays, consequently, is meaningful worship for believers that is also sensitive to seekers. We plan each service knowing seekers will be present. We are sensitive to their needs and concerns, but we don't plan the service exclusively for them.

We assume that God is opening them to new possibilities such as worship. Though they do not yet fully believe, because God is already working in them, we feel they can have a meaningful worship experience. For us that's enough. In 1 Corinthians 14, Paul says that proper worship should be so powerful that unbelievers will fall on their faces and worship God. They will say, "There really must be a God!"

We tell our people that our worship will be a safe place to bring their friends. We're not going to offend them. In fact, we're going to celebrate the fact that they're investigating. But at the same time we want to unabashedly worship the Savior.

For example, we use terms a seeker can understand. We want them to be uninhibited as they sample worship—as if they were taking a test drive. We also encourage believers to translate the language we use into deeper expressions of worship. For instance, when we say *celebration*, they should understand *worship*. A *Scripture study* means a *sermon*, and *investigate* or *think through* means *consider the commitment this calls for.*

3. *The process is as important as the product.* We want people to accept Christ, but we want to honor the validity of their journey to him as well. So we celebrate the process of people coming to Christ and growing in him. We will not allow ourselves to be alarmed if their lifestyles or practices are inconsistent with our own. Instead, we rejoice when they move in the direction of committed discipleship.

God uses different things to bring people along. We're content just to be part of the process, helping them grow to the next step. We don't ask, "Do they fit our mold?" but, "What is it God wants them to experience through this church?"

Some lifelong Christians have joined our new church. But since they've adopted this value, they view the church as a process too.

They're not going to evaluate its success in terms of numbers, programs, and money. They don't expect the new church immediately to offer all the services of an established church. We're all in process.

4. *We build people, not programs.* A statement of purpose answers the question, "What kind of things are we trying to do?" But in terms of people-vision, we first ask, "What kind of people are we trying to build?"

We want people to become the Michael Jordans of Christianity. We want them to be impact players—in their work, in their homes, and in their neighborhoods. It's not that we want only the super-talented; we want ordinary people to make a difference wherever they are. It might be that their pain and weakness makes as much of a difference as their success and triumph.

For instance, one woman, sexually abused as a child, helped begin a support group for people with similar pasts. Her contribution to the group became a redeeming outlet for her own recovery. "Starting this group," she said, "has finally helped me deal with the pain I went through."

5. *When we study and serve, the Holy Spirit will produce joy in our lives.* One man came to me when his wife suddenly abandoned him. I could support him in his grief, but because we were a small church, I couldn't refer him to a pastoral staff counselor or a supportive singles' ministry.

Instead, I told him about our value statements and reminded him that the best thing I could do was give him an opportunity for study and service so the Holy Spirit could produce joy in his life.

"You know," I said, "if you're really going to get past this grief to find real joy, you're going to need some opportunities to serve and to study. It might be that the very things you find painful are the things that will give you strength to reach others."

In a month or two, he was involved in a small group where he was able to help another person facing the same kind of problem. He took his eyes off of his own pain and need and became caught up in the vision, impacting the lives of others. In doing so his deeper needs for fulfillment and purpose were met.

Discovering the joy of service, however, is a value that has to compete with other legitimate experiences. In my most recent church plant, the mothering church provided funding and a "hunting license" to recruit a core group from among church members.

I found, though, that the members attending the mother church attended there because they liked its many programs and evangelical thrust. Few were receptive to the idea of a new church outreach until I told them about the values the new church would emphasize. Only then was the gravitational pull of the mother church weakened for some. Soon I had a core who were willing to switch churches, sacrifice, and commit themselves to a new church.

This emphasis on values, however, goes against the grain of much teaching about church growth and especially church planting. In fact, I found that if I wanted to be passionate about these values, I had to abandon my misconceptions about church growth and adopt a new frame of reference. Here are five principles that have helped me do that.

Don't seek out just anybody

When starting a church with next to nothing, the temptation is to do whatever is necessary to get anybody in—as long as they're warm bodies in the pew. But that's not necessarily best for the church. Some people can divert the church from its purpose.

Consumers. These people come with primarily one thing in mind: they are shopping for the church that will best meet their needs. But they're not that interested in becoming *investors* in the mission of the church. Unless I can change these consumers into investors, they will distort the values of the church.

The best tools I've found to encourage people to buy into the church are the values expressed in the church's vision. I use vision statements to tell people the reason we meet needs: not because we care so much about their immediate needs but because we care about fulfilling the vision for this church, which aims to fulfill people's deepest longings. "We want you to join and be part of this church," we say, "because as you do, your larger needs will be met." This approach turns consumers into investors. They discover they can be part of something close to the heart of God, and they can be part of a mission larger than themselves.

Antagonists. It's better to have empty pews (or in our case, chairs) than seats filled with antagonists. Empty pews usually leave the church's vision intact. But the wrong kind of people tamper with our values and exert a negative influence on the church. New churches

seem especially vulnerable to antagonists, who are frequently looking for new power bases. They are black holes of spiritual energy,
sucking out the resolve of those around them.

One man visited our new church and responded enthusiastically
to its ministry. He eagerly found new friends and became part of our
core group. Because he blended in so agreeably, I didn't adequately
explain the church's values and vision.

Some time later he handed me a five-page, typed statement ad-
vocating a radically different worship style for the church. "Either this
church will have to change," he said, "or I'm going to have to leave."
But of course it wasn't that simple. He began to lobby his friends in
the church with whom he had gained confidence. When he eventually left the church, everyone close to him felt the pain of his withdrawal.

When I recruit someone like that, I'm recruiting trouble. As an
optimist, I might think my personality and ministry would win him
over. But such people demand too much of my energy. They under-
cut what I'm doing. If people are not open to the vision I've laid out,
there's no reason to try to get them to sign on.

It can be a temptation to accommodate their views, especially if
they seem to be just a degree or two off our vision. But an angle of
just a degree, stretched out far enough, can become a major gap. That
minor discrepancy in the beginning may become a major source of
contention three years later.

That's why I think the sympathetic or nurturing pastor may *not* be
the best kind of church planter. The pastor with a shepherd's heart
may find it difficult to resist this temptation. The first time someone
balks at his vision, his pastoral instincts take over: "Well, this vision
is not as cut and dried as it sounds. We can adapt to your concerns."
When a pastor embraces the shepherding, caring role at the expense
of his vision he will undermine his ability to lead.

Those who are different. Some people are not mean-spirited,
they're simply different—they don't share our values. But if people
who have other values come to our church, they won't have the co-
hesiveness to stick through difficult times. It doesn't matter how
much they like me or benefit from my ministry. They need to go
where they can invest in the vision.

Woodridge, for example, has a set of values more consistent with
my Baptist theology. If I were to start an Episcopalian church, how-

ever, I would need to have a different set of values:

Where our statement says we're contemporary and progressive, if I were an Episcopalian I might emphasize *heritage*. Or talk about *time-tested truth*. Another vision word might be *diversity*: "We celebrate diversity in people's thinking." I might also use the word *mystery*: "Though we grapple to understand coherently the complexities of life, as spiritual people we leave room for mystery, for the fact that God works in ways we can't fully comprehend."

What I would *not* say, is: "We Episcopalians have two sacraments and *The Book of Common Prayer*." Rather, "We have continuity with history. When you sit in our church, there's a sense of timelessness. Words that the apostles used are spoken again." In this way, instead of defending liturgy, I've stated our values and vision.

If core Christian beliefs are at the center, I don't judge one set of values to be better than the other. They're just different. No single church can fully reflect God's multifaceted passion. It would be a mistake for me to recruit someone whose values and personality would better fit another tradition. I would only make them unhappy, and ultimately, our church would suffer because of their unhappiness.

Don't duplicate success

Newly planted churches sometimes fall into the trap of trying to clone themselves to "successful" churches. But clones almost never work. More likely, what works in one setting will probably have to be reworked in another.

Woodridge was birthed by a large, established church, Wooddale Church of Eden Prairie, a suburb of Minneapolis. But Woodridge can't be a clone of Wooddale. Daughter churches will likely have a genetic mix: in our case, Woodridge has mixed the Wooddale approach with the community church philosophy, something our team of church planters in central Wisconsin had worked with. We're similar in that both churches are intentional about ministry, committed to excellence and evangelism.

We're distinct, however, in that Woodridge is more entrepreneurial. Because of where we are in our development, we are more process-oriented. We've inherited a view of ministry from others, but we've developed it on our own.

Because we're not trying to duplicate something that's already successful, we've been able to maintain a positive self-image. We're doing something new! If we were to compare ourselves with the mother church, we'd start feeling pretty discouraged. Instead, our positive attitude about our uniqueness is contagious. New people can sense the upbeat outlook.

A church planter should, first and foremost, be an entrepreneur. Church planting calls for someone who is a nonconformist, a self-starter, and an innovative leader. Someone may be a natural sales-person, but the church planter should be something more, someone who would say, "If I'm going to sell insurance, then I want to start an agency, not just sell the product."

Don't trust tested techniques

A major mistake made in church planting is to seek the perfect program or strategy: "Oh, full-color brochures! Now I've got it. That's why Woodridge could start with all those people."

The brochure helped, but even if we had never printed it, I believe we would have grown.

More than techniques, a new church needs values. Values keep us in line. Church growth can be cancerous growth if the methods used are unbiblical. Values help us clarify the kinds of growth that are healthy. Values determine the methods we use.

Recently I asked our leadership team to evaluate a letter I intended to send to our regular attenders. I wanted to motivate people to stronger commitments of time and money. The leaders, however, asked me to show how the letter was in line with our values. One leader even pulled out our church's value statement and told me to rewrite the letter using the statement as a guide.

Whenever people start a church by modeling programs after some other church, they should first ask themselves if they have the same underlying values that motivated those programs in the first place.

Don't let individuals eclipse vision

Some people accuse me of neglecting individual needs. "You're sacrificing people to feed the vision," they say. Many pastors have a more shepherding attitude than I have: they want to meet the needs of people. They try to sense the direction people want to go.

As a church planter, on the other hand, I'm more likely to say, "Here's the vision God has given us to fulfill. We have to do whatever it takes to realize that vision, even if it means losing a few individuals along the way."

I have to be careful that I'm not misunderstood at this point. People *are* important. People are why Christ died. But when I allow a dysfunctional person to strangle a church's calling, I undermine God's purpose for us. Sometimes I have to risk alienating one person for the good of the whole. Still that can be painful, and there's a part of me that regrets it whenever it happens.

Don't lead by consensus

Consensus is highly valued in our country. In the church we see attempts to lead by consensus. That almost never works for a new church.

The problem is that often the vision of the new church, when drawn up by group consensus, won't be the same vision necessary to reach the community. It may not always take a leader to decide on where to go (although it usually does); it does take a leader to get a group there.

I have never seen strong values come out of a committee. Values, to be held passionately, require a point person. Normally the pastor has to be that point person, inspiring values that reflect God's heart for the community. Committees function best when they ratify the value statements of the leader.

Sometimes pastors feel they would be dictatorial if they were to propose the values. But proposing what God desires to do is not the same as controlling or manipulating others. Strong leaders surely must be sensitive to the people they lead, especially if they want to generate commitment from people. Still, they must lead.

What has worked for me is to state my values, selling the vision in sermons, classes, and conversations. In fact, seldom does a day go by that I don't bring at least one conversation around to value statements. And they're part of almost every sermon that I give.

When I first developed a passion for these values, I wondered if it wouldn't be risky to start a new church based purely on this kind of vision. What if people disagreed with my values? What if no one wanted a contemporary, progressive new church, for example? What if I failed to attract people?

It seemed shortsighted to launch a work without the proven methods of defining community needs and developing strategies and programs to meet those needs. I felt as if I was throwing out my box of church recipes.

To my surprise (and delight), these values—the things I felt defined God's heart for my work—attracted people. When I gave them a vision based on passionately held values, some, frankly, balked. But many became committed and have helped found and shape churches that continue to develop faithful and steadfast disciples of Jesus Christ.

29

Measuring Success

*One facet of success is to maintain a realistic
but hopeful attitude.*

—Stuart Briscoe

W hen I was a young businessman in England, a group of church
leaders got together in a major city to plan how they could
sponsor an evangelist and hold meetings.

An older gentleman, something of a self-appointed archbishop,
rose to address the assembly. He gave a stirring speech decrying the
idea of making plans to increase the number of believers. He ended
with a rhetorical flourish: "God has called us to be faithful, not
successful!"

"Amen!" responded the assembly. The group then voted to scrap
the evangelistic enterprise.

They had mistakenly concluded that faithfulness and success
are diametrically opposed. Unfortunately, that's not an uncommon
assumption.

The issues of size and success are inseparable for many pastors.
For some bigger is better, with success defined as continued growth
in membership, giving, and attendance. The larger the church, they
reason, the more people reached with the gospel. These leaders exhibit the creative, pragmatic, and aggressive entrepreneurial spirit
that has served American society so well.

Others equate success with "quality" ministry, in particular, effective personal care and nurture. Such leaders worry that increased
growth will diminish the close-knit nature of the congregation. Their
primary concern is that the sick are visited, the hurting are comforted,

and that everyone knows each other's name on Sunday morning.

Which paradigm represents "successful" ministry?

I cannot answer that question concisely. For me, success, like a diamond, is multifaceted. The best I can do is show you different facets of the diamond, all of which together make up the luster of pastoral success.

The difference church culture makes

If we are going to be successful pastors, how our congregations measure success determines to some extent how we must measure it. This varies according to the community we serve.

My older son ministers in a small town of good, solid, reliable people who have been there forever (and will likely remain there forever). One measure of success there is the ability to conduct meaningful funerals. Love and personal nurture top their list of expectations for a pastor. So they measure a pastor by his willingness to visit the elderly, care for the sick and grieving, and continue the programs they've grown to love.

The town faces difficult economic conditions, so the leadership is naturally wary of taking risks. If a pastor can simply maintain the status quo in the face of a declining population, he will be considered a success.

My son is sensitive to that, yet he has managed over a five-year period to help them develop a more dynamic vision for the future. I categorize that as great success.

My youngest son serves in a major metropolitan area. His ministry is primarily to young professionals, and the leaders in his church are movers and shakers, successful businessmen with national and international positions. They tend to have vision, drive, and creativity. Their basic approach to ministry is, "Let's go for it!"

They appreciate my son's drive and initiative, and though he's a young man, they offer him strong support. Given their expectations of a pastor, he too is experiencing success.

My situation differs from both my sons. I minister in what some term a megachurch setting. Most of my elders have joined the church since I became pastor over twenty years ago. As a result, they look to me for leadership initiative. While they function as a strong board, they tend to take their cues from my feelings on a matter. Because we work well together, I consider our relationship a success.

Faithful despite fears

One way I measure success is by asking myself three or four times a year, *What did I do, even if I didn't particularly want to, that I knew I should?* Fulfilling one's responsibilities is a major part of success, especially when we overcome apprehensions to do so.

Shortly after I arrived at Elmbrook Church, one of the men largely responsible for bringing me to the church was killed in an accident. Because I had already grown to love him dearly, the idea of performing his funeral was enormously intimidating. What made the situation even more difficult was that all his relatives spoke only German.

But in the providence of God, I had previously ministered in Germany and had gained some comprehension of the language. I was able to conduct some of the service in German. His family seemed deeply touched.

At the end of the day I felt incredible exhilaration. I had faced my fears and fulfilled my biblical responsibility. To me one measure of success is to do what I think is right and good for my people, regardless of my feelings.

Fulfilling your primary roles

Another measure for me has to do with fulfilling my pastoral roles. Sorting through the various roles that we are expected to fulfill successfully is daunting: prophet, counselor, administrator, preacher, teacher, and on and on.

I've found it helpful, though, to keep my job simple. For me, Scripture describes two essential roles, which are valid regardless of the size or location of the church.

Pastor/Teacher. Occasionally I meet pastors who face gridlock with their board. They complain that they can't agree on anything.

I'll often reply by asking, "Well, who is their pastor/teacher?"

"I am," the discouraged minister will reply.

"What are you teaching them?"

They begin to see the point. God has afforded them a weekly platform to shape the thinking of their board and the church in a biblical fashion. Over a long period, sound biblical instruction, taught in a gracious spirit, should diminish disagreements and acrimony.

When I came to Elmbrook, I had neither pastoral training nor previous experience. The board members and I were starting from scratch in our ministry relationship.

"The only thing I know at the moment is a great book on the church called the Bible," I admitted. "I will try to teach it faithfully and accurately. Let us study it together and try to figure out what the church is supposed to be."

I told them I would undoubtedly make mistakes and challenged them to tell me when I was in error. "All I ask," I said, "is that you not criticize me behind my back. Come to me with your Bible in hand, and we'll discuss the matter." A pastor and congregation can only achieve community to the extent they are prepared to put aside preconceptions and submit every idea to this common point of appeal.

One time, a woman who was upset with me said, "Pastor, I want you to hear me out. But please, don't drag the Bible into this thing!"

I heard her out, but eventually I had to bring the Bible into the conversation. We had no other point of reference.

Shepherd. I measure my success by how well I am tending the flock, and especially in a larger church, by how well I am caring for the leaders who themselves are caring for others. I want to be a patient, caring pastor to my people.

One failure I most regret at Elmbrook had nothing to do with a building project or a doctrinal issue, but when I failed in my role as shepherd.

One couple in the church was utterly convinced the church needed a library—immediately. While I did nothing to encourage or discourage their enthusiasm, I doubted whether it was the right time for such an undertaking. We were a new church. A library simply wasn't at the top of my priorities.

But their passion for the project knew no bounds. Time and again the man pressed me to join his card-catalogue crusade. Each time I gently declined. "No, I can't get involved in this."

The man would not be dissuaded. He insisted that I take a public stand in favor of the project. The more I asked him not to push, the more pressure he exerted. My frustration rose.

One day he cornered me and would no longer take no for an

answer. He demanded that I throw my support behind the idea and quit rebuffing him. I exploded: "I'm getting angry, very angry with you," I seethed. "This has gone on for weeks. I'm worn out and fed up with your behavior." With that, I turned and walked away in a huff.

As far as I can remember, this is the only time in my two decades at Elmbrook that I have ever spoken so harshly with a parishioner. I still ache when I recall the incident. I hardly displayed the heart of a shepherd. Yet, even as I walked away I thought, *This should not be. Two brothers in Christ should never get in such an adversarial position that they completely lose their tempers.*

That night I went home and began work on a sermon. Sitting with my Bible open and pen ready, I waited, but the words wouldn't come. The spiritual wells within me were pumping only sand. I knew instinctively what was causing the blockage.

So I took out a fresh piece of paper and wrote a letter, apologizing to this man. I took pains to admit how I had acted wrongly and to specify how I felt he had acted improperly. I suggested we meet with a third deacon to iron out the matter, which we eventually did.

Looking back on the incident, it was a failure. My actions were inexcusable, and a fracture in the body of Christ had occurred. Fortunately, it was mended, the couple remained in our church, and today we enjoy superb library facilities, with individuals working on graduate degrees using our resources.

Maintaining realism, sustaining hope

Two dangers exist for pastors when it comes to setting standards for success. One is to shoot for the moon. The other is to throw in the towel.

If I suffer chronic disappointment or disillusionment over my ministry, it might indicate I've been expecting too much, too soon. I need to ask myself the question, *What's disappointing me? Is it the failings of people in the congregation? Or is it my unrealistic expectations?*

For years, during our annual missions conference, I would go through emotional contortions because so few people seemed interested in world missions. We'd offer splendid speakers and activities all week, but relatively few people would attend, at least compared with Sunday morning attendance.

I just couldn't understand the lack of enthusiasm. After visiting a foreign country, when I boarded a plane for the States I would inevitably turn and say to the missionaries, "Boy, I wish I could stay and help you. There's so much to be done." Then, when I returned home and planned a missions conference, people would stay home and watch a sitcom.

I would get so discouraged about this, my wife, Jill, would dread being around me during missions week. I would make matters worse by scolding the people who did turn out for the conference: "We've got to be more committed to missions!" Fortunately, Jill took me aside once and said, "Stuart, don't shout at *them*. They are the ones who showed up."

Gradually, as I gained a bit more sense, I realized that some people will never seek more out of their faith than what's in it for them. The church is comprised exclusively of sinners; unfortunately that includes me. In that sense, it's unwise to expect too much of others or myself. I've resolved not to abandon such people, just as a father doesn't abandon children who are disappointingly slow in development. Neither will I seek to make them perfect according to my timetable.

On the other hand, there's a danger of lowering our expectations too far, and thus losing hope. When I meet a stunning setback, it's always a temptation to abandon the project.

As Elmbrook grew, our system of church government, which had worked well when we were a smaller church, became cumbersome and inefficient. So after much thought, I sat down at a typewriter and drafted a proposal to restructure our governing system. The plan flowed effortlessly onto paper, and I couldn't wait to share it with others.

First I presented it to the staff, who wholeheartedly endorsed it. *Wonderful*, I thought. *This is going to sail through the church.*

Next step was the deacons. While the proposal did have its controversial aspects for them (the deacons would be asked to vote themselves into extinction), it seemed like an eminently rational plan they could support.

The deacons responded with passion but not the sort I had hoped for. The discussion degenerated into one of the most difficult board meetings of my entire career.

The chairman of the board, a calm and thoughtful man, said, "I have read your plan, Stuart, and it's positively un-American. Only a Britisher could have written such a document." And that was one of the more charitable statements made that evening! The deacons ripped the document to shreds.

But then one of the board members said, "Any jackass can kick down a barn, but it takes a craftsman to build one. Do we have any craftsmen here tonight?"

The room grew quiet. He went on: "It appears our pastor has made a genuine attempt to deal with a serious problem. Maybe some of us should do the same."

After further discussion, the men responded as any good board would—they created a subcommittee to study the problem. But as a sign of their displeasure, they stacked the committee with those most vehemently opposed to my proposal. The smell of embalming fluid filled the room. I concluded the plan was dead.

I was leaving the next morning for seven weeks of ministry in India, so I asked the board to put one of my associates on the task force. While I was away, the only news I received on the committee's work was a humorous note from my associate added to a letter from Jill: "P.S. We've decided to go with an Episcopal form of church government, and you've been unanimously elected archbishop!"

When I returned, I learned to my amazement that the entire subcommittee, having had time to examine the alternatives, now supported the plan 100 percent. We took it to the board, and they passed it unanimously.

Intending to move slowly and involve a large number of people in the discussion, the board mapped out a twelve-month plan to present the new system to the congregation. We scheduled numerous question-and-answer sessions, small group meetings, and educational forums to familiarize the people with the proposal.

Six months into the plan, many said, "Can't we just vote on it right now? Let's do it." In the end only one family voted against the proposal. They left the church but returned six months later.

I had mentally thrown in the towel on this proposal. Fortunately, by God's grace, it rose from the canvas. One facet of success for me, then, is to maintain a realistic but hopeful attitude as I minister.

Looking for progress

Another facet of success is progress—not perfection, but progress.

For instance, success is often measured by a congregation meeting a giving goal. Yet, in most instances, the goals we set are purely arbitrary. Who is to say if a 10 percent or 30 percent increase is too much or too little? The more important question to me is, "Are people progressing in their understanding and expression of biblical stewardship and worship and service?"

The largest Thanksgiving offering we ever received was the result of a presentation by a young woman who had worked on relief trucks in Kenya. She showed her pictures and then brought out a coffee can, filling it with corn to illustrate how little each person had to eat on a daily basis. The people opened their hearts and their wallets that day, and we received a large offering for World Relief, more than we had ever previously given for such a project. It was not the large amount that impressed me but that we had made progress in our ability to give sacrificially.

Take another example: when I finished preaching one series on sexual values, various people came to staff members and said such things as, "We're living together, please help us," or "I've lost my virginity, and I'm feeling desolate." The staff reported a sudden increase in the number of people seeking help in this area. They were responding to the prompting of God's Spirit in their lives, and that kind of progress is a facet of pastoral success.

Diamonds are forever

Who is more successful: the pastor who grows a large church or the one who maintains a church in a stagnant area? The pastor who preaches to thousands or the one who lovingly cares for individuals one by one? The pastor who impatiently pushes people to deeper discipleship or the pastor who patiently accepts the shortcomings of his people?

Yes.

Faithfulness, shepherding, teaching, patience, perseverance, growth, progress—these are some of the facets of the diamond of success. Each alone won't bring glory to God, but together they make a lustrous offering to him.

30

Staying Motivated

A motivated Christian is a relaxed and grateful Christian.

—Ben Patterson

One of the most remarkable plants in nature is the *ibervillea sonorae*. It can exist for seemingly indefinite periods without soil or even water. As Annie Dillard tells the story, one was kept in a display case in the New York Botanical Garden for seven years without soil or water. For seven springs it sent out little anticipatory shoots looking for water. Finding none, it simply dried up again, hoping for better luck next year.

Now that's what I call being motivated: hanging on, keeping on when it's not easy.

But motivation can run out, even for the *ibervillea sonorae*. In the eighth year of no soil and water, the rather sadistic folks at the New York Botanical Garden had a dead plant on their hands.

Most pastors know what it's like to find themselves past their seventh season, bereft of soil, thirsty, and waiting for the eighth spring. No more motivation; barely enough energy to send out another anticipatory shoot. With most of us, however, it happens seven or eight times each year. Would that we could last like that tough little desert plant.

Ministry's twin sins

Sometimes it's simple fatigue that finally takes its toll. Too much work, a lingering illness, or poor diet come singly or in combination, and we find ourselves desperately in need of a good night's sleep, a day off, a walk in the park, or a shot of penicillin. That's all. Simple fatigue, simple treatment, and we snap back like a rubber band.

But there may be a deeper meaning to our loss of motivation. It can stem from a loss of direction in the ministry. Preaching, teaching, training, counseling, and administrating may become intolerably burdensome because we have somehow forgotten why we are doing them. This weariness comes close to the deadly sin of sloth or acedia. Simple fatigue says, "I know I should be doing this, but I just can't seem to generate the energy." Acedia says, "Why? What's the difference?"

"Acedia is all of Friday consumed in getting out the Sunday bulletin," says Richard John Neuhaus in *Freedom for Ministry.* "Acedia is three hours dawdled away on *Time* magazine, which is then guiltily chalked up to 'study.' Acedia is evenings without number obliterated by television, evenings neither of entertainment nor of education, but of narcotized defense against time and duty. Above all, acedia is apathy, the refusal to engage the pathos of other lives and of God's life with them."

A physician friend of mine gave me an article from the *Journal of Internal Medicine*, which dealt with the psychological state conducive to illness called the "giving up, given up complex." It is found in people who lose the reasons for living; who are saying of their existence, "Why? What's the difference?" Acedia can make bodies vulnerable to disease and pastors terminally tired of the church.

Curiously, loss of motivation can produce what appears to be the opposite of sloth or acedia: hyperactivity. But in reality, it is just another dimension of the same loss of direction and sense of "why" that saps us of our ability to do the "what" of ministry. "Hyperactivity and sloth are twin sins," says Neuhaus, and rightly so. The only real difference is the anxious, frenetic shape hyperactivity takes.

Many pastors are no longer truly activated to do the work of the kingdom. Like children lost in a forest, the more lost they feel, the faster they run. Hyperactivity is to authentic motivation what junk food is to a nourishing diet. It gives the feeling of satisfaction while starving the person to death. In the New Testament it is the "Ephesian Syndrome" described in Revelation 2:17. The first love is gone, and now all that is left is the form and the trappings. This may be the sickness most preyed upon by the innumerable seminars offered on the techniques of church leadership. People who have forgotten "why" become obsessed with "how." Where once there was creativity and tenderness born of deep love, there is now only the sex manual.

Clerical works-righteousness

The twin sins of acedia and hyperactivity can be expanded into triplets with the addition of a third: hubris. Hubris, or pride, was the word the Greeks used to speak of presumption, the folly of trying to be like the gods. This vice, rather than stemming from a loss of direction in the ministry, is the loss par excellence. For the Christian, hubris is anything we do to try to save ourselves. For pastors, it is anything we do to try to save the church: *clerical works-righteousness.*

Hubris is bad enough by itself, but it also sets us up for acedia and hyperactivity. I know. One of the greatest crises I have faced in my own ministry came concerning my preaching. I had noticed a pattern developing in my weeks. Sunday afternoon through Monday morning I would be depressed. Monday afternoon through Wednesday evening I would feel fine. Thursday I would begin to feel irritable. The irritability would build on Friday, and on Saturday I would be almost impossible to live with. Sunday morning found me filled with energy but totally out of touch with my family or anyone else. My energy level would peak during worship, and then I'd drop exhausted back into depression Sunday afternoon.

Week after week this cycle repeated itself. After a few months, I found myself vacillating between frenetic activity and paralyzing sloth—sometimes within the same day. It just wasn't fun being a preacher any more. That concerned me greatly because I never doubted God called me to preach. Something had to be done, because I couldn't see myself going through those cycles and mood changes for the next thirty or forty years of my life.

After much prayer, study, and hard thought, it dawned on me that each week I was trying to preach the greatest sermon ever heard, the kind that generations after me would read and admire and discuss. I wasn't satisfied to offer God and my people my best from the pulpit. I demanded superstardom.

Of course, superstardom escaped me. My depression each Sunday afternoon grew out of the disparity between what I sought and what I deserved. My sermonizing was clerical works-righteousness. It sapped me of authentic motivation, leaving me alternately asking the "What's the difference?" of acedia, and proclaiming the "I am driven" of hyperactivity.

With the exception of simple fatigue, all loss of motivation is a form of forgetfulness. It is losing touch with the "why" of ministry, being cut off from the Vine whose branches we are; and then keeping busy enough or noisy enough or narcotized enough to not have to face up to the fundamental disjointedness of our lives.

First-love revival

There is only one antidote to forgetfulness, and that is remembrance. In John Bunyan's *Pilgrim's Progress*, the pilgrims were leaving the Delectable Mountains after having been warned by the shepherds to beware of the Enchanted Ground. The overwhelming desire there would be to fall asleep, never to awake. And just as the shepherds told them, the drowsiness became nearly unbearable. Hopeful pleaded for a nap, just one little rest. But Christian made him talk. He asked him the question, "By what means were you led to go on this pilgrimage?" By telling the story, Hopeful kept talking and kept walking.

It is remembrance that keeps Christians awake; and the supreme act of Christian worship, the Lord's Supper, draws us into fellowship with Christ by remembering his mercy and love for us. It is a love feast spread out upon a redeemed and quickened memory.

Motivation to minister, then, is recovered only by a revived first love in response to the resurrected Christ's command to *"Remember the height from which you have fallen!"* (Revelation 2:5, emphasis mine).

Sometimes remembrance takes no more than a few moments of quiet reflection over the things God has done in your life. More often, it means an intensified effort to a more disciplined life of prayer, study, and rigorous thought. For me, when motivation goes, these three are the last things I want to do. "If only I could get motivated" I rationalize, "then I could begin praying, studying, and thinking again." So I sit and wait for it to happen—for motivation to somehow descend upon me like tongues of fire at Pentecost.

It never works that way. The more I need to pray, study, and think, the less I feel like doing it. But do it I must. As the song says, "Them that gots is them that gets." I am convinced that the choices I make when I don't feel motivated are the most crucial of my Christian walk. C. S. Lewis touched on this when he had the devil Screwtape advise his nephew Wormwood that God will sometimes overwhelm us with his presence and motivating power early in our Christian experience, but that he never allows that to happen too long. His goal is to get us to stand on our own two legs, "to carry out from the will alone duties which have lost all relish." Screwtape observes that during such "tough periods, much more than during the peak periods," we are growing into the creatures God wants us to be.

A call to remember is a call to get back to basics and back to the people God has given to us. Acedia, hyperactivity, and hubris isolate us from our congregation.

Each week I conduct a "sermon group." Five or six people meet with me to do two things: critique my last sermon and discuss the text I'll be preaching on next.

Face-to-face contact with real people struggling with me over the meaning and application of God's Word motivates me tremendously; it can carry me along when I'm not particularly excited about preaching. Knowing I will be critiqued introduces a kind of salutary terror into my preparation I would not normally have. Besides, it's good theology. Preaching should always grow out of a context of dialogue within a community. Jesus' did. Paul's did. What they had to say was not little gospel pills dropped out of the sky on an anonymous crowd, but vigorous conversation between God and specific people living in concrete situations.

Among the people God would want us to stay close to are our colleagues in ministry. These men and women know, as no one else, the difficulties of sustaining a pure motivation in the ministry. A high priority in my choice of commitments is a covenant prayer group of fellow pastors. There are times when we just get together and gripe. More often than not, however, when one of us is "down" the others are "up" and can offer encouragement and advice. When things are bad for me, it seems that they have never been good, and that they are good nowhere else in the universe, either. My brothers and sisters in the ministry often serve as good agents of remembrance for me, reminding me of why I am here, and therefore what I am to do.

Relaxed motivation

One last thing needs to be said about remembrance. It has to do with the sovereignty of God. Martin Luther said he took great comfort from knowing that as he sat and enjoyed his mug of Wittenberg beer, the kingdom of God kept marching on. That assurance was a great motivator to hard work. He could relax and rest periodically, and therefore go back to work with greater élan. More important, when he did work, he knew nothing was wasted or lost because God was sovereign over everything.

That's how it should be for us. A motivated Christian is a relaxed and grateful Christian; grateful because of what God has done in the death and resurrection of Christ, and relaxed because of his hope in God's sure dénouement of all history in his Son. Because the motivated Christian has been freed from the bondage of the past and anxiety over the future, he can get down to the work at hand in the present.